Laboratory Manual

Human Biology

Eleventh Edition

Laboratory Manual

Human Biology

Eleventh Edition

Sylvia S. Mader

Boston   Burr Ridge, IL   Dubuque, IA   New York   San Francisco   St. Louis
Bangkok   Bogotá   Caracas   Kuala Lumpur   Lisbon   London   Madrid   Mexico City
Milan   Montreal   New Delhi   Santiago   Seoul   Singapore   Sydney   Taipei   Toronto

LABORATORY MANUAL TO ACCOMPANY HUMAN BIOLOGY, ELEVENTH EDITION

Published by McGraw-Hill, a business unit of The McGraw-Hill Companies, Inc., 1221 Avenue of the Americas, New York, NY 10020.

Some ancillaries, including electronic and print components, may not be available to customers outside the United States.

This book is printed on acid-free paper.

3 4 5 6 7 8 9 0 WDQ/WDQ 10

ISBN 978–0–07–723513–0
MHID 0–07–723513–4

Publisher: *Janice Roerig-Blong*
Executive Editor: *Michael S. Hackett*
Director of Development: *Kristine Tibbetts*
Senior Developmental Editor: *Lisa A. Bruflodt*
Marketing Manager: *Tamara Maury*
Project Coordinator: *Mary Jane Lampe*
Lead Production Supervisor: *Sandy Ludovissy*
Designer: *Laurie B. Janssen*
Cover Designer: *Christopher Reese*
(USE) Cover Image: © *Chris Noble/Gettyimages*
Senior Photo Research Coordinator: *Lori Hancock*
Photo Research: *Evelyn Jo Johnson*
Compositor: *Electronic Publishing Services Inc., NYC*
Typeface: *11/13 Slimbach*
Printer: *Quad/Graphics Dubuque, IA*

The credits section for this book begins on page CR-1 and is considered an extension of the copyright page.

Some of the laboratory experiments included in this text may be hazardous if materials are handled improperly or if procedures are conducted incorrectly. Safety precautions are necessary when you are working with chemicals, glass test tubes, hot water baths, sharp instruments, and the like, or for any procedures that generally require caution. Your school may have set regulations regarding safety procedures that your instructor will explain to you. Should you have any problems with materials or procedures, please ask your instructor for help.

www.mhhe.com

Contents

Applications for Daily Living

Preface

To the Instructor

The laboratory exercises in this manual are coordinated with *Human Biology*, a text that has two primary functions: (1) to show how the human body works, and (2) to show the relationship of humans to other living things in the biosphere.

This laboratory manual can be adapted to a variety of course orientations and designs. There are a sufficient number of laboratories to permit a choice of activities over the length of the course. Many activities may be performed as demonstrations rather than as student activities, thereby shortening the time required to cover a particular concept.

The Exercises

All exercises have been tested for student interest, preparation time, estimated time of completion, and feasibility. The following features are particularly appreciated by adopters.

Integrated Opening. Each laboratory begins with a list of learning objectives organized according to the major sections of the laboratory. The major sections of the laboratory are numbered on the opening page and in the laboratory text material. This organization will help students better understand the goals of each laboratory session. New to this edition, the integrated opening contains pre-lab questions.

Self-Contained Content. Each laboratory contains all the background information necessary to understand the concepts being studied and to answer the questions asked. This feature will reduce student frustration and increase learning.

Human Emphasis. This manual accompanies *Human Biology*, so it is fitting that the laboratories would have a human emphasis. This emphasis has been significantly improved in this edition. It is no longer necessary to include "Human" in the title of the labs because they all have a human orientation.

Student Activities. A color bar is used to designate each student activity. Some student activities are observations and some are experimental procedures. An icon appears whenever a procedure requires time before results can be viewed. Sequentially numbered steps guide students as they perform an activity.

Laboratory Safety. Special attention has been given to increasing laboratory safety, and the listing on page viii will assist instructors in their efforts to make the laboratory experience a safe one.

New Artwork. The art in the manual underwent significant revision from the last edition. Still, new art has been added that is also clear and illustrates the content effectively for the student.

New to the Eleventh Edition

All laboratories have been revised to increase pedagogy and student interest. Pre-lab questions now appear in the Integrated Opening. If students can answer these questions, they have prepared themselves for the laboratory. The introductions have take-home messages pertinent to human biology.

The many additional questions that occur throughout the lab ensure that students will have a meaningful laboratory experience. Also, students are more motivated when they know that the concepts they are learning are relevant and can be applied to their daily lives. Relevancy was assured in two ways:

First, the human emphasis of this manual has significantly been improved in this edition. It was a pleasure to revise each lab to make it more appropriate to a student enrolled in a human biology course.

Second, each lab now includes a greater number of applications. Frequent applications appear throughout the lab, and one particular application is now featured in almost every laboratory. The featured application is entitled, "Application for Daily Living."

I am pleased to report that the revision of these labs are of particular interest:

Laboratory 1, "Scientific Method," is new to this edition. Students participate in developing an experiment that tests a hypothesis concerning pulse rate following exercise. The entire class comes to a conclusion based on collective data at the end of the experiment.

Laboratory 3, "Chemical Composition of Cells," runs tests on "foods" in the same manner as a Food and Drug Administration employee would do. From that perspective, students discover how to test "foods" for proteins, carbohydrates, and fats.

Laboratory 6, "Organization of the Body," is new to this edition. The emphasis is on learning the placement of the human organs by observing a human torso model and by either observing, doing a virtual dissection, or actually dissecting a fetal pig, as is judged appropriate by the instructor.

Laboratory 7, "Cardiovascular System," new to this edition, begins with learning the anatomy of the heart, followed by the blood vessels. Then, students observe blood pressure before and after exercise as a follow-up to Laboratory 1.

Laboratory 10, "Urinary and Reproductive Systems," has been rewritten to emphasize differences between male and female anatomy through observation of models. Instructions are also given for observing, doing a virtual dissection, or actually dissecting a fetal pig, as is judged appropriate by the instructor.

Laboratory 11, "Homeostasis," has been reorganized and the lab now begins with capillary exchange and moves from there to an improved study of how the lungs, liver, and kidneys contribute to homeostasis. As before, students do a simulated urinary analysis, and the lab ends with a new expanded summary.

Laboratory 13, "Nervous System and Senses," was rewritten to allow for more student involvement and better comprehension of basic concepts. After a study of the central nervous system, students perform a number of exercises involving the senses.

Laboratory 14, "Development," is new to this edition. Human development is stressed as students of necessity examine embryonic development in other organisms. "Development of Human Organs" is a new section that precedes an expanded study of fetal development.

Laboratory 16, "Patterns of Genetic Inheritance," is a new human oriented lab in which students determine their genotypes for traits, and then they solve genetics problems based on their traits. They also determine the chances of a couple having children with described genetic disorders. After a study of pedigrees, students construct one from scratch.

Customized Editions

The 19 laboratories in this manual are available as individual "lab separates," so instructors can custom-tailor a manual to their particular course needs.

Laboratory Resource Guide

The *Laboratory Resource Guide* is essential for instructors and laboratory assistants and is available free to adopters of the *Laboratory Manual* at www.mhhe.com/maderhuman11e. Aside from helping instructors get ready for each week's laboratory session, all questions are answered in the *Laboratory Resource Guide,* including the pre-lab and the Laboratory Review questions.

To the Student

Special care has been taken in preparing the *Laboratory Manual for Human Biology* so that you will *enjoy* the laboratory experience as you *learn* from it. The instructions and discussion are written clearly so you can understand the material while working through it. Student aids are designed to help you focus on important aspects of each exercise. Where time is a factor in successfully completing an exercise, icons are used to alert you to effective time management strategies.

Student Learning Aids

Student learning aids are carefully integrated throughout each laboratory.

The *Learning Outcomes* set the goals of each laboratory session and help you review the material for a laboratory practical or any other type of exam. The major topics are numbered, and the learning outcomes are grouped according to these topics on the opening page of the laboratory. This numbering system is also used in the pages that follow so that you can study the laboratory in terms of the outcomes presented.

There is a pre-lab question for each major topic. When you can answer the prelab questions, you are prepared for a meaningful laboratory experience.

The *Introduction* gives an overview of the laboratory session and includes background information required to comprehend upcoming experiments.

Throughout, *color bars* highlight Observations and Experimental Procedures and call your attention to exercises that require your active participation. An *icon* indicates a timed exercise. Appropriate space is available for recording answers to questions and the results of investigations and experiments.

Each laboratory ends with a set of *review questions* covering the day's work.

The appendix at the end of the laboratory manual provides useful information on the metric system. Practical examination answer sheets are also provided.

Laboratory Preparation

1. *Read* each exercise before coming to the laboratory.
2. *Study* the introductory material and the experimental procedures. To obtain a better understanding, *read* the corresponding chapter in your text. If your text is *Human Biology,* by Sylvia S. Mader, see the text *chapter reference* in the table of contents at the beginning of the *Laboratory Manual.*
3. Answer the pre-lab questions.

Explanations and Conclusions

Throughout the laboratory, you are often asked to formulate explanations or conclusions. To do so, you will need to synthesize information from a variety of sources, including the following:

1. Your experimental results and/or the results of other groups in the class. If your data are different from other groups in your class, do not erase your answer; add the other answers in parentheses.
2. Your knowledge of underlying principles. Obtain this information from the laboratory introduction or the appropriate section of the laboratory and the corresponding chapter of your text.
3. Your understanding of how the experiment was conducted and/or the materials that were used. *Note:* Ingredients can be contaminated or procedures incorrectly followed, resulting in reactions that seem inappropriate. If this occurs, consult with other students and your instructor to see if you should repeat the experiment.

In the end, be sure you are truly writing an explanation or conclusion and not just restating the observations made.

Color Bars, Icon, and Safety Boxes

Observation—An activity in which you observe models or slides and make identifications or draw conclusions. Observations are designated with a tan color bar.

Experimental Procedure—An activity in which a series of laboratory steps is followed to achieve a learning outcome. Experimental procedures are identified with a green color bar.

Time—An icon is used to designate when time is needed for an experimental procedure. Allow the designated amount of time for this activity. Start these activities at the beginning of the laboratory, proceed to other activities, and return to these when the designated time is up.

Safety—An icon is used to designate when particular caution is needed. Your health and safety are of utmost concern, and you should follow the directive.

Laboratory Review

Each laboratory ends with approximately 10–20 short-answer questions that will help you determine if you have accomplished the outcomes for the laboratory. The answers to these questions are found in the *Laboratory Resource Guide.*

Student Feedback

If you have any suggestions for how this laboratory manual could be improved, you can send your comments to

The McGraw-Hill Companies
Introductory Biology
501 Bell Street
Dubuque, Iowa 52001

Acknowledgments

We gratefully acknowledge the following reviewers for their assistance in the development of this lab manual:

Dave Cox, *Lincoln Land Community College*
Edwin Klibaner, *Touro College*
Jennifer E. McCoy, *Wichita State University*
Dean O'Grady, *Morrisville State College*
Tom Pitzer, *Florida International University*
Nick Roster, *Northwestern Michigan College*
Deborah Schulman, *Cleveland State University*
Chad Thompson, *Westchester Community College*
Jamey Thompson, *Hudson Valley Community College*

Laboratory Safety

The following is a list of practices required for safety purposes in the biology laboratory and in outdoor activities. Following rules of lab safety and using common sense throughout the course will enhance your learning experience by increasing your confidence in your ability to safely use chemicals and equipment. Pay particular attention to oral and written safety instructions given by the instructor. If you do not understand a procedure, ask the instructor, rather than a fellow student, for clarification. Be aware of your school's policy regarding accident liability and any medical care needed as a result of a laboratory or outdoor accident.

The following rules of laboratory safety should become a habit:

1. Wear safety glasses or goggles during exercises in which glassware and chemical reagents are handled, or when dangerous fumes may be present, creating possible hazards to eyes or contact lenses.
2. Assume that all reagents are poisonous and act accordingly. Read the labels on chemical bottles for safety precautions and know the nature of the chemical you are using. If chemicals come into contact with skin, wash immediately with water.
3. **DO NOT**
   a. ingest any reagents.
   b. eat, drink, or smoke in the laboratory. Toxic material may be present, and some chemicals are flammable.
   c. carry reagent bottles around the room.
   d. pipette anything by mouth.
   e. put chemicals in the sink or trash unless instructed to do so.
   f. pour chemicals back into containers unless instructed to do so.
   g. operate any equipment until you are instructed in its use.
   h. dispose of biological or chemical wastes in regular classroom trash receptacles.
4. **DO**
   a. note the location of emergency equipment such as a first aid kit, eyewash bottle, fire extinguisher, switch for ceiling showers, fire blanket(s), sand bucket, and telephone (911).
   b. be familiar with the experiments you will be doing before coming to the laboratory. This will increase your understanding, enjoyment, and safety during exercises. Confusion is dangerous. Completely follow the procedure set forth by the instructor.
   c. keep your work area neat, clean, and organized. Before beginning, remove everything from your work area except the lab manual, pen, and equipment used for the experiment. Wash hands and desk area, including desk top and edge, before and after each experiment. Use clean glassware at the beginning of each exercise, and wash glassware at the end of each exercise or before leaving the laboratory.
   d. wear clothing that, if damaged, would not be a serious loss, or use aprons or laboratory coats, because chemicals may damage fabrics.
   e. wear shoes as protection against broken glass or spillage that may not have been adequately cleaned up.
   f. handle hot glassware with a test tube clamp or tongs. Use caution when using heat, especially when heating chemicals. Do not leave a flame unattended; do not light a Bunsen burner near a gas tank or cylinder; do not move a lit Bunsen burner; do keep long hair and loose clothing well away from the flame; do make certain gas jets are off when the Bunsen burner is not in use. Use proper ventilation and hoods when instructed.
   g. read chemical bottle labels; be aware of the hazards of all chemicals used. Know the safety precautions for each.
   h. stopper all reagent bottles when not in use. Immediately wash reagents off yourself and your clothing if they spill on you, and immediately inform the instructor. If you accidentally get any reagent in your mouth, rinse the mouth thoroughly, and immediately inform your instructor.
   i. use extra care and wear disposable gloves when working with glass tubing and when using dissection equipment (scalpels, knives, or razor blades), whether cutting or assisting.
   j. administer first aid immediately to clean, sterilize, and cover any scrapes, cuts, and burns where the skin is broken and/or where there may be bleeding. Wear bandages over open skin wounds.
   k. report all accidents to the instructor immediately, and ask your instructor for assistance in cleaning up broken glassware and spills.
   l. report to the instructor any condition that appears unsafe or hazardous.
   m. use caution during any outdoor activities. Watch for snakes, poisonous insects or spiders, stinging insects, poison oak, poison ivy, and so on. Be careful near water.
   n. wash your hands thoroughly after handling any preserved biological specimens.

I understand the safety rules as presented above. I agree to follow them and all other instructions given by the instructor.

Name: _____   Date: _____

Laboratory Class and Time: _____

1

Scientific Method

Learning Outcomes

1.1 Using the Scientific Method
- Outline the steps of the scientific method.
- Distinguish among observations, hypotheses, conclusions, and theories.
Question: Explain what a scientist means by the term "theory."

1.2 Observations Concerning Heart Rate
- Observe and describe the rhythmical beating of the heart.
- Read the data presented by the laboratory manual about the heartbeat.
Question: How do scientists carry out the first step of the scientific method?

1.3 Formulating Hypotheses
- Formulate a hypothesis based on the observations.
Question: Why is a hypothesis called a tentative explanation?

1.4 Performing an Experiment and Coming to a Conclusion
- Design an experiment that can be repeated by others.
- Reach a conclusion based on observation and experimentation.
Question: In science, a conclusion is based on the data. Explain.

Application for Daily Living: The Stress Test

Introduction

In everyday life we are often called upon to make observations and use our past experiences to come to a hypothesis that can be tested. For example, suppose you flipped the switch, but the light didn't come on. Most likely you would hypothesize that the bulb has burnt out, the socket isn't working, or there has been a power outage. Each of these possibilities could be tested until you have come to a conclusion that allows the problem to be fixed. In today's laboratory, we want to experience firsthand the manner in which a scientist uses these same steps to come to a conclusion.

1.1 Using the Scientific Method

Science differs from other human ways of knowing and learning by its process, which can be varied because it can be adjusted to where and how a study is being conducted. Still, the scientific process often involves the use of the scientific method. In today's laboratory, we will use the scientific method to come to a conclusion about the heartbeat rate. As depicted in Figure 1.1, the scientific method involves making observations, formulating hypotheses, doing experiments, and coming to a conclusion. Many conclusions on the same topic allow scientists to develop a scientific theory.

Figure 1.1 Flow diagram for the scientific method.
On the basis of observations, a scientist formulates a hypothesis. The hypothesis is tested by further experiments and/or observations. The scientist then concludes whether the results support or do not support the hypothesis. The return arrow shows that scientists often choose to retest the same hypothesis or test a related hypothesis. Conclusions from many different but related experiments may lead to the development of a scientific theory.

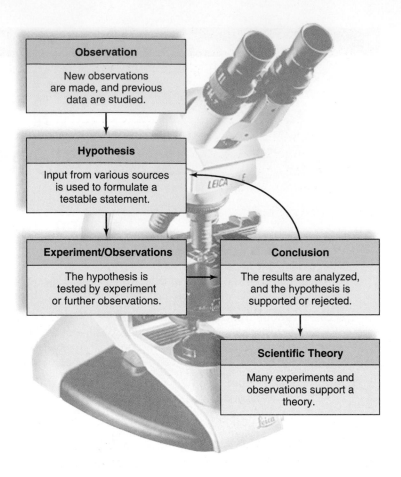

Observation
New observations are made, and previous data are studied.

Hypothesis
Input from various sources is used to formulate a testable statement.

Experiment/Observations
The hypothesis is tested by experiment or further observations.

Conclusion
The results are analyzed, and the hypothesis is supported or rejected.

Scientific Theory
Many experiments and observations support a theory.

Making observations: As a first step in their study of a topic, scientists use all their senses and also instruments, such as a microscope, to make observations. Observations can also include something you read, such as the information given on page 3 about the beating of the heart. If you want to learn more about the heartbeat rate, you could do a Google search of the Web or talk to a nurse or doctor about the heartbeat. Scientists keep notes about their observations, as you will be asked to do. Why is it helpful for a scientist to begin by making observations? _____

_____

Formulating a hypothesis: Based on their observations, scientists come to a tentative explanation about what it is they are investigating. Having observed the beating of the heart and having done a little literary research, you will be asked to formulate a hypothesis about the influence of exercise on the heartbeat rate. Why is a hypothesis sometimes called an "educated guess?"

_____

Testing your hypothesis: After formulating a hypothesis, a scientist experimentally tests the hypothesis. A well-designed experiment must have a control, a sample or event that is not exposed to the testing procedure. If the control and the test produce the same results, either the procedure is flawed or the hypothesis is wrong. What is the purpose of a control? _____

_____

The results of your experiment are called **data.** Data are any factual information that comes to light because of your experiment or perhaps further observations you have made. It is important for a scientist to keep accurate records of all their data. When another person repeats the experiment, their data should be the same or something is amiss. Why must a scientist keep complete records of an experiment? _____

Conclusion: The data will either support or not support the hypothesis. A scientist can report that the hypothesis has been shown to be false but does not say that a hypothesis has been shown to be true. After all, some fault might be found with the method of collecting data. Why don't scientists say they have proven their hypothesis true? _____

_____

Theory: A "theory" in science is an encompassing conclusion based on many individual conclusions in the same field. For example, the cell theory states that all organisms are composed of cells. The cell theory is based on observations made by many scientists over many years who have observed a countless variety of living things. We will not be developing any theories today. How is a scientific theory different from a conclusion? _____

_____

1.2 Observations Concerning Heart Rate

You will follow the procedure for the scientific method outlined in Figure 1.1. The first step in this procedure is to make observations about the topic you are proposing to study.

Observation: The Human Heart

1. Your instructor will show a short video of the heart beating. After viewing the video and studying Figure 1.2, do your observations suggest that the human heartbeat sends blood rhythmically into the blood vessels of the cardiovascular system? _____

2. In his text, *Functional Human Anatomy*, James E. Crouch writes:

    The heart is a pump which is of primary importance in the maintenance of the flow and pressure of the blood in the closed cardiovascular system. Its contractions start in the early days of embryonic development and must continue for the duration of the individual's life. For the contractions to cease even for a few minutes, would

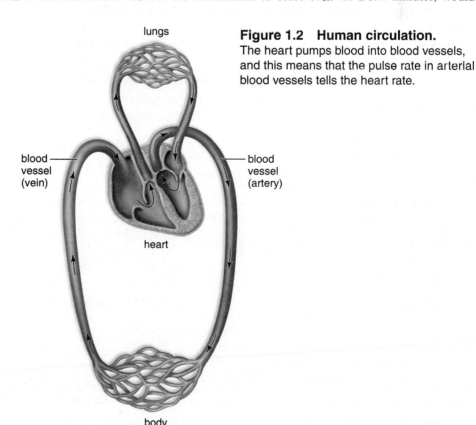

Figure 1.2 Human circulation.
The heart pumps blood into blood vessels, and this means that the pulse rate in arterial blood vessels tells the heart rate.

cause serious damage, or would be fatal. The heart beat occurs at an average rate of 72 times per minute and add up to about 100,000 times a day or about 2,600,000,000 beats in a lifetime of seventy years. If you clench and open your fist alternately at the rate of 72 times per minute, the muscles involved will "feel" tired after about 2 minutes....[1]

3. When you take an aerobics exercise class, your instructor may ask you to periodically take your pulse rate. The pulse rate indicates how fast the heart is beating. In your experience, does the heart rate and pulse rate increase upon exercise? _____

1.3 Formulating Hypotheses

Now that you have made some observations of the beating heart, had some literary input, and recalled past experiences, it is time to formulate a hypothesis about the heart rate and exercise.

1. Think of an exercise a subject could do in the laboratory at a slow speed and a fast speed.

   Record your choice here: _____

2. After a class discussion and input from your instructor, everyone will have the subject do some type of exercise for the same length of time during the experiment. Together you will decide what is meant by a "slow speed" and "fast speed" exercise and the time limit for each. Three minutes of exercise are suggested. Record the class decision about type of exercise to be done and for how long:

   Slow exercise/time: *Fast exercise/time:*

   _____   _____

3. Formulate a hypothesis here that tells how you expect the heart rate to be affected by the chosen slow and fast exercise per length of time:

   Hypothesis: The heart rate will _____

1.4 Performing an Experiment and Coming to a Conclusion

Variables

1. Variables are differences in your experimental procedure or results. Two variables of value are the experimental variable and the dependent variable. The **experimental variable** is what you purposely change to get your results. What is your experimental variable?

   _____

   The **dependent variables** are the variables that the hypothesis predicts will be influenced by the experimental variable. What will be a dependent variable in your experiment?

   _____

2. The experimenter tries to avoid other variables that could affect the results. For example, if a scientist were doing an experiment with plants, s/he would always use the same type plant, the same type pots, and subject the plants to the same treatment under the same circumstances. Otherwise, the experiment has too many variables (differences) to make your results meaningful: The results might be due to differences in treatment other than the one being tested. What are some possible variables that could unfortunately affect the reliability of your results? _____

   _____

[1]Crouch, James E. 1985. *Functional Human Anatomy*, 4th ed. Philadelphia. Lea & Febiger, p. 399.

3. Subject variability is often a concern when doing experiments with humans. Just as all the people signed up for an aerobics class are different (Fig. 1.3), so are the people taking a human biology course. Then, too, we have to consider that some subjects are used to doing exercise and some are not. This is one reason to pool our results as a class. The hope is that if subjects are randomly chosen, and the results are averaged, then differences between subjects may cancel themselves out. Skill of the experimenter is another variable that we have to consider, and the experimenters should practice taking the pulse rate in the same manner before the experiment begins.

Figure 1.3   An aerobics class.
Just as the individuals taking an aerobics class are varied in their appearance, so participants in a scientific study are different in their physiological characteristics.

Experimental Design

1. It's time to consider what the experimenter is to do. The experimenters will take pulse rate measurements at the wrist using the radial artery, which pulses every time the heart beats.

    Location of the Radial Artery The radial artery is located on the thumb side of the wrist, a little below the base of the thumb. If you are right handed, use the tips of your index and third finger of your right hand to find the radial artery on your left wrist. (Left-handed people should do the opposite.) You should be able to feel the pulsing of the artery.

    Choose a timepiece to use, preferably a stopwatch, but if this is not available, use a watch with a second hand as a way to tell the number of seconds.

    To take a measurement, use only the tips of your index and third finger. Holding gently, begin counting the pulse with "zero," and count for 10 seconds. Multiply by six, and the answer is your pulse rate per minute. Record your results:

    Counts per 10 seconds _____ × 6 = _____ pulse rate per minute.

    When taking the pulse rate after exercising, begin as soon as the subject stops. If you let time pass, the pulse rate will slow, and your count will not be accurate. As a precautionary measure, consult Table 1.1. If the subject experiences a high pulse rate during slow exercise, they should not continue with the fast exercise portion.

2. As mentioned, every experiment needs to have a control; in this instance, data from a subject that does not experience exercise. You could use the pulse of a student who will not be asked to exercise, or you could use the pulse of each subject, as long as you let the subject recover well from slow exercise before they undergo fast exercise. What would be the pros and cons of

    each method of providing a control? _____

    _____

    _____

    To generate enough data, we will use the second method and assume that pulse rate before slow and again, after recovery, before fast exercise is the control sample (see Table 1.2).

Table 1.1 Physical Fitness Evaluation Chart for the Canadian Home Fitness Test

Ten-Second Pulse Rate

Age (yr)	After First Three Minutes of Exercise	After Second Three Minutes of Exercise
15–19	If 30 or more, stop. Given your personal fitness level, further exercise is not recommended.	If 27 or more, you have a minimum personal fitness level. If 26 or less, you have the recommended personal fitness level.
20–29	If 29 or more, stop. Given your personal fitness level, further exercise is not recommended.	If 26 or more, you have a minimum personal fitness level. If 25 or less, you have the recommended personal fitness level.
30–39	If 28 or more, stop. Given your personal fitness level, further exercise is not recommended.	If 25 or more, you have a minimum personal fitness level. If 24 or less, you have the recommended personal fitness level.
40–49	If 26 or more, stop. Given your personal fitness level, further exercise is not recommended.	If 24 or more, you have a minimum personal fitness level. If 23 or less, you have the recommended personal fitness level.
50–59	If 25 or more, stop. Given your personal fitness level, further exercise is not recommended.	If 23 or more, you have a minimum personal fitness level. If 22 or less, you have the recommended personal fitness level.
60–69	If 24 or more, stop. Given your personal fitness level, further exercise is not recommended.	If 23 or more, you have a minimum personal fitness level. If 22 or less, you have the recommended personal fitness level.

From R. J. Shephard, et. al., "Development of the Canadian Home Fitness Test," originally published in *Canadian Medical Association Journal*, 114:675–79, 1976. Copyright © 1976 Canadian Medical Association, Ottowa, Canada. Reprinted by permission.

Experimental Procedure: Increase in Heart Rate Following Slow and Fast Exercise

Scientists explicitly describe an experiment so that anyone would be able to perform the experiment also. Summarize here your complete experimental design for the benefit of anyone else who wishes to do the experiment exactly as you did. Include information concerning how the subjects were chosen; the experimental variable (what the subjects did); and how the results, called the data, will be gathered.

Repeat the experiment as many times as desirable. Scientists always repeat their experiment as many times as possible.

1. The members of your class will work in groups. Each group will contain at least one experimenter and one subject. You may switch off and be the experimenter for one round of the experiment and the subject for another round of the experiment. Record your results in Table 1.2

Table 1.2 Increase in Heart Rate Following Slow and Fast Exercise Per Group

	Pulse Rate/min Before Exercise	Pulse Rate/min Slow Exercise	Pulse Rate/min Before Exercise	Pulse Rate/min Fast Exercise
First Subject				
Second Subject				

2. Your instructor or designated members of the class will collect the data, average the results, and tell you what data to record in Table 1.3.

Table 1.3 Increase in Heart Rate Following Slow and Fast Exercise Per Class				
	Pulse Rate/min Before Exercise	Pulse Rate/min Slow Exercise	Pulse Rate/min Before Exercise	Pulse Rate/min Fast Exercise
Class average				

Conclusion: Heart Rate Following Exercise

- Did the results of your experiment support the hypothesis, per your group? _____
  per class? _____
- Why or why not? _____

Application for Daily Living

The Stress Test

A high pulse rate could be an indication of heart irregularities. Another test that may be ordered is a cardiac stress test, which examines a series of ECGs as the patient exercises (Fig. 1.4). An abnormal ECG, which measures the electrical activity of the heart, is suggestive of an impending heart attack. One out of every five deaths in the United States is due to a heart attack, and there are over 1 million new and recurrent heart attacks per year. Heart attack is a fairly common occurrence, so it is often a good idea to determine the chances of having one.

During a stress test, the level of exercise is increased in three-minute stages of ever-increasing incline and speed. The American Heart Association recommends a stress test as the first choice for patients with medium risk of coronary heart disease based on risk factors, such as smoking and family history of cardiac disorders. Over the past 20 years, more modern methods have been devised to test whether the heart is functioning properly, but they are more expensive methods and more invasive than a stress test.

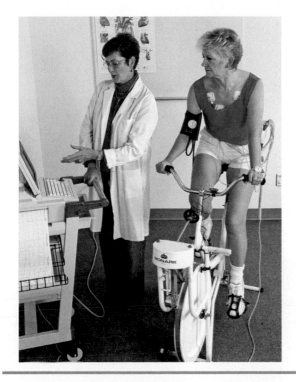

Figure 1.4 The stress test.
As a patient rides a bike, a technician takes her blood pressure while viewing the ECGs on the computer screen.

_____ 1. Which is more comprehensive, a conclusion or a theory?

_____ 2. What is a tentative explanation of observed phenomena?

_____ 3. What do you call the information scientists collect when doing experiments and making observations?

_____ 4. What step in the scientific method follows experiments and observations?

_____ 5. What do you call a sample that goes through all the steps of an experiment and does not contain the factor being tested?

Indicate whether statements 6 and 7 are hypotheses, conclusions, or scientific theories.

_____ 6. The data show that vaccines protect people from disease.

_____ 7. All living things are made of cells.

_____ 8. The heart rate is the same as what other cardiovascular system rate?

_____ 9. What is the function of a beating heart?

_____ 10. What is the normal heart rate when at rest?

_____ 11. What is your evidence that a beating heart is critical to our good health?

Thought Questions

12. To save time, Dale decides to have Nancy do the slow exercise test and Henry the fast exercise test. Criticize Dale's procedure.

13. How does the method you use to decide what to wear differ from that of the scientific method?

Human Biology Website

The companion website for _Human Biology_ provides a wealth of information organized and integrated by chapter. You will find practice tests, animations, and much more that will complement your learning and understanding of general biology.

www.mhhe.com/maderhuman11

McGraw-Hill Access Science Website

An online encyclopedia of science and technology that provides information, including videos, that can enhance the laboratory experience.

www.accessscience.com

2

Light Microscopy

Learning Outcomes

2.1 Light Microscopes versus Electron Microscopes
- Describe three differences between the compound light microscope and the electron microscope.
Question: Greater magnification enlarges the subject, but just as important is, what other attribute of a microscope? Explain.

2.2 Stereomicroscope (Binocular Dissecting Microscope)
- Identify the parts of and tell how to focus the stereomicroscope.
Question: If you wanted to examine the external features of a fly, you might decide to use a stereomicroscope. Why?

2.3 Use of the Compound Light Microscope
- Name and give the function of the basic parts of the compound light microscope.
- List the steps for bringing an object into focus with the compound light microscope.
- Describe how the image is inverted by the compound light microscope.
- Calculate the total magnification and the diameter of field of view for both low- and high-power lens systems.
- Explain how a slide of colored threads provides information on the depth of field.
Question: What's the difference between low power and high power when using the compound light microscope?

2.4 Microscopic Observations
- Name and describe three types of cells studied in this exercise.
Question: What is there about a live *Euglena* that makes it difficult to study microscopically?

Application for Daily Living: Microscopic Diagnoses

Introduction

This laboratory introduces you to the features, functions, and use of the stereomicroscope and the compound light microscope. Transmission and scanning electron microscopes are explained, and micrographs produced by using these microscopes are shown throughout these exercises. The stereomicroscope and the scanning electron microscope view the surface and/or the three-dimensional structure of an object. The compound light microscope and the transmission electron microscope can view only extremely thin sections of a specimen. If a subject was sectioned lengthwise for viewing, the interior of the projections at the top of the cell, called cilia, would appear in the micrograph (Fig. 2.1*b*). A lengthwise cut through any type of specimen is called a **longitudinal section (l.s.).** On the other hand, if the subject was sectioned crosswise below the area of the cilia, you would see other portions of the interior of the subject (Fig. 2.1*c*). A crosswise cut through any type of specimen is called a **cross section (c.s.).**

Figure 2.1 Longitudinal and cross sections.
a. Transparent view of a cell. **b.** A longitudinal section would show the cilia at the top of the cell. **c.** A cross section shows only the interior where the cut is made.

a. Cell

b. Longitudinal section

c. Cross section

2.1 Light Microscopes versus Electron Microscopes

Biological objects can be small, so we often use a microscope to view them. Many types of instruments, ranging from the hand lens to the electron microscope, are effective magnifying devices. A short description of two types of light microscopes and two types of electron microscopes follows.

Light Microscopes

Light microscopes use visible light rays magnified and focused by means of lenses. The **stereomicroscope** (binocular dissecting microscope) is designed to study entire objects in three dimensions at low magnification. The **compound light microscope** is used for examining small or thinly sliced sections of objects under higher magnification than that of the stereomicroscope. The term **compound** refers to the use of two sets of lenses: the ocular lenses located near the eyes and the objective lenses located near the object. Illumination is from below, and visible light passes through clear portions but does not pass through opaque portions. To improve contrast, the microscopist uses stains or dyes that bind to cellular structures and absorb light. Figure 2.2*a* is a **photomicrograph,** a photograph of an image produced by a compound light microscope.

Figure 2.2   Comparative micrographs.
Micrographs of a lymphocyte, a type of white blood cell. **a.** A photomicrograph (light micrograph) shows less detail than a **(b)** transmission electron micrograph (TEM). **c.** A scanning electron micrograph (SEM) shows the cell surface in three dimensions.

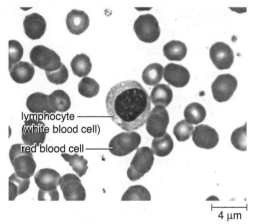

lymphocyte
(white blood cell)
red blood cell

⊢ 4 µm ⊣

a. Photomicrograph or light micrograph (LM)

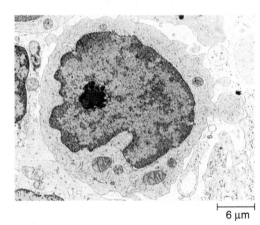

⊢ 6 µm ⊣

b. Transmission electron micrograph (TEM)

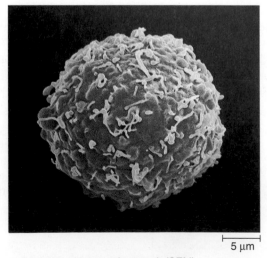

⊢ 5 µm ⊣

c. Scanning electron micrograph (SEM)

Electron Microscopes

Electron microscopes use a beam of electrons magnified and focused on a photographic plate by means of electromagnets. The **transmission electron microscope** is analogous to the compound light microscope. The object is ultra-thinly sliced and treated with heavy metal salts to provide contrast. Figure 2.2*b* is a micrograph produced by this type of microscope. The **scanning electron microscope** is analogous to the dissecting light microscope. It gives an image of the surface and dimensions of an object, as is apparent from the scanning electron micrograph in Figure 2.2*c*.

   The micrographs in Figure 2.2 demonstrate that much smaller objects can be viewed with electron microscopes than with compound light microscopes. The difference between these two types of microscopes, however, is not simply a matter of magnification; it is also the electron microscope's ability to show detail. The electron microscope has greater resolving power. **Resolution** is the minimum distance between two objects at which they can still be seen, or resolved, as two separate objects. The use of high-energy electrons rather than light gives electron microscopes a much greater resolving power because two objects much closer together can still be distinguished as separate points. Table 2.1 lists several other differences between the compound light microscope and the transmission electron microscope.

Table 2.1 Comparison of the Compound Light Microscope and the Transmission Electron Microscope	
Compound Light Microscope	**Transmission Electron Microscope**
1. Glass lenses	1. Electromagnetic lenses
2. Illumination by visible light	2. Illumination due to a beam of electrons
3. Resolution $\cong$ 200 nm	3. Resolution $\cong$ 0.1 nm
4. Magnifies to 2,000$\times$	4. Magnifies to 1,000,000$\times$
5. Costs up to tens of thousands of dollars	5. Costs up to hundreds of thousands of dollars

2.2 Stereomicroscope (Binocular Dissecting Microscope)

The stereomicroscope (binocular dissecting microscope) allows you to view objects in three dimensions at low magnifications. It is used to study entire small organisms, any object requiring lower magnification, and opaque objects that can be viewed only by reflected light. It is also called a stereomicroscope because it produces a three-dimensional image.

Identifying the Parts

After your instructor has explained how to carry a microscope, obtain a stereomicroscope and a separate illuminator, if necessary, from the storage area. Place it securely on the table. Plug in the power cord, and turn on the illuminator. There is a wide variety of stereomicroscope styles, and your instructor will discuss the specific style(s) available to you. Regardless of style, the following features should be present:

1. **Binocular head:** Holds two eyepiece lenses that move to accommodate for the various distances between different individuals' eyes.
2. **Eyepiece lenses:** The two lenses located on the binocular head. What is the magnification of your eyepieces? _____ Some models have one **independent focusing eyepiece** with a knurled knob to allow independent adjustment of each eye. The nonadjustable eyepiece is called the **fixed eyepiece.**
3. **Focusing knob:** A large black or gray knob located on the arm; used for changing the focus of both eyepieces together.

4. **Magnification changing knob:** A knob, often built into the binocular head, used to simultaneously change magnification in both eyepieces. This may be a **zoom** mechanism or a **rotating lens** mechanism of different powers that clicks into place.
5. **Illuminator:** Used to illuminate an object from above; may be built into the microscope or separate.

Locate each of these parts on your stereomicroscope, and label them on Figure 2.3.

Focusing the Stereomicroscope

1. Place a plastomount that contains small organisms in the center of the stage.
2. Adjust the distance between the eyepieces on the binocular head so that they comfortably fit the distance between your eyes. You should be able to see the object with both eyes as one three-dimensional image.

Figure 2.3 Stereomicroscope.
Label this microscope with the help of the text material.

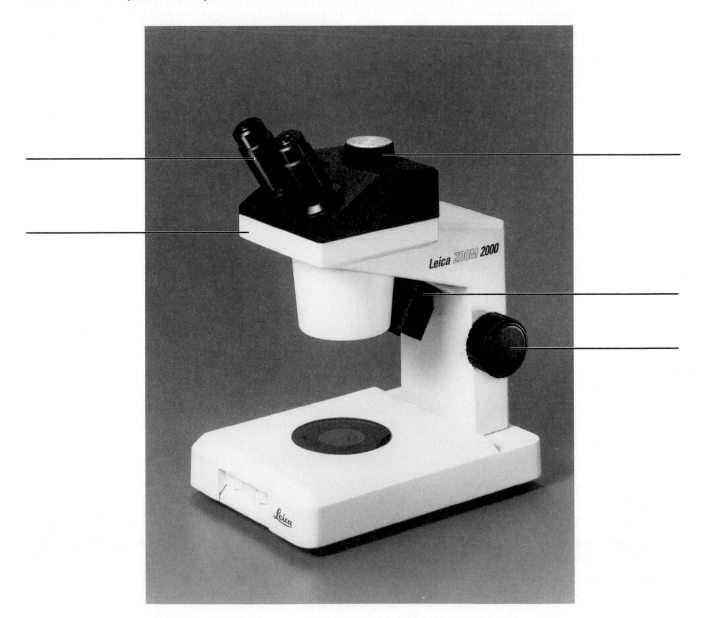

3. Use the focusing knob to bring the object into focus.

4. Does your microscope have an independent focusing eyepiece? _____ If so, use the focusing knob to bring the image in the fixed eyepiece into focus, while keeping the eye at the independent focusing eyepiece closed. Then adjust the independent focusing eyepiece so that the image is clear, while keeping the other eye closed. Is the image inverted? _____

5. Turn the magnification changing knob, and determine the type of mechanism on your microscope. A zoom mechanism allows continuous viewing while changing the magnification. A rotating lens mechanism blocks the view of the object as the new lenses are rotated. Be sure to click each lens firmly into place. If you do not, the field will be only partially visible. What type of mechanism is on your microscope? _____

6. Set the magnification changing knob on the lowest magnification. Sketch the object in the following circle as though this represents your entire field of view:

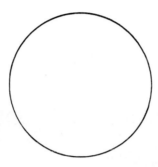

7. Rotate the magnification changing knob to the highest magnification. Draw another circle within the one provided to indicate the reduction of the field of view.

8. Experiment with various objects at various magnifications until you are comfortable with using the binocular dissecting microscope.

9. When you are finished, return your stereomicroscope and illuminator to their correct storage areas.

Conclusions: Microscopy

- Which two types of microscopes view the surface of an object? _____

- Which two types of microscopes view objects that have been sliced and treated to improve contrast? _____

- Of the microscopes just mentioned, which one resolves the greater amount of detail?

_____

2.3 Use of the Compound Light Microscope

As mentioned, the name **compound light microscope** indicates that it uses two sets of lenses and light to view an object. The two sets of lenses are the ocular lenses located near the eyes and the objective lenses located near the object. Illumination is from below, and the light passes through clear portions but does not pass through opaque portions. This microscope is used to examine small or thinly sliced sections of objects under higher magnification than would be possible with the stereomicroscope.

Identifying the Parts

Obtain a compound light microscope from the storage area, and place it securely on the table. *Identify the following parts on your microscope, and label them in Figure 2.4.*

1. **Eyepieces (ocular lenses):** What is the magnifying power of the ocular lenses on your microscope? _____

2. **Body tube:** Holds nosepiece at one end and eyepiece at the other end; conducts light rays.

3. **Arm:** Supports upper parts and provides carrying handle.

4. **Nosepiece:** Revolving device that holds objectives.

5. **Objectives** (objective lenses):

   a. **Scanning power objective:** This is the shortest of the objective lenses and is used to scan the whole slide. The magnification is stamped on the housing of the lens. It is a number

Figure 2.4 Compound light microscope.

Compound light microscope with binocular head and mechanical stage. Label this microscope with the help of the text.

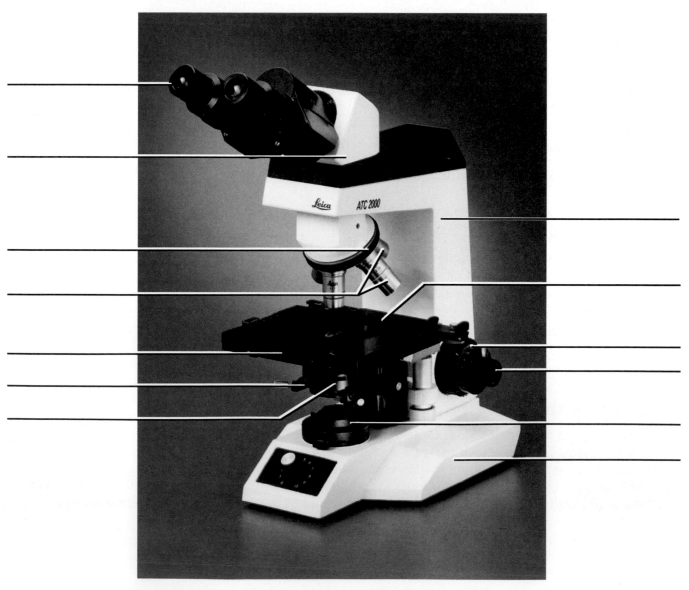

followed by an $\times$. What is the magnifying power of the scanning lens on your microscope? _____

   b. **Low-power objective:** This lens is longer than the scanning lens and is used to view objects in greater detail. What is the magnifying power of the low-power objective lens on your microscope? _____

   c. **High-power objective:** If your microscope has three objective lenses, this lens will be the longest. It is used to view an object in even greater detail. What is the magnifying power of the high-power objective lens on your microscope? _____

   d. **Oil immersion objective** (on microscopes with four objective lenses): Holds a 95$\times$ (to 100$\times$) lens and is used in conjunction with immersion oil to view objects with the greatest magnification. Does your microscope have an oil immersion objective? _____ If this lens is available, your instructor will discuss its use when the lens is needed.

6. **Coarse-adjustment knob:** Knob used to bring object into approximate focus; used only with low-power objective.
7. **Fine-adjustment knob:** Knob used to bring object into final focus.
8. **Condenser:** Lens system below the stage used to focus the beam of light on the object being viewed.
9. **Diaphragm** or **diaphragm control lever:** Controls amount of light used to view the object.
10. **Light source:** An attached lamp that directs a beam of light up through the object.
11. **Base:** The flat surface of the microscope that rests on the table.
12. **Stage:** Holds and supports microscope slides.
13. **Stage clips:** Hold slides in place on the stage.
14. **Mechanical stage** (optional): A movable stage that aids in the accurate positioning of the slide.

   Does your microscope have a mechanical stage? _____

15. **Mechanical stage control knobs** (optional): Two knobs usually located below the stage. One knob controls forward/reverse movement, and the other controls right/left movement.

Rules for Microscope Use

Observe the following rules for using a microscope:

1. The lowest power objective (scanning or low) should be in position both at the beginning and at the end of microscope use.
2. Use only lens paper for cleaning lenses.
3. Do not tilt the microscope as the eyepieces could fall out, or wet mounts could be ruined.
4. Keep the stage clean and dry to prevent rust and corrosion.
5. Do not remove parts of the microscope.
6. Keep the microscope dust-free by covering it after use.
7. Report any malfunctions.
8. Do not use coarse focus when viewing a specimen with the high-power objective.

Focusing the Microscope—Lowest Power

1. Turn the nosepiece so that the *lowest*-power lens is in straight alignment over the stage.
2. Always begin focusing with the *lowest*-power objective lens (4× [scanning] or 10× [low power]).
3. With the coarse-adjustment knob, lower the stage (or raise the objectives) until it stops.
4. Place a slide of the letter *e* on the stage, and stabilize it with the clips. (If your microscope has a mechanical stage, pinch the spring of the slide arms on the stage, and insert the slide.) Center the *e* as best you can on the stage or use the two control knobs located below the stage (if your microscope has a mechanical stage) to center the *e*.
5. Again, be sure that the lowest-power objective is in place. Then, as you look from the side, decrease the distance between the stage and the tip of the objective lens until the lens comes to an automatic stop or is no closer than 3 mm above the slide.
6. While looking into the eyepiece, rotate the diaphragm (or diaphragm control lever) to give the maximum amount of light.
7. Using the coarse-adjustment knob, slowly increase the distance between the stage and the objective lens until the object—in this case, the letter *e*—comes into view, or focus.
8. Once the object is seen, you may need to adjust the amount of light. To increase or decrease the contrast, slightly rotate the diaphragm.
9. Use the fine-adjustment knob to sharpen the focus if necessary.
10. Practice having both eyes open when looking through the eyepiece, as this greatly reduces eyestrain.

Inversion

Inversion refers to a microscopic image that is upside down and reversed.

Observation: Inversion

1. Draw the letter *e* as it appears on the slide (with the unaided eye, not looking through the eyepiece). _____

2. Draw the letter *e* as it appears when you look through the eyepiece. _____

3. What differences do you notice? _____

4. Move the slide to the right. Which way does the image appear to move? _____
   Explain. _____

Focusing the Microscope—Higher Powers

Compound light microscopes are **parfocal**—once the object is in focus with the lowest power, it should also be almost in focus with the higher power.

1. Bring the object into focus under the lowest power by following the instructions in the previous section.
2. Make sure that the letter *e* is centered in the field of the lowest objective.
3. Move to the next higher objective (low power [10×] or high power [40×]) by turning the nosepiece until you hear it click into place. Do not change the focus; parfocal microscope objectives will not hit normal slides when changing the focus if the lowest objective is initially in focus. (If you are on low power [10×], proceed to high power [40×] before going on to step 4.)
4. If any adjustment is needed, use only the *fine*-adjustment knob. (*Note:* Always use only the fine-adjustment knob and not the coarse-adjustment knob with high power.)
5. On a drawing of the letter *e*, draw a circle around the portion of the letter that you are now seeing with high-power magnification. _____
6. When you have finished your observations of this slide (or any slide), rotate the nosepiece until the lowest-power objective clicks into place, lower the stage, and then remove the slide.

Total Magnification

Total magnification is calculated by multiplying the magnification of the ocular lens (eyepiece) by the magnification of the objective lens.

Observation: Total Magnification

Calculate total magnification figures for your microscope, and record your findings in Table 2.2.

Table 2.2 Total Magnification			
Objective	**Ocular Lens**	**Objective Lens**	**Total Magnification**
Scanning power (if present)	×	×	×
Low power	×	×	×
High power	×	×	×

Field of View

A microscope's field of view is the circle visible through the lenses. The diameter of field is the length of the field from one edge to the other. Like any other measurement in science, the diameter of the field is measured using metric units. The metric system has tremendous advantages because all conversions are in units of ten. Table 2.3 provides the metric units for length. The basic unit of length is the meter (m), and Table 2.3 tells you how the other units of length relate to the meter. You would use a meter to measure your car or this classroom. Examine a meter stick on display. It is divided into centimeters (cm) and millimeters (mm). Look at 1 mm, and imagine dividing up that amount of space into 1,000 micrometers (μm). A meter is much too large a unit for microscopy. The units appropriate for microscopic use are highlighted in Table 2.3. They are:

1.0 millimeter (mm) = 1,000 micrometers (μm) = 1,000,000 nanometers (nm)

For light microscopy, the most useful unit of these is μm, and you will be asked to convert millimeters into micrometers by multiplying by 1,000 in the exercises that follow.

Table 2.3 Metric Unit Values						
Unit	**Symbol**	**Value (m)**	**Value (cm)**	**Value (mm)**	**Value (μm)**	**Value (nm)**
Meter	m	1.0 m	100 cm	1,000 mm	1,000,000 μm	1,000,000,000 nm
Centimeter	cm	0.01 m	1.0 cm	10 mm	10,000 μm	10,000,000 nm
Millimeter	mm	0.001 m	0.1 cm	1.0 mm	1,000 μm	1,000,000 nm
Micrometer	μm	0.000001 m	0.0001 cm	0.001 mm	1.0 μm	1,000 nm
Nanometer	nm	0.000000001 m	0.0000001 cm	0.000001 mm	0.001 μm	1.0 nm

Low Power (10×) Diameter of Field

1. Place a clear, plastic metric ruler across the stage so that the edge of the ruler is visible as a horizontal line along the diameter of the low-power (not scanning) field. Be sure that you are looking at the millimeter side of the ruler.

2. Estimate the number of millimeters, to tenths, that you see along the field: _____ mm. (*Hint:* Start with one of the millimeter markers at the edge of the field.) Convert the number to micrometers: _____ μm. This is the **low-power diameter of field (lpd)** for your microscope in micrometers.

High Power (40×) Diameter of Field

1. To compute the **high-power diameter of field (hpd),** substitute these data into the formula given:
   a. lpd = low-power diameter of field (in micrometers) = _____ μm
   b. lpm = low-power total magnification (from Table 2.2) = _____ ×
   c. hpm = high-power total magnification (from Table 2.2) = _____ ×

$$hpd = lpd \times \frac{lpm}{hpm}$$

$$hpd = (\quad μm) \times \frac{(\quad)}{(\quad)} = _____ μm$$

Conclusion: Total Magnification and Field of View

- What unit of metric measurement is most useful for light microscopy? _____ Use the micrometer row in Table 2.3 to convert 1 μm to millimeters. 1 μm = _____ mm Use the meter row to convert 1 m to μm. 1 m = _____ μm

- Does low power or high power have a larger field of view (allowing you to see more of the object)? _____

- Does low power or high power have a smaller field but magnifies to a greater extent?
_____

- To locate small objects on a slide, first find them under _____; then place them in the center of the field before rotating to _____.

2.4 Microscopic Observations

In this part of the laboratory session, you will have an opportunity to first examine a prepared slide and then two slides you will prepare yourself.

Human Blood Cells

Human blood contains red blood cells that transport oxygen about the body and white blood cells that fight infection. You will have no difficulty finding the red blood cells on the slide because they are numerous (see Fig. 2.2*a*).

Observation: Human Blood Cells

1. Obtain a prepared slide of human blood, and mount it on the microscope stage. Use the method you learned previously to bring the red blood cells into focus. Practice observing

different parts of the slide and switching to high power. Can you find a white blood cell? White blood cells are generally much larger than red blood cells.

2. Red blood cells are small, only 7–8 μm in diameter, and their small size can account for why there are so many in the blood. Blood is a liquid tissue, and this gives us an opportunity to tell you that a liter (L) is the basic unit of liquid measurement in science. The metric system is uniform. Table 2.3 can be used to describe the units of liquid measurement, as long as you appropriately change the terms.

Instead of these terms:	Use:
meter (m)	liter (L)
centimeter (cm)	centiliter(cL)
millimeter (mm)	milliliter (mL)
micrometer (μm)	microliter (μL)

There are generally 4–6 million red blood cells in a microliter (μL). To appreciate this quantity, observe these items on display: Liter graduate cylinder, so called because there are markings on the glass, most likely for mL. To measure a μL, you need to use a micropipette, which will be on display also. If so advised by your instructor, use the micropipette to measure a μL and disperse this quantity into a beaker.

3. As a part of a physical exam, doctors will sometimes order a differential blood cell count. This count is done microscopically, and the results indicate whether the patient has the normal number of each type blood cell in the blood.

Wet Mounts

When a specimen is prepared for observation, the object should always be viewed as a **wet mount**. A wet mount is prepared by placing a drop of liquid on a slide or, if the material is dry, by placing it directly on the slide and adding a drop of water or stain. The mount is then covered with a coverslip, as illustrated in Figure 2.5. Dry the bottom of your slide before placing it on the stage.

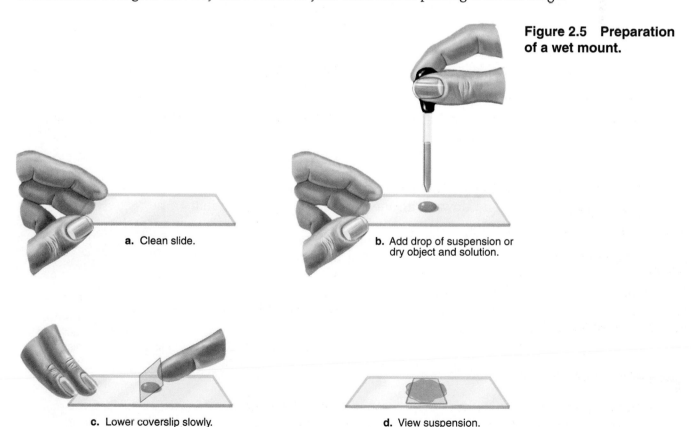

Figure 2.5 Preparation of a wet mount.

a. Clean slide.

b. Add drop of suspension or dry object and solution.

c. Lower coverslip slowly.

d. View suspension.

Human Epithelial Cells

Epithelial cells cover the body's surface and line its cavities.

1. Obtain a prepared slide, or make your own as follows:
    a. Obtain a prepackaged flat toothpick (or sanitize one with alcohol or alcohol swabs).
    b. Gently scrape the inside of your cheek with the toothpick, and place the scrapings on a clean, dry slide. Discard used toothpicks in the biohazard waste container provided.
    c. Add a drop of very weak *methylene blue* or *iodine solution,* and cover with a coverslip.
2. Observe under the microscope.
3. Locate the nucleus (the central, round body), the cytoplasm (interior), and the plasma membrane (outer cell boundary). *Label Figure 2.6.*
4. Your epithelial slides are biohazardous, so they must be disposed of as indicated by your instructor.

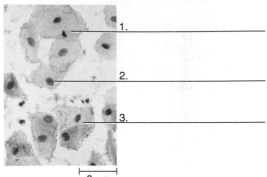

3 μm

Figure 2.6   Cheek epithelial cells.
Label the nucleus, the cytoplasm, and the plasma membrane.

Euglena

Examination of *Euglena* (a unicellular organism with a flagellum to facilitate movement) will test your ability to observe objects with the microscope, to use depth of field, and to control illumination to heighten contrast.

1. Make a wet mount of *Euglena* by using a drop of a *Euglena* culture and adding a drop of Protoslo® (methyl cellulose solution) onto a slide. The Protoslo slows the organism's swimming.
2. Mix thoroughly with a toothpick, and add a coverslip.
3. Scan the slide for *Euglena:* Start at the upper left-hand corner, and move the slide forward and back as you work across the slide from left to right. The *Euglena* may be at the edge of the slide because they show an aversion to Protoslo. Use Figure 2.7 to help identify *Euglena.*
4. Experiment by using scanning, low-power, and high-power objective lenses; by focusing up and down with the fine-adjustment knob; and by adjusting the light so that it is not too bright.
5. Compare your *Euglena* specimens with Figure 2.7. Can you distinguish between the anterior and posterior ends? (The anterior end has a red eye spot.) _____ Does *Euglena* move forward or backward?

_____

Does *Euglena* have internal structures?

_____

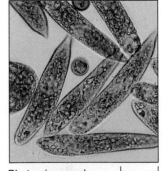

Photomicrograph   20 μm

Figure 2.7 Euglena.
Euglena is a unicellular, flagellated organism.

Microscopic Diagnoses

Microscopic examination of discharges, tissues, and the blood play an important part of a physical exam. We have already mentioned that your doctor may order a differential blood cell count when he or she believes it will help diagnose your illness. Or, he or she may microscopically examine a discharge if you may have a particular bacterial sexually transmitted disease (STD).

The Pap test, which women have during a routine gynecological exam, is a low-cost, easy microscopic examination of cells taken from the cervix located at the entrance to the womb. Pap tests look for abnormal cells in the lining of the cervix to determine if they are precancerous or cancerous. The more abnormal the appearance of the cells, the greater the concern (Fig. 2.8).

To do a Pap test, a physician merely takes a sample of cells from the cervix, which is then microscopically examined for signs of abnormality. Pap tests are credited with preventing over 90% of deaths from cervical cancer.

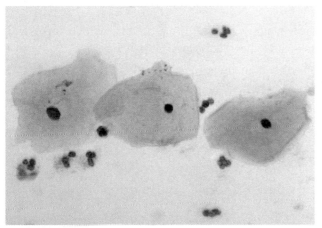

a. Normal Pap test slide

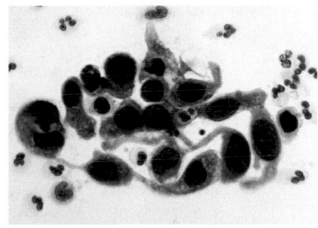

b. Abnormal Pap test slide

Figure 2.8 Pap test.
A Pap test is a microscopic examination of cells from the cervix at the entrance to the womb. **a.** The cells are normal and cancer is not present. **b.** The cells are abnormal and cancer is present.

_____ 1. 11 mm equals how many cm?

_____ 2. 950 mm equals how many m?

_____ 3. 2.1 liters equals how many ml?

_____ 4. Which type of microscope would you use to view a *Euglena* swimming in pond water?

_____ 5. What are the ocular lenses?

_____ 6. Which objective always should be in place when beginning to use the microscope and also when putting it away?

_____ 7. A total magnification of 100× requires the use of the 10× ocular lens with which objective?

_____ 8. Which part of a microscope controls the amount of light?

_____ 9. What word is used to indicate that if the object is in focus at low power it will also be in focus at high power?

_____ 10. If the thread layers are red, brown, green, from top to bottom, which layer will come into focus first if you are using the microscope properly?

_____ 11. What adjustment knob is used with high power?

_____ 12. If a *Euglena* is swimming to the left, which way should you move your slide to keep it in view?

_____ 13. What is the final item placed on a wet mount before viewing with a light microscope?

_____ 14. What type of object do you study with a stereomicroscope?

_____ 15. Why is a stereomicroscope also called a binocular dissecting microscope?

Thought Questions

16. A virus is 50 nm in size. Which type of microscope should be used to view it? Why?

17. What advantages does the metric system provide over English units of measure?

3

Chemical Composition of Cells

Learning Outcomes

3.1 Proteins
- Identify the test for the presence of protein, and tell how to-conduct the test.
- Relate the manner in which amino acids join to form a polypeptide (protein).
- Cite examples of typical structural and functional proteins, and describe their respective functions.

Question: When testing a food for protein, what test might you use and how would you do the test?

3.2 Carbohydrates
- Identify the test for the presence of starch and the test for the presence of sugars.
- Explain how monosaccharides, such as glucose, relate to disaccharides and polysaccharides.

Question: Why is it a good idea to avoid foods high in sugars?

3.3 Lipids
- Describe a simple test for the detection of fat.
- State the structural composition of a common lipid, such as fat, and explain the difference between a naturally occurring saturated/unsaturated fat and a trans fat.

Question: Why is butter solid at room temperature, while an oil is a liquid even when placed in the refrigerator?

3.4 Testing Foods and Unknowns
- Explain a procedure for testing the same food for all three components—proteins, carbohydrates, and fats.

Question: Explain why it would not be possible to use one test tube and test a food for proteins, carbohydrates, and lipids all at once.

Application for Daily Living: Nutrition Labels

Introduction

The U.S. Food and Drug Administration is charged with the task of assuring that our foods are safe and wholesome. Investigators and inspectors visit more than 15,000 facilities a year, overseeing that food products are not contaminated and are labeled truthfully. About 3,000 products a year are found to be unfit for consumers and are withdrawn from the marketplace, so the task of testing foods is a necessary one.

Food products contain three major components: proteins, carbohydrates, and lipids. Today you will learn how to test a

food for the presence of these components. You will also learn how proteins, carbohydrates, and lipids are constructed and, therefore, why they give a positive test with particular reagents. A positive test indicates that a component is present, and a negative test indicates that a component is not present.

Your laboratory instructor may advise you to set up parts of the lab procedure in advance to ensure your ability to complete the exercise. A clock icon will alert you to sections where prior setup may be warranted.

In this laboratory exercise heating the water bath in advance for the test for sugars (page 30) may save valuable time.

3.1 Proteins

Proteins have numerous functions in cells. Some are present for functional reasons, while others provide structural integrity.

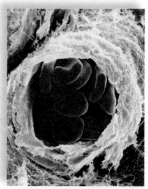

Antibodies are functional proteins that combine with disease-causing pathogens as part of the body's immune response.

Transport proteins combine with and move substances from place to place. Hemoglobin packed inside red blood cells transports oxygen throughout the body. Albumin is another protein in our blood that performs several important roles including fatty acid transport.

Hemoglobin is a protein

Regulatory proteins control cellular metabolism in some way. For example, the hormone insulin regulates the amount of glucose in blood so that cells have a ready supply of energy.

Enzymatic proteins speed chemical reactions. A reaction that could take days or weeks to complete can happen within an instant if the correct enzyme is present. Amylase is an enzyme that speeds the breakdown of starch in the mouth and small intestine.

Structural proteins include keratin, found in hair, and myosin, found in muscle.

Amino Acids and Peptides

Hair is a protein

Proteins are long chains of **amino acids** joined together. About 20 different common amino acids are found in cells. All amino acids have an acidic group (—COOH) and an amino group (H_2N—), each linked to a central carbon by a separate covalent bond. Amino acids differ by the **R group** (rest of molecule) attached to the central carbon atom. The R groups have varying compositions, sizes, shapes, and chemical activities.

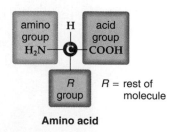

Amino acid

A chain of two or more amino acids is called a **peptide,** and the bond between the two amino acids is called a **peptide bond.** A **polypeptide** is a long chain of amino acids. A protein can be comprised of one or more polypeptides.

When you digest your food, the **protein** component is broken down to amino acids, and then your body uses these amino acids to synthesize peptides and your proteins.

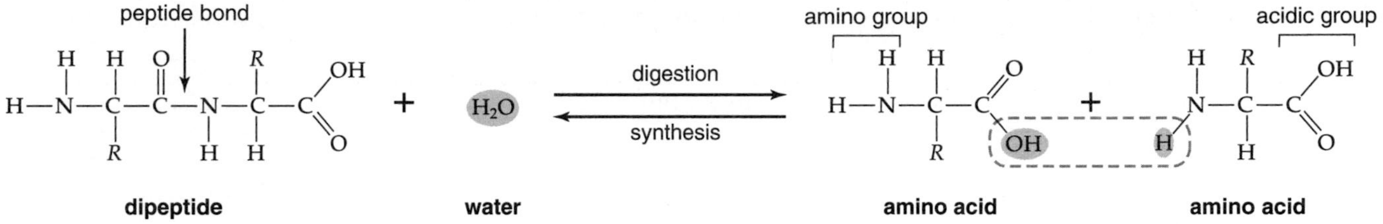

Figure 3.1 Peptide bond.
Peptide bond formation between amino acids creates a dipeptide. In a polypeptide, many amino acids are held together by multiple peptide bonds. During a digestion reaction, water is added, and the peptide bond is broken. The synthesis reaction involves the removal of one water molecule.

Test for Proteins

Biuret reagent (blue color) contains a strong solution of sodium or potassium hydroxide (NaOH or KOH) and a small amount of dilute copper sulfate ($CuSO_4$) solution. The reagent changes color in the presence of proteins or peptides because the peptide bonds of the protein or peptide chemically combine with the copper ions in Biuret reagent.

> ⚠ **Biuret reagent** Biuret reagent is highly corrosive. Exercise care in using this chemical. If any should spill on your skin, wash the area with mild soap and water. Follow your instructor's directions for its disposal.

In this reaction, the range of positive results described in Table 3.1 occurs when copper ions react with different amino groups, deforming the adjacent polypeptide chains and causing a resultant change in color.

Table 3.1 Positive Test for Protein and Peptides		
	Protein	**Peptides**
Biuret reagent (blue)	Purple	Pinkish-purple

If a positive result occurs and protein is present, what color will appear after using the Biuret test? _____

If a negative result occurs and protein is not present, what color will remain after using the Biuret test? _____

Chemical Composition of Cells   Laboratory 3   **25**

In this procedure you will be running a test for protein, much as an employee of the Food and Drug Administration would do. Egg white is composed of the protein called **albumin.** Therefore, albumin can be present in a number of different foods.

Before running the tests, answer these questions.

1. Choose which of these substances would be in the test tube if you detected protein: albumin, starch, water, Biuret reagent. _____

2. Which substances listed would you include in a control test tube? _____

    Why (see page 5)? _____

3. Why might you run another test using starch in the test tube instead of the food expected to

    contain protein? _____

    If the results were negative, would it suggest that Biuret reagent is specific for

    protein? _____

The Procedure

With a millimeter ruler and a wax pencil, label and mark three clean test tubes at the 1 cm level. After filling a tube, cover it with Parafilm, and swirl well to mix. (Do not turn upside down.) The reaction is almost immediate.

Tube 1   1. Fill to the mark with *protein (albumin) solution* and add about 5 drops of *Biuret reagent.*
            2. Record the final color in Table 3.2.
*Tube 2   1. Fill to the mark with *distilled water* and add about 5 drops of *Biuret reagent.*
            2. Record the final color in Table 3.2.
Tube 3   1. Fill to the mark with *starch solution* and add about 5 drops of *Biuret reagent.*
            2. Record the final color in Table 3.2.

If your results are not as expected, offer an explanation. _____
Then inform your instructor, who will advise you how to proceed.

Table 3.2 Biuret Test

Tube	Contents	Final Color	Conclusions
1.	Protein		
2.	Distilled water		
3.	Starch		

Conclusions: Test for Proteins

- From your test results, did you conclude that protein is present in any of the three test solutions? Enter your conclusions in Table 3.2. Explain your data and conclusions.

    _____

- Based on your results, is Biuret reagent a valid test for protein? _____

    Explain._____

*To test an unknown for a protein, use this procedure. Instead of water, use the unknown. If protein is present, a pinkish-purple color appears.

3.2 Carbohydrates

Carbohydrates include starch, glycogen, and sugars. Starch and sugar are major components of baked goods, such as breads, cakes, and cookies. Flour contains starch, but starch does not taste sweet. The disaccharide, called **sucrose,** which does taste sweet, is often added to baked goods. Although we enjoy the sweet taste of sucrose, research has shown it is detrimental to our health. Researchers at the Harvard School of Public Health found that subjects who consumed sugar-sweetened sodas more than once per day for eight years exhibited an 80% increased risk of the illness diabetes mellitus. Also, they gained 17 pounds on the average, showing the link between sugar consumption and obesity. Obese individuals tend to suffer from cardiovascular disease more than those of normal weight.

Starch and Glycogen

When you digest your food, the starch component from plants is broken down to maltose and then maltose is digested to **glucose,** the sugar found in your blood.

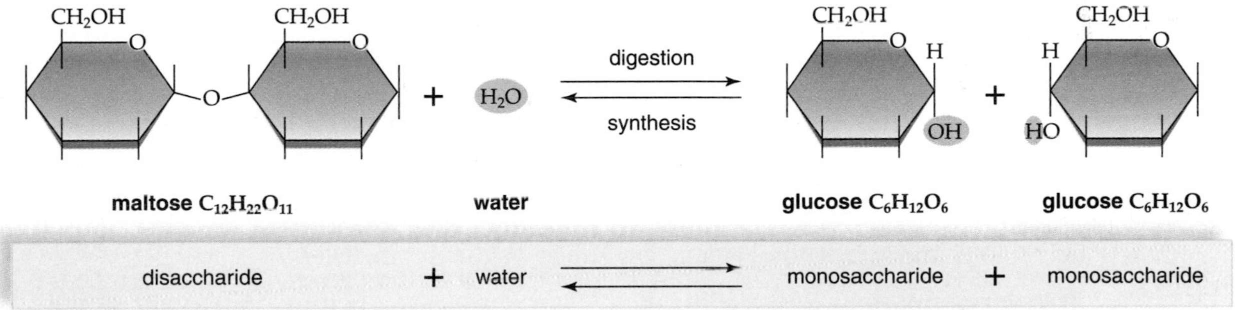

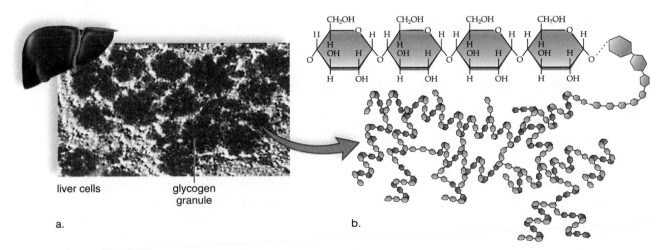

maltose $C_{12}H_{22}O_{11}$ **water**   **glucose $C_6H_{12}O_6$**   **glucose $C_6H_{12}O_6$**

disaccharide + water ⇄ monosaccharide + monosaccharide

Figure 3.2 Maltose, a disaccharide.
During a digestion reaction, the components of water are added, and the bond is broken. During a synthesis reaction, a bond forms between the two glucose molecules, the components of water are removed, and maltose results.

Your body stores excess glucose as glycogen, often called animal starch, in the liver. Both glycogen and starch are long chains of glucose molecules; therefore, they are **polysaccharides** (Fig. 3.2).

liver cells   glycogen granule

a.   b.

Figure 3.3 Glycogen.
Glycogen is a polysaccharide composed of many glucose units. **a.** Photomicrograph of glycogen granules in liver cells. **b.** Structure of glycogen. Glycogen is a very branched molecule.

Test for Starch

The test for starch is to add an iodine solution. If the substance contains starch, the color shifts from brown to a deep purple to black, as noted in Table 3.3. This positive result is explained thus: Iodine molecules lodge in the coiled structure of starch. This causes a change in the way that iodine molecules are able to reflect light and the color we observe.

Table 3.3 Positive Test for Starch	
	Starch
Iodine solution (brown)	Black

Experimental Procedure: Test for Starch

In this procedure, you will be running a test for starch much as an employee of the Food and Drug Administration would do. Starch, as you know, is present in a number of different baked goods.
   Before running the tests, answer these questions.

1. Choose which of these substances would be in a test tube if you detected starch: starch, albumin, water, iodine. _____

2. Which substances listed would you include in a control test tube? _____
    Why? _____

3. Why might you run another test using albumin in the test tube instead of the food expected to contain starch? _____

The Procedure

With a wax pencil, label and mark four clean test tubes at the 1 cm level.

Tube 1   **1.** It is very important to shake the *starch suspension* well before taking your sample. After shaking, fill this tube to the mark with the 1% starch suspension. Add five drops of *iodine solution.*
           2. Note the final color change, and record your results in Table 3.4.

*Tube 2 **1.** Fill to the mark with *water,* and add five drops of *iodine solution.*
           2. Note the final color change, and record your results in Table 3.4.

Tube 3   **1.** Add a few drops of *potato juice* to the test tube. (Obtain the juice by adding water and crushing a small piece of potato with a mortar and pestle. Clean mortar and pestle after using.) Add five drops of *iodine solution.*
           2. Note the final color change, and record your results in Table 3.4.

Tube 4   **1.** Fill to the mark with *albumin solution,* and add five drops of *iodine solution.*
           2. Note the final color change, and record your results in Table 3.4.

If your results are not as expected, offer an explanation. _____
Then inform your instructor, who will advise you how to proceed.

*To test an unknown for starch, use this procedure. Instead of water, use the unknown. If starch is present, a blue-black color appears.

Table 3.4 Iodine (IKI) Tests for Starch

Tube	Contents	Color	Conclusions
1	Starch suspension		
2	Water		
3	Potato juice		
4	Albumin solution		

Conclusions: Test for Starch

- From your test results, draw conclusions about whether starch is present in each tube. Write these conclusions in Table 3.4. Explain your data and conclusions.

_____

- Based on your results, is iodine a valid test for starch? _____

  Explain. _____

Experimental Procedure: Microscopic Study of Potato

1. With a sharp razor blade, carefully slice a very thin piece of potato. Place it on a microscope slide, add a drop of *water* and a coverslip, and observe under low power with your compound light-microscope. Compare your slide with the photomicrograph of starch granules (Fig. 3.4). Find the cell wall (large, geometric compartments) and the starch grains (numerous clear, oval-shaped objects).
2. Without removing the coverslip, place two drops of *iodine solution* onto the microscope slide so that the iodine touches the coverslip. Draw the iodine under the coverslip by placing a small piece of paper towel in contact with the water on the **opposite** side of the coverslip.
3. Microscopically examine the potato again on the side closest to where the iodine solution was applied.

   What is the color of the small oval bodies? _____

   What is the chemical composition of these oval bodies? _____

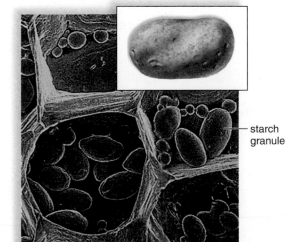

starch granule

250 μm

Figure 3.4 Starch.
Photomicrograph of starch granules in potato cells.

Test for Sugars

Monosaccharides and some disaccharides will react with **Benedict's reagent** after being heated in a boiling water bath. The color change can range from green to red, and increasing concentrations of sugar will give a continuum of colored products (Table 3.5). This experiment tests for the presence (or absence) of varying amounts of sugars in a variety of materials and chemicals.

Table 3.5 Benedict's Reagent (Some Typical Reactions)

Chemical	Chemical Category	Benedict's Reagent (After Heating)
Water	Inorganic	Blue (no change)
Glucose	Monosaccharide (carbohydrate)	Varies with concentration: very low—green low—yellow moderate—yellow-orange high—orange very high—orange-red
Maltose	Disaccharide (carbohydrate)	Varies with concentration—see "Glucose"
Starch	Polysaccharide (carbohydrate)	Blue (no change)

Experimental Procedure: Test for Sugars

Heating the water bath in advance may maximize your efficient use of time.
With a wax pencil, label and mark four clean test tubes at the 1 cm level. Save your tubes for comparison with Section 3.4.

Tube 1 1. Fill to the mark with *glucose solution*, and then add about 5 drops of *Benedict's reagent*.
        2. Heat in a boiling water bath for 5 to 10 minutes, note any color change, and record in Table 3.6.

*Tube 2 1. Fill to the mark with *water*, and then add about 5 drops of *Benedict's reagent*.
         2. Heat in a boiling water bath for 5 to 10 minutes, note any color change, and record in Table 3.6.

Tube 3 1. Place a few drops of *onion juice* in the test tube. (Obtain the juice by adding water and crushing a small piece of onion with a mortar and pestle. Clean mortar and pestle after using.)
        2. Fill to the mark with *water*, and then add about 5 drops of *Benedict's reagent*.
        3. Heat in a boiling water bath for 5 to 10 minutes, note any color change, and record in Table 3.6.

Tube 4 1. Fill to the mark with *starch suspension*, and then add about 5 drops of *Benedict's reagent*.
        2. Heat in a boiling water bath for 5 to 10 minutes, note any color change, and record in Table 3.6.

> ⚠ **Benedict's reagent** Benedict's reagent is highly corrosive. Exercise care in using this chemical. If any should spill on your skin, wash the area with mild soap and water. Follow your instructor's directions for disposal of this chemical..

*To test an unknown for sugars, use this procedure. Instead of water, use the unknown. If sugar is present, a green to orange-red color appears.

Table 3.6 Benedict's Reagent Test

Tube	Contents	Color (After Heating)	Conclusions
1	Glucose solution		
2	Water		
3	Onion juice		
4	Starch suspension		

Conclusions: Test for Sugar

- From your test results, conclude whether sugar is present and enter your conclusions in Table 3.6. Explain your data and conclusions.

_____

_____

- Based on your results, is Benedict's reagent a valid test for sugar? _____

  Explain. _____

  _____

3.3 Lipids

A number of different molecules, including fats and oils, are grouped together as **lipids** because they are insoluble in water. Fats and oils differ by their fatty acid content. A **fatty acid** consists of a long hydrocarbon chain and ends in an acid group (Fig. 3.5). The hydrocarbon chain can have bonds that differ like this:

Unsaturated	Saturated	Trans fats
(oils)	(butter)	(hydrogenated oils)

An unsaturated fatty acid has no double bonds between the carbon atoms, while an unsaturated fatty acid does have double bonds between certain of the carbon atoms. Saturated fatty acids are found in a solid fat, such as butter, while unsaturated fatty acids are found in liquid oils. They are liquid because the double bond creates a kink that prevents close packing of hydrocarbon chains. Saturated fats, but not unsaturated oils, encourage the development of plaque in the arteries of the body, leading to cardiovascular disease. Even more harmful than naturally occurring saturated fats are the so-called trans fats, found in vegetable oils that have been partially hydrogenated to make them more solid. Partial hydrogenation does not saturate all bonds. Instead, some hydrogen atoms end up on different sides of the chain. Processed and fast foods are apt to contain trans fats.

Fats and Oils

When you digest your food, fats and oils are broken down to one molecule of glycerol and three fatty acids (Fig. 3.5). Later, your body rejoins these molecules to form fat, which is a long-term energy source.

Figure 3.5   A fat.
During a digestion reaction, water is added, and the bonds are broken. A fat molecule forms when glycerol joins with three fatty acids as three water molecules are removed during a synthesis reaction.

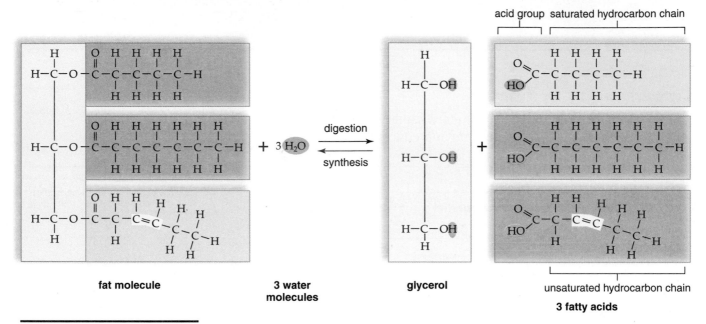

fat molecule   3 water molecules   glycerol   3 fatty acids

Test for Fats and Oils

Fats and oils do not evaporate from brown paper; instead, they leave an oily spot.

Experimental Procedure: Test for Fats and Oils

*1. Place a small drop of *water* on a square of brown paper. Describe the immediate effect. _____

2. Place a small drop of *vegetable oil* on a square of brown paper. Describe the immediate effect.

3. Wait at least 15 minutes for the paper to dry. Evaluate which substance penetrates the paper and which is subject to evaporation. Record your observations in Table 3.7.

Table 3.7   Test for Fats and Oils

Sample	Observations	Conclusions
Water spot		
Oil spot		

*To test an unknown for fats and oils, use this procedure. Instead of water, use the unknown. If fats and oils are present, an oily spot appears.

Conclusions: Test for Fats and Oils

- Based on your results, add your conclusions to Table 3.7.
- Is this an adequate test for fats and oils? _____ Why or why not? _____

_____

Adipose Tissue

Adipose tissue stores fat droplets. Fat is a long-term energy source for humans. Also, adipose tissue is found beneath the skin, where it helps insulate and keep the body warm. It also forms a protective cushion around various internal organs.

Observation: Adipose Tissue

1. Obtain a slide of adipose tissue, and view it under the microscope at high power. Refer to Figure 3.6 for help in identifying the structures.
2. Notice how the fat droplets push the cytoplasm to the edges of the cells.

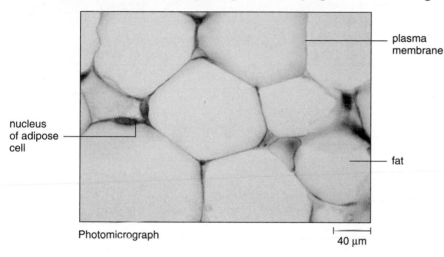

nucleus of adipose cell

plasma membrane

fat

Photomicrograph

40 μm

Figure 3.6   Adipose tissue.
The cells are so full of fat that the nucleus is pushed to one side.

3.4 Testing Foods and Unknowns

It is common for us to associate the term *organic* with the foods we eat. While we may recognize foods as being organic, often we are not aware of what specific types of compounds are found in what we eat. In the following Experimental Procedure, you will use the same tests you used previously to determine the composition of everyday materials (unknowns).

Figure 3.7   Carbohydrate foods.

Figure 3.8   Lipid foods.

Figure 3.9   Protein foods.

Experimental Procedure: Testing Foods and Unknowns

Your instructor will provide you with several everyday foods including unknowns and your task is to:

1. Develop instructions for a procedure that will allow you to test the foods for proteins (page 25), carbohydrates (pages 28 and 30), and lipids (page 32) using the tests from this laboratory manual.

_____

_____

_____

_____

2. Have your instructor okay your procedure, and then conduct the necessary tests.
3. Record your results as positive or negative in Table 3.8.

Table 3.8 Testing Foods and Unknowns				
Sample Name	Sugar (Benedict's)	Starch (Iodine)	Protein (Biuret)	Lipid (Brown Paper)
Unknown A				
Unknown B				

Conclusions: Testing Foods and Unknowns

- Did any food test positive for only one of the organic compounds? _____ Explain. _____
- What types of foods would you expect to test positive for more than one of the organic compounds studied in this laboratory? _____
- What type of carbohydrate might be found in an unknown food source that would test positive for the iodine test but negative for the Benedict's test? _____

_____

Nutrition Labels

For good health, the diet should be balanced and should not contain an overabundance of either protein, sugars, or fat. Everyone should become familiar with reading nutrition labels and a portion of one is shown in Figure 3.10.

It is very important to note the serving size and servings per container. For comparison purposes, you need to compare the same serving sizes. The % daily values are based on an intake of 2,000 calories per day. A Calorie is an indication of the amount of energy provided, and the number of Calories taken in should match the number required per day, unless you wish to gain weight.

Most people are extremely interested in the amount of fat provided by a food. One serving of this food provides 18% of the total fat-required for the day. If you find this excessive, you could look for another macaroni and cheese that supplies less total fat and less saturated fat. If you decide that you prefer this product, you might wish to balance it with a food that contains very little fat and one that provides a carbohydrate that contains fiber. This food contains no fiber. Complex carbohydrates containing fiber, such as those found in whole grains, are recommended and not those that contain simply starch.

Making wise decisions about the foods we buy can lead to a longer and more healthy life.

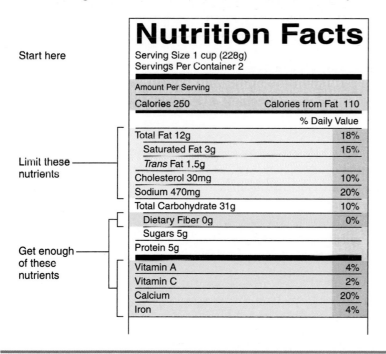

Figure 3.10   Sample nutrition label for macaroni and cheese.
As of January 2006, foods must include the quantity of trans fat. There is no % daily value for trans fats, and they should be avoided. See page 31.

_____ 1. What type of bond joins amino acids to make peptides?

_____ 2. What type of protein speeds chemical reactions?

_____ 3. What group is different between types of amino acids?

_____ 4. If iodine solution turns blue-black, what substance is present?

_____ 5. If Benedict's reagent turns red, what substance is present?

_____ 6. When you digest food, starch is broken down to what molecule?

_____ 7. Is starch a monosaccharide or a polysaccharide?

_____ 8. What is the function of fat in humans?

_____ 9. What molecules are released when fat undergoes digestion?

_____ 10. What type of organic molecule is not soluble in water?

_____ 11. Name two organic molecules that are acids?

_____ 12. If Biuret reagent turns purple, what substance is present?

_____ 13. A student adds iodine solution to egg white and waits for a color change. How long will the student have to wait?

_____ 14. To test whether a sample contains glucose, what test should be done?

Thought Questions

15. Why is it necessary to shake a bottle of salad dressing before adding it to a salad?

16. An unknown sample is tested with both Biuret reagent and Benedict's reagent. Both tests result in a blue color. What has been learned? Why are these called negative results?

17. Starch and water are mixed together as ingredients for making gravy. Why doesn't starch react with water to produce monosaccharides?

Human Biology Website

The companion website for _Human Biology_ provides a wealth of information organized and integrated by chapter. You will find practice tests, animations, and much more that will complement your learning and understanding of general biology.

www.mhhe.com/maderhuman11

McGraw-Hill Access Science Website

An online encyclopedia of science and technology that provides information, including videos, that can enhance the laboratory experience.

www.accessscience.com

4

Cell Structure and Function

Learning Outcomes

4.1 Anatomy of a Human Cell
- Using a model or drawing, identify the parts of a human cell and state a function for each part.

Question: Why is it beneficial for different parts of the cell to have specific functions?

4.2 Diffusion of Solutes
- Describe the process of diffusion as a physical phenomenon independent of the plasma membrane.
- Describe which solutes can cross the plasma membrane by diffusion and which cannot cross the plasma membrane by diffusion.

Question: Why is it beneficial for a cell when needed substances can cross the plasma membrane by diffusion?

4.3 Osmosis: Diffusion of Water Across the Plasma Membrane
- Predict the effect that solutions of different tonicities have on red blood cells.

Question: Why is 0.9% the usual tonicity of intravenous solutions?

4.4 Enzyme Activity
- Explain why enzymes have the ability to speed chemical reactions in cells.
- List some factors that can affect the speed of enzymatic reactions.

Question: Why is a warm body temperature advantageous to metabolism?

Application for Daily Living: Inborn Errors of Metabolism and Organelles

Introduction

We are accustomed to observing the outward appearance of human beings and rarely have an opportunity to become aware that humans are composed of cells, small entities assisted in their metabolic endeavors by their structure. We stay alive because cells are constantly carrying on enzymatic reactions within and outside of their organelles. In today's laboratory, we review the structure and function of organelles, subcompartments of a cell, before observing how its outer boundary, the plasma membrane, serves as a selective barrier. Finally, we will marvel at the rapidity of an enzymatic reaction, even at room temperature.

⏰ Planning Ahead

The tonicity experiment using potato strips (page 44) requires that the experiment run for one hour. Your instructor may advise you to set this experiment up in advance so that you will have adequate time to complete the experiment in the time allotted for this laboratory.

Figure 4.1 Human (animal) cell.

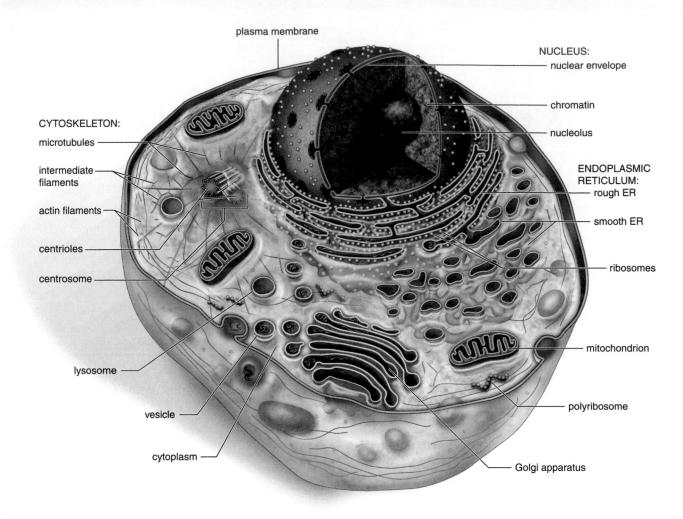

4.1 Anatomy of a Human Cell

Figure 4.1 shows that an animal cell is partitioned into a number of compartments. Just like a house works more efficiently when each room has a specialized function, so does a cell with different compartments for varied functions. With the help of Table 4.1 identify the following structures.

Composition and Function	Structure
9 + 2 pattern of microtubules; responsible for the movement of the cell	_____
Stack of membranous saccules; functions in processing, packaging, and distribution of molecules	_____
Membranous sacs; storage and transport of substances	_____
Have a double membrane; responsible for cellular respiration	_____
Composed of protein and RNA in two subunits; responsible for protein synthesis	_____
Phospholipid bilayer; selectively allows molecules into and out of a cell	_____

Table 4.1 Human (Animal) Cell

Name	Composition	Function
Plasma membrane	Phospholipid bilayer with embedded proteins	Selective passage of molecules into and out of cell
Nucleus	Nuclear envelope surrounding nucleoplasm, chromatin, and nucleolus	Storage of genetic information
Nucleolus	Concentrated area of chromatin, RNA, and proteins	Ribosomal formation
Ribosome	Protein and RNA in two subunits	Protein synthesis
Endoplasmic reticulum (ER)	Membranous saccules and canals	Synthesis and/or modification of proteins and other substances
Rough ER	Studded with ribosomes	Protein synthesis
Smooth ER	Having no ribosomes	Various; lipid synthesis in some cells
Golgi apparatus	Stack of membranous saccules	Processing, packaging, and distribution of molecules
Vesicle	Membranous sacs	Storage and transport of substances
Lysosome	Membranous vesicle containing digestive enzymes	Intracellular digestion
Mitochondrion	Inner membrane (cristae) within outer membrane	Cellular respiration
Cytoskeleton	Microtubules, intermediate filaments, and actin filaments	Shape of cell and movement of its parts
Cilia and flagella	9+2 pattern of microtubules	Movement of cell
Centrosome	Dense area that contains centrioles	Microtubule organizing center
Centriole	9 + 0 pattern of microtubules	Formation of basal bodies, which give rise to cilia and flagella

Concentrated area of chromatin, RNA, and proteins; involved in ribosomal formation _____

Composed of microtubules in a 9 + 0 pattern; forms basal bodies, which give rise to cilia and flagella _____

Central body where genetic information is stored _____

Membranous vesicle containing digestive enzymes _____

Composed of microtubules, actin filaments, and intermediate filaments; responsible for the shape of the cell and movement of its parts _____

Membranous saccules and canals having no ribosomes; has various functions _____

4.2 Diffusion of Solutes

Diffusion is the random movement of molecules from the area of higher concentration to the area of lower concentration until they are equally distributed. A **solution** contains both solutes (solid particles) and solvent (a liquid, most often water).

Environmental Factors and Diffusion of Solutes

If you spray a deodorant in one corner of the room, it will soon spread to fill the room because diffusion has occurred. (Notice, therefore, that diffusion can occur independently of a plasma membrane.) Environmental factors such as temperature and the resistance of the medium can affect the speed of diffusion. Air offers little resistance to random motion of molecules, followed by a liquid, and then by any type of a solid.

Observation: Environmental Factors and Diffusion

You will calculate the speed of diffusion (1) through a semisolid gel and (2) through a liquid. Hypothesize whether you expect diffusion to occur faster through a semisolid or through a liquid, and give a reason for your hypothesis. _____

_____

Diffusion Through a Semisolid

1. Observe a petri dish containing 1.5% gelatin (or agar) to which a crystal of potassium permanganate ($KMnO_4$) was added previously (time zero) in the center depression.
2. Record *time zero* and the *final time* (now) in Table 4.2. Calculate the length of time in hours and minutes; then convert the entire time to hours. _____ hrs
3. Using a ruler placed over the petri dish, measure (in mm) the movement of color from the center of the depression outward in one direction. _____ mm
4. Calculate the speed of diffusion. _____ mm/hr. (Divide the number of millimeters by the number of hours.)
5. Record all data in Table 4.2.

Diffusion Through a Liquid

1. Add water to a glass petri dish.
2. Place the petri dish over a thin, flat ruler.
3. With tweezers, add a crystal of potassium permanganate ($KMnO_4$) directly over a millimeter measurement line. Note the *time zero* in Table 4.2.
4. After 10 minutes, note the distance the color has moved (Fig. 4.2). Record the *final time, length of time,* and *distance moved* in Table 4.2.
5. Multiply the length of time and the distance moved by 6 to calculate the *speed of diffusion.* _____ mm/hr. Record in Table 4.2.

Figure 4.2 Process of diffusion.
Diffusion is apparent when dye molecules have equally dispersed.

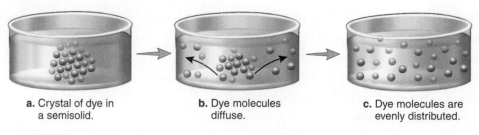

a. Crystal of dye in a semisolid.

b. Dye molecules diffuse.

c. Dye molecules are evenly distributed.

Table 4.2 Speed of Diffusion

Medium	Time Zero	Final Time	Length of Time (hrs)	Distance Moved (mm)	Speed of Diffusion (mm/hr)
Semisolid					
Liquid					

Conclusions: Diffusion

- Why did the dye molecules move rather than stay where they were originally? _____
- In which experiment was diffusion the fastest? _____
- What accounts for the difference in speed? _____

The Plasma Membrane and Diffusion of Solutes

The plasma membrane regulates the passage of molecules into and out of cells. It is said to be **selectively permeable,** because only small, noncharged molecules can diffuse across the plasma membrane without assistance (Fig. 4.3a). Carriers, proteins embedded in plasma membrane, can assist the passage of molecules across a membrane. Each carrier is specific to a particular molecule. During facilitated transport, a carrier assists a molecule diffusing across the membrane (Fig. 4.3b). During active transport, a carrier assists a molecule moving the opposite to diffusion: from lower concentration outside the cell to higher concentration inside the cell and energy is required (Fig. 4.3c). In other words, energy is not required when a molecule is diffusing down its concentration gradient and, otherwise, energy is required.

Figure 4.3 Passage of molecules across a plasma membrane.
a. During diffusion, molecules move from the higher to the lower concentration. **b.** During facilitated transport, carrier proteins transport molecules from the higher to the lower concentration. **c.** During active transport, molecules move from the lower to the higher concentration; a protein carrier and energy are required.

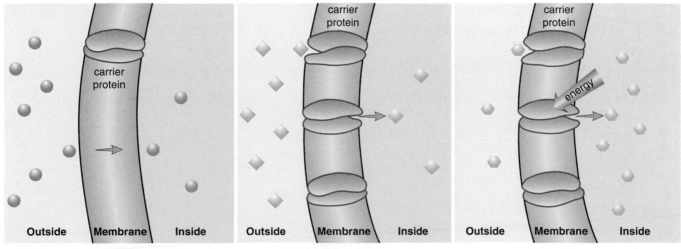

a. Diffusion

b. Facilitated transport

c. Active transport

In this experiment, an artificial membrane is used to simulate the plasma membrane; the artificial membrane is also semipermeable. Only certain molecules can cross the membrane. The artificial membrane contains no carriers to assist the movement of molecules across the membrane.

Notice in Figure 4.4 that glucose (small molecule) and starch (large molecule) will be inside the membranous bag and iodine (small molecule) will be outside the bag. Hypothesize which molecules will cross the membrane and in which direction they will move. (For direction, use the terminology "to inside the bag" or "to outside the bag.") _____

_____

Figure 4.4 Diffusion experiment.

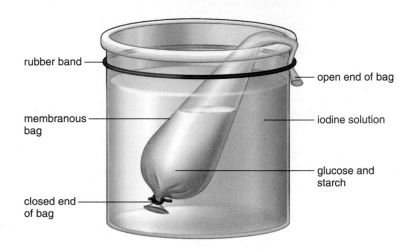

rubber band

open end of bag

membranous bag

iodine solution

glucose and starch

closed end of bag

Diffusion Through a Selectively Permeable Membrane

The artificial membrane used in the following experiment simulates the plasma membrane. Small molecules can freely diffuse across the plasma membrane, but large substances cannot cross the membrane.

At the start of this procedure:

1. Cut a piece of membranous tubing approximately 12 cm long. Soak the tubing in water until it is soft and pliable.
2. Close one end of the tubing with a rubber band or string.
3. Add four full droppers of *glucose solution* to the bag.
4. Add four full droppers of *starch solution* to the bag.
5. Hold the open end while you mix the contents of the bag. Rinse off the outside of the bag with water.
6. Record the color of the bag contents in Table 4.3.
7. Fill a beaker 2/3 full with *water*.
8. Add droppers of *iodine solution* (*IKI*) to the water in the beaker until an amber (tealike) color is apparent.
9. Record the color of the solution in the beaker in Table 4.3.
10. Place the bag in the beaker with the open end hanging over the edge. Secure the open end of the bag to the beaker with a rubber band as shown (Fig. 4.4). Make sure the contents do not spill into the beaker.

At the end of this procedure (approximately 5 minutes):

11. You will note a color change. Record the color of the bag contents and the beaker contents in Table 4.3.
12. Mark off a test tube at 1 cm and 3 cm.
13. Remove the dialysis bag from the beaker and dispose of it in the manner directed by your instructor.
14. Fill the test tube to the first mark with the beaker contents. Add *Benedict's reagent* to the 3 cm mark. Heat in a boiling water bath for 5–10 minutes, observe any color change, and record your results as positive or negative in Table 4.3. (Refer to Table 3.4.)

> ⚠ **Benedict's reagent** Benedict's reagent is highly corrosive. Exercise care in using this chemical. If any should spill on your skin, wash the area with mild soap and water. Follow your instructor's directions for disposal of this chemical.

Table 4.3   Diffusion Through a Membrane

		At Start of Experiment	At End of Experiment		
	Contents	Color	Color	Benedict's Test (+) or (−)	Conclusion
Bag	Glucose Starch				
Beaker	Water Iodine				

Conclusions: Plasma Membrane and Diffusion of Solutes

- Based on the color change noted in the bag, conclude what solute diffused across the membrane from the beaker to the bag, and record your conclusion in Table 4.3.
- From the results of the Benedict's test on the beaker contents, conclude what solute diffused across the membrane from the bag to the beaker, and record your conclusion in Table 4.3.
- Which solute did not diffuse across the membrane from the bag to the beaker? _____

    Explain. _____

4.3 Osmosis: Diffusion of Water Across the Plasma Membrane

Osmosis is the diffusion of water across a selectively permeable membrane. Just like any other molecule, water follows its concentration gradient and moves from a region of higher concentration to a region of lower concentration.

Tonicity is the relative concentration of solute (particles) and solvent (water) outside the cell compared to inside the cell.[1] An **isotonic solution** has the same concentration of solute (and therefore of water) as the cell. When cells are placed in an isotonic solution, there is no net movement of water. A **hypertonic solution** has a higher solute (therefore, lower water) concentration than the cell. When cells are placed in a hypertonic solution, water moves out of the cell into the solution. A **hypotonic solution** has a lower solute (therefore, higher water) concentration than the cell. When cells are placed in a hypotonic solution, water moves from the solution into the cell.

The next two Experimental Procedures explore tonicity using potato strips and red blood cells.

---

[1]Percent solutions are grams of solute per 100 ml of solvent. Therefore, a 10% solution is 10 g of sugar with water added to make up 100 ml of solution.

This procedure runs for one hour. Prior setup can maximize your time efficiency.

1. Cut two strips of potato, each about 7 cm long and 1 1/2 cm wide.
2. Label two test tubes 1 and 2. Place one *potato strip* in each tube.
3. Fill tube 1 with *water* to cover the potato strip.
4. Fill tube 2 with 10% *sodium chloride* (*NaCl*) to cover the potato strip.
5. After one hour, observe each strip for limpness (water loss) or stiffness (water gain). Which tube has the limp potato strip? _____ Why did water diffuse out of the potato strip? _____ Which tube has the stiff potato strip? _____ Why did water diffuse into the potato strip?

_____

_____

Red Blood Cells (Animal Cells)

A solution of 0.9% NaCl is isotonic to red blood cells. In such a solution, red blood cells maintain their normal appearance (Fig. 4.5a). A solution greater than 0.9% NaCl is hypertonic to red blood cells. In such a solution, the cells shrivel up, a process called **crenation** (Fig. 4.5b). A solution of less than 0.9% NaCl is hypotonic to red blood cells. In such a solution, the cells swell to bursting, a process called **hemolysis** (Fig. 4.5c).

Complete Table 4.4 by following these instructions. In the second column, state whether the solution is isotonic, hypertonic, or hypotonic to red blood cells. In the third column, hypothesize the effect on the shape of the cell after being in this solution. In the fourth column, explain why you hypothesized this outcome. Base your explanation on the movement of water.

Table 4.4 Effect of Tonicity on Red Blood Cells			
Concentration (NaCl)	**Tonicity**	**Effect on Cells**	**Explanation**
0.9%			
Higher than 0.9%			
Lower than 0.9%			

Figure 4.5 Tonicity and red blood cells.

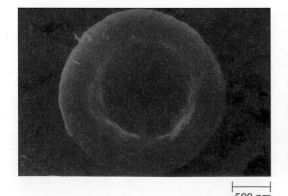

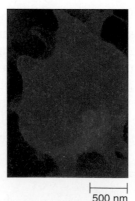

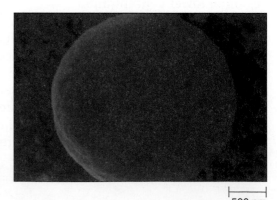

a. Isotonic solution. Red blood cell has normal appearance due to no net gain or loss of water.

b. Hypertonic solution. Red blood cell shrivels due to loss of water.

c. Hypotonic solution. Red blood cell fills to bursting due to gain of water.

Three stoppered test tubes on display have the following contents:

> **Animal tissues** Do not remove the stoppers of test tubes during this procedure.

Tube 1: 0.9% NaCl plus a few drops of sheep blood
Tube 2: 10% NaCl plus a few drops of sheep blood
Tube 3: 0.9% NaCl plus distilled water and a few drops of sheep blood

1. In the second column of Table 4.5, record the tonicity of each tube, in relation to a red blood cell.
2. Shake each tube as shown in Figure 4.6*a*. Then place the tube in front of your lab manual as shown in Figure 4.6*b*. Determine whether you can see the print on the page. Record your findings in the third column of Table 4.5.

Table 4.5 Tonicity and Print Visibility			
Tube	**Tonicity**	**Print Visibility**	**Explanation**
1			
2			
3			

Conclusion: Tonicity in Red Blood Cells

- Explain in the fourth column of Table 4.5 why you can or cannot see the print. Base your explanation on what happened to the cells at these tonicities.

Figure 4.6 Proof of hemolysis.
a. Shake the tube as shown here. **b.** Once the red blood cells burst, you can read print placed behind a tube of diluted blood.

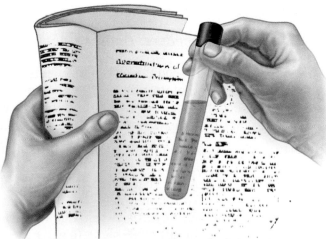

stopper

a. Gently invert tube several times.

b. Determine whether print is readable through tube.

4.4 Enzyme Activity

Enzymes are organic catalysts that speed metabolic reactions, either degradation or synthesis (Fig. 4.7). Each enzyme has a three-dimensional shape that accommodates its substrate(s), the reactant(s) in the enzyme's reaction. This shape, therefore, determines the specificity of the enzyme and is important to the action of the enzyme. While the shape of the enzyme and its substrate are compatible, the favored model for enzyme action suggests that the enzyme initially interacts with its substrate, changes shape slightly to improve the interaction, and then proceeds with a more efficient reaction. Certain environmental effects ensure that enzymes can function speedily. A warm temperature, sufficient enzyme and substrate concentrations, and the correct pH are all important. Each enzyme has a pH at which the speed of the reaction is optimum. Any pH higher or lower than the optimum affects the shape of the enzyme, leading to reduced activity.

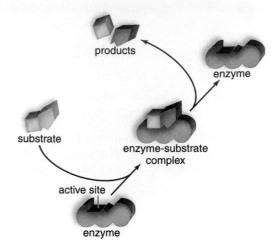

Figure 4.7 Enzymatic action.
During degradation, the substrate is broken down into smaller products.

Experiment with the Enzyme Catalase

In the Experimental Procedure that follows, you will be working with the enzyme catalase. **Catalase** is present in cells, where it speeds the breakdown of the toxic chemical hydrogen peroxide (H_2O_2) to water and oxygen:

$$2H_2O_2 \xrightarrow{\text{catalase}} 2H_2O + O_2$$

hydrogen peroxide   water   oxygen

In this example, the enzyme is catalase; the substrate that fits within the active site of the enzyme is hydrogen peroxide; and the products are water and oxygen. Catalase performs a useful function in organisms because hydrogen peroxide is harmful to cells. Hydrogen peroxide is a powerful oxidizer that can attack and denature cellular molecules such as DNA. Knowing its harmful nature, humans use hydrogen peroxide as a commercial antiseptic to kill germs. In reduced concentration, hydrogen peroxide is a whitening agent used to bleach hair and teeth. It is also used industrially to clean most anything from tubs to sewage.

Experimental Procedure: Catalase Activity

This Experimental Procedure tests the effects of pH on the activity of catalase. Potato will be the source of catalase. As the reaction occurs, easily observable bubbling will develop. Mark and label two clean test tubes at 2 cm and 6 cm.

> ⚠ **Protective eyewear** Protective eyewear should be worn for this procedure. HCl is a strong caustic acid, and NaOH is a strong caustic base. Exercise care in using these chemicals, and follow your instructor's directions for disposal of these tubes. If any acid or base should spill on your skin, rinse immediately with water.

Tube 1:
1. Fill to the 2 cm mark with *distilled water*. (This is neutral pH.)
2. Add a macerated cube (1 cc) of *potato*.
3. Wait 3 minutes.
4. Add *hydrogen peroxide* to the 6 cm mark. Record bubbling in Table 4.6 using 0 (no bubbling) or + signs (e.g., +, + +, + + +, most bubbling).

Tube 2: 1. Carefully fill to the 2 cm mark with *hydrochloric acid* (5M HCl). (This is acidic pH.)
2. Add a macerated cube (1 cc) of *potato*.
3. Wait 3 minutes.
4. Add *hydrogen peroxide* to the 6 cm mark. Record bubbling in Table 4.6.

Table 4.6	Effect of pH on Catalase Activity		
Tube	Contents	Bubbling	Explanation
1	Distilled water; Potato, macerated; Hydrogen peroxide		
2	Hydrochloric acid; Potato, macerated; Hydrogen peroxide		

Conclusions: Catalase Activity

• From your test results, decide which pH is preferred by catalase, neutral or acidic. Write your explanations for your results in Table 4.6.

• What happens to an enzyme if the pH is too far removed from its preferred pH? _____

_____

Application for Daily Living

Inborn Errors of Metabolism and Organelles

We tend to associate illness with particular organs and we talk about heart disease, liver disease, and so forth. However, it would be more correct to associate illness with particular cellular organelles.

Inborn errors of metabolism are due to inheritance of faulty enzymes, traceable to mutations that occur in the nucleus, a major compartment of cells. In several instances, organelles are at fault. Lysosomal storage diseases are due to the inability to break down a particular molecule due to a missing enzyme. Tay-Sachs disease occurs when an undigested substance collects in nerve cells, leading to retarded development of a child and early death. Another problem researchers are aware of is the likelihood of malfunctioning mitochondria as we age. Mitochondrial DNA defects can cause a number of degenerative human diseases due to a decreased ability of mitochondria to produce ATP.

_____ 1. What is the function of rough endoplasmic reticulum?

_____ 2. Which organelle carries on intracellular digestion?

_____ 3. What is the function of the nucleus?

_____ 4. Which organelle is responsible for protein synthesis?

_____ 5. What term is used to describe the movement of molecules from an area of higher concentration to an area of lower concentration?

_____ 6. What is the name for the movement of water across a selectively permeable membrane?

_____ 7. Is 10% NaCl isotonic, hypertonic, or hypotonic to red blood cells?

_____ 8. What appearance will red blood cells have when they are placed in 0.0009% NaCl?

_____ 9. How does water move when cells are placed in a hypertonic solution?

_____ 10. In general, what does the wrong pH do to the shape of an enzyme?

_____ 11. If an enzyme reaction is exposed to an unfavorable pH, what happens to the speed of the reaction?

_____ 12. What is a pH of 7 called?

Thought Questions

13. If a dialysis bag filled with water is placed in a starch solution, what do you predict will happen to the weight of the bag over time? Why?

14. Ocean water is hypertonic to the internal environment of the body. Predict what would happen to an individual who consumes large quantities of ocean (salt) water.

Human Biology Website

The companion website for *Human Biology* provides a wealth of information organized and integrated by chapter. You will find practice tests, animations, and much more that will complement your learning and understanding of general biology.

www.mhhe.com/maderhuman11

McGraw-Hill Access Science Website

An online encyclopedia of science and technology that provides information, including videos, that can enhance the laboratory experience.

www.accessscience.com

5

Body Tissues

Learning Outcomes

5.1 Tissues Form Organs
- Use a portion of the digestive tract to show that organs can contain four different types of tissue: epithelial, connective, muscular, and nervous tissues.

Question: Give an example of the levels of organization in the body.

5.2 Epithelial Tissue
- Identify slides and models or diagrams of various types of epithelium.
- Tell where a particular type of epithelium is located in the body, and state a function.

Question: Where in the digestive tract would you find epithelial tissue? What various functions could it have along the tract?

5.3 Connective Tissue
- Identify slides and models or diagrams of various types of connective tissue.
- Tell where a particular connective tissue is located in the body, and state a function.

Question: Name six types of connective tissue and give a location for each type in the body.

5.4 Muscular Tissue
- Identify slides and models or diagrams of three types of muscular tissue.
- Tell where each type of muscular tissue is located in the body, and state a function.

Question: Associate each type of muscular tissue with (a) particular organ(s) in the body.

5.5 Nervous Tissue
- Identify a slide and model or diagram of a neuron.
- Tell where nervous tissue is located in the body, and state a function.

Question: Which part of a neuron do you expect to see concentrated in the brain?

Application for Daily Living: Tissue Engineering

Introduction

In our last laboratory, we studied a generalized cell, one that has no particular specialization. The cells in our body are usually specialized in structure and function, and these specialized cells congregate together in a **tissue.** So, for example, muscular tissue contains muscle cells that all have the same appearance and perform the same task. That is, each muscle cell can contract, and because of this, muscular tissue can contract.

While some **organs** of the body are known for having a particular type of tissue—for example, the brain contains nervous tissue and a muscle contains muscular tissue—other organs have several types of tissues. We will begin this laboratory by taking a look at a portion of the digestive tract, which has several types of tissues. This will help you realize that tissues are not isolated in the body; instead, they are a part of a specialized organ.

5.1 Tissues Form Organs

There are only four types of tissues in the body: epithelial, connective, muscular, and nervous. To simplify matters, epithelial tissues form protective coverings; connective tissues connect other tissues; muscular tissues contract; and nervous tissues are sensitive to stimuli. Each of these tissues does not occur in a vacuum. They are integral parts of an organ. We will take as our example a portion of the digestive tract shown in Figure 5.1.

The inner layer of the tract is called the mucosa. The mucosa is an inner lining of eplithelial cells, some of which secrete mucus. Epithelium performs a protective function; the mucus protects the other layers of the tract. Occasionally along the tract, some epithelial cells are glandular and secrete digestive juices.

Beneath the epithelial lining, the submucosa is a connective tissue layer. Connective tissue binds together other tissues. As is often the case, blood vessels and nerves run along within the connective tissue layer.

Next, the muscularis has two layers of muscle tissue and the contraction of these layers mix food and digestive juices. It also pushes the food along the tract. Muscles don't contract unless they are stimulated to do so by nerves; nerves occur between the two layers of muscle.

Finally, the serosa is connective tissue that supports the digestive organs within the abdominal cavity.

Figure 5.1 Wall of the gastrointestinal tract.
The wall of the gastrointestinal tract contains the four layers noted.

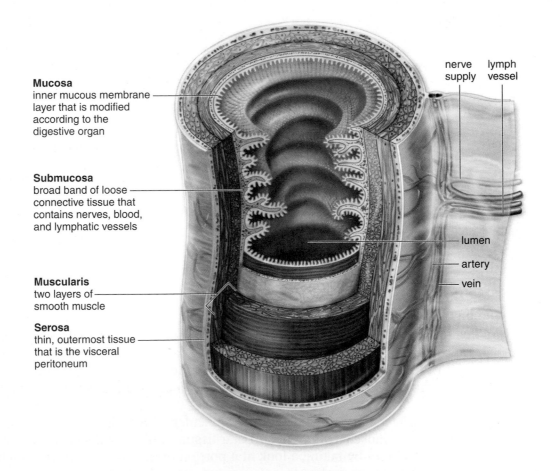

Mucosa
inner mucous membrane layer that is modified according to the digestive organ

Submucosa
broad band of loose connective tissue that contains nerves, blood, and lymphatic vessels

Muscularis
two layers of smooth muscle

Serosa
thin, outermost tissue that is the visceral peritoneum

nerve supply

lymph vessel

lumen

artery

vein

You can apply what you know about the tissues in the digestive tract to any other organ in the body. No matter where you find these tissues, what do you expect them to do?

Tissue:	General Function:
Epithelial tissue	_____
Connective tissue	_____
Muscular tissue	_____
Nervous tissue	_____

In the next laboratory, we will study the various systems of the body and learn that each **organ system,** such as the digestive system, contains several different types of organs, such as the esophagus, stomach, small intestine, and large intestine. Use the digestive system to illustrate the levels of organization of the human body from an organ system to cells:

Name of organ system: _____

Name of organs: _____

Types of tissues in each organ: _____

Type of cell in each tissue type: _____

5.2 Epithelial Tissue

Epithelial tissue (epithelium) forms a continuous layer, or sheet, over the entire body surface and most of the body's inner cavities. Externally, it forms a covering that protects the animal from infection, injury, and drying out. Some epithelial tissues produce and release secretions. Others absorb nutrients.

The name of an epithelial tissue includes two descriptive terms: the shape of the cells and the number of layers. The three possible shapes are *squamous, cuboidal,* and *columnar*. With regard to layers, an epithelial tissue may be simple or stratified. **Simple** means that there is only one layer of cells; **stratified** means that cell layers are placed on top of each other. Some epithelial tissues are **pseudostratified,** meaning that they only appear to be layered. Epithelium may also have cellular extensions called **microvilli** or hairlike extensions called **cilia.** In the latter case, "ciliated" may be part of the tissue's name.

Figure 5.2 Simple squamous epithelium.
Simple squamous epithelium lines blood vessels and various tracts.

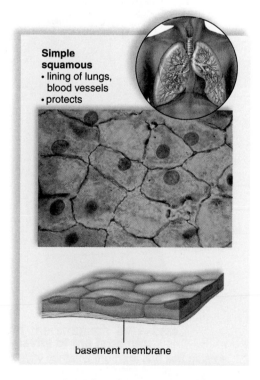

Simple squamous
• lining of lungs, blood vessels
• protects

basement membrane

Observation: Simple and Stratified Squamous Epithelium

Simple Squamous Epithelium

Simple squamous epithelium is a single layer of thin, flat, many-sided cells, each with a central nucleus. It lines internal cavities, the heart, and all the blood vessels. It also lines parts of the urinary, respiratory, and male reproductive tracts.

1. Study a model or diagram of simple squamous epithelium (Fig. 5.2). What does *squamous* mean?

_____

2. Examine a prepared slide of squamous epithelium. Under low power, note the close packing of the flat cells. What shapes are the cells?

_____

3. Under high power, examine an individual cell, and identify the plasma membrane, cytoplasm, and nucleus.

Stratified Squamous Epithelium

As would be expected from its name, stratified squamous epithelium consists of many layers of cells. The innermost layer produces cells that are first cuboidal or columnar in shape, but as the cells push toward the surface, they become flattened.

The outer region of the skin, called the epidermis, is stratified squamous epithelium. As the cells move toward the surface, they flatten, begin to accumulate a protein called **keratin,** and eventually die. Keratin makes the outer layer of epidermis tough, protective, and able to repel water.

The linings of the mouth, throat, anal canal, and vagina are stratified epithelium. The outermost layer of cells surrounding the cavity is simple squamous epithelium. In these organs, this layer of cells remains soft, moist, and alive.

1. Examine a slide of skin, and find the portion of the slide that is stratified squamous epithelium.

2. Approximately how many layers of cells make up this portion of skin? _____

3. Which layers of cells best represent squamous epithelium? _____

Observation: Simple Cuboidal Epithelium

Simple cuboidal epithelium is a single layer of cube-shaped cells, each with a central nucleus. It is found in tubules of the kidney and in the ducts of many glands, where it has a protective function. It also occurs in the secretory portions of some glands, where the tissue produces and releases secretions.

1. Study a model or diagram of simple cuboidal epithelium (Fig. 5.3).
2. Examine a prepared slide of simple cuboidal epithelium. Move the slide until you locate

   cube-shaped cells that line a lumen (cavity). Are these cells ciliated? _____

Figure 5.3   Simple cuboidal epithelium.
Simple cuboidal epithelium lines kidney tubules and the ducts of many glands.

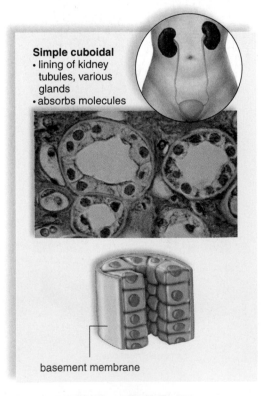

Simple cuboidal
• lining of kidney tubules, various glands
• absorbs molecules

basement membrane

Simple columnar epithelium is a single layer of tall, cylindrical cells, each with a nucleus near the base. This tissue, which lines the digestive tract from the stomach to the anus, protects, secretes, and allows absorption of nutrients.

1. Study a model or diagram of simple columnar epithelium (Fig. 5.4).
2. Examine a prepared slide of simple columnar epithelium. Find tall and narrow cells that line a lumen. Under high power, focus on an individual cell. Identify the plasma membrane, the cytoplasm, and the nucleus. Epithelial tissues are attached to underlying tissues by a basement membrane composed of extracellular material containing protein fibers.
3. The tissue you are observing contains mucus-secreting cells. Search among the columnar cells until you find a **goblet cell,** so named because of its goblet-shaped, clear interior. This region contains mucus, which may be stained a light blue. In the living animal, the mucus is discharged into the gut cavity and protects the lining from digestive enzymes.

Observation: Pseudostratified Ciliated Columnar Epithelium

Pseudostratified ciliated columnar epithelium appears to be layered, while actually all cells touch the basement membrane. Many cilia are located on the free end of each cell (Fig. 5.5). In the human trachea, the cilia wave back and forth, moving mucus and debris up toward the throat so that it cannot enter the lungs. Smoking destroys these cilia, but they will grow back if smoking is discontinued.

1. Study a model or diagram of pseudostratified ciliated columnar epithelium (Fig. 5.5).
2. Examine a prepared slide of pseudostratified ciliated columnar epithelium. Concentrate on the part of the slide that resembles the model. Identify the cilia.

Figure 5.4 Simple columnar epithelium.
Simple columnar epithelium lines the digestive tract. Goblet cells among the columnar cells secrete mucus.

Figure 5.5 Pseudostratified ciliated columnar epithelium.
Pseudostratified ciliated columnar epithelium lines the trachea. The cilia help keep the lungs free of debris.

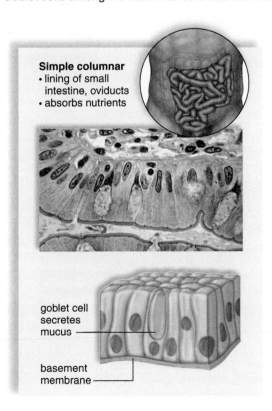

Simple columnar
• lining of small intestine, oviducts
• absorbs nutrients

goblet cell secretes mucus

basement membrane

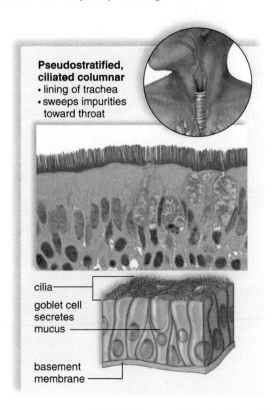

Pseudostratified, ciliated columnar
• lining of trachea
• sweeps impurities toward throat

cilia

goblet cell secretes mucus

basement membrane

5.3 Connective Tissue

Connective tissue joins different parts of the body together. There are four general classes of connective tissue: connective tissue proper (loose fibrous, dense fibrous, and adipose), bone, cartilage, and blood. All types of connective tissue consist of cells surrounded by a matrix that usually contains fibers. Elastic fibers are composed of a protein called elastin. Collagenous fibers contain the protein collagen.

Observation: Loose and Dense Fibrous Connective Tissue

There are several different types of connective tissue. We will study loose fibrous connective tissue, dense fibrous connective tissue, adipose tissue, bone, cartilage, and blood. **Loose fibrous connective tissue** supports epithelium and many internal organs, such as muscles, blood vessels, and nerves (Fig. 5.6). Its presence allows organs to expand. **Dense fibrous connective tissue** contains many collagenous fibers packed together, as in tendons, which connect muscles to bones, and in ligaments, which connect bones to other bones at joints (Fig. 5.7).

1. Examine a slide of loose fibrous connective tissue, and compare it with Figure 5.7. What is the function of loose fibrous connective tissue? _____

2. Examine a slide of dense fibrous connective tissue, and compare it with Figure 5.8. What two types of structures in the body contain dense fibrous connective tissue?

_____

Figure 5.6   Loose fibrous connective tissue.
Loose fibrous connective tissue supports epithelium and many internal organs.

Figure 5.7   Dense fibrous connective tissue.
Dense fibrous connective tissue is found in tendons and ligaments.

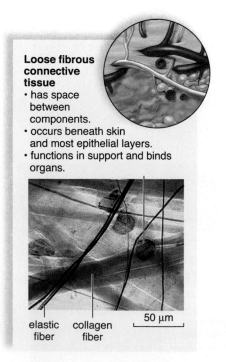

Loose fibrous connective tissue
• has space between components.
• occurs beneath skin and most epithelial layers.
• functions in support and binds organs.

elastic fiber   collagen fiber   50 µm

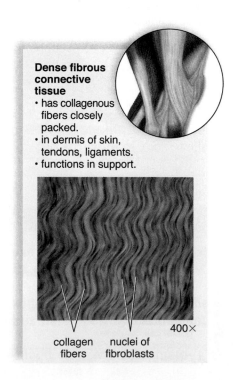

Dense fibrous connective tissue
• has collagenous fibers closely packed.
• in dermis of skin, tendons, ligaments.
• functions in support.

collagen fibers   nuclei of fibroblasts   400×

Observation: Adipose Tissue

In **adipose tissue,** the cells have a large, central, fat-filled vacuole that causes the nucleus and cytoplasm to be at the perimeter of the cell (Fig. 5.8). Adipose tissue occurs beneath the skin, where it insulates the body, and around internal organs, such as the kidneys and heart. It cushions and helps protect these organs.

1. Examine a prepared slide of adipose tissue. Why is the nucleus pushed to one side? _____

_____

2. State a location for adipose tissue in the body. _____

_____

  What are two functions of adipose tissue at this location? _____

_____

Observation: Compact Bone

Compact bone is found in the bones that make up the skeleton. It consists of **osteons** (Haversian systems), with a **central canal,** and concentric rings of spaces called **lacunae,** connected by tiny crevices called **canaliculi.** The central canal contains a nerve and blood vessels, which service bone. The lacunae contain bone cells called **osteocytes,** whose processes extend into the canaliculi. Separating the lacunae is a matrix that is hard because it contains minerals, notably calcium salts. The matrix also contains collagenous fibers.

1. Study a model or diagram of compact bone (Fig. 5.9). Then look at a prepared slide and identify the central canal, lacunae, and canaliculi.

2. What is the function of the central canal and canaliculi? _____

_____

Figure 5.8   Adipose tissue.
Adipose tissue is composed of cells filled with fat droplets.

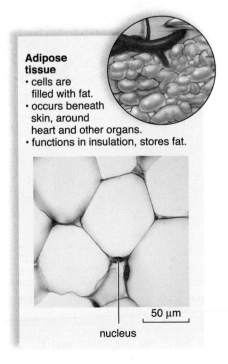

Adipose tissue
• cells are filled with fat.
• occurs beneath skin, around heart and other organs.
• functions in insulation, stores fat.

50 μm

nucleus

Figure 5.9   Compact bone.
Compact bone contains osteons, in which osteocytes within lacunae are arranged in concentric circles.

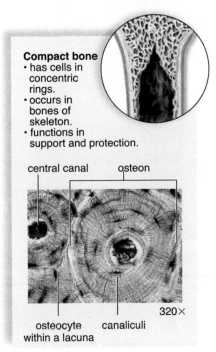

Compact bone
• has cells in concentric rings.
• occurs in bones of skeleton.
• functions in support and protection.

central canal   osteon

320×

osteocyte   canaliculi
within a lacuna

Observation: Hyaline Cartilage

In **hyaline cartilage,** cells called **chondrocytes** are found in twos or threes in lacunae. The lacunae are separated by a flexible matrix containing weak collagenous fibers.

1. Study the diagram and photomicrograph of hyaline cartilage in Figure 5.10. Then study a prepared slide of hyaline cartilage, and identify the matrix, lacunae, and chondrocytes.
2. Compare slides of compact bone and hyaline cartilage. Which of these types of connective tissue is more organized?

_____ Why? _____

3. Which of these two types of connective tissue lends more support to body parts? _____

_____

Figure 5.10 Connective tissues associated with the knee.
The human knee provides examples of most types of connective tissue.

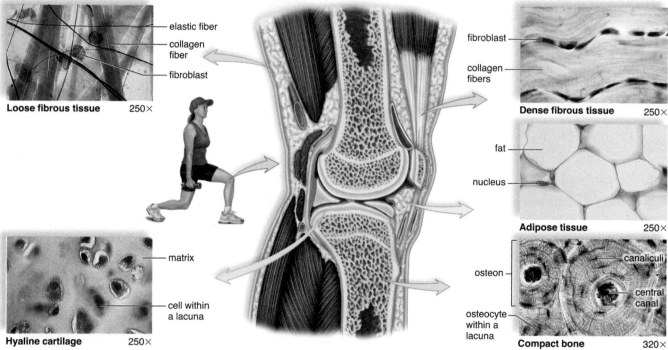

Loose fibrous tissue   250×
- elastic fiber
- collagen fiber
- fibroblast

Dense fibrous tissue   250×
- fibroblast
- collagen fibers

Adipose tissue   250×
- fat
- nucleus

Hyaline cartilage   250×
- matrix
- cell within a lacuna
  - has cells in lacunae.
  - occurs in nose and walls of respiratory passages; at ends of bones, including ribs.
  - functions in support and protection.

Compact bone   320×
- canaliculi
- central canal
- osteon
- osteocyte within a lacuna

Blood is a connective tissue in which the matrix is an intercellular fluid called **plasma. Red blood cells** (erythrocytes) carry oxygen combined with the respiratory pigment hemoglobin. **White blood cells** (leukocytes) fight infection. Also present in blood are many small bodies, the **platelets,** which play a major role in clot formation.

1. Study a prepared slide of human blood. With the help of Figure 5.11, identify the numerous red blood cells and the less numerous but larger white blood cells, which appear faint because of the stain. As you scan your slide on high power, also look for the small platelets, the small objects scattered between the blood cells.
2. Try to identify a neutrophil, the most common type of white blood cell. A neutrophil has a multilobed nucleus. Try to identify a lymphocyte, the next most common type of white blood cell. A lymphocyte is the smallest of the white blood cells, with a spherical or slightly indented nucleus.

Figure 5.11 Blood cells.
Red blood cells are more numerous than white blood cells. White blood cells can be separated into five distinct types. If you have blood work done that includes a complete blood count (CBC), the doctor is getting a count of each of these types of WBCs. (**a–e:** Magnification ×1,050)

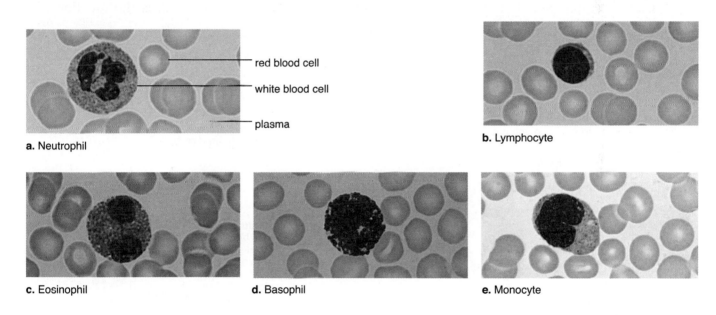

a. Neutrophil

red blood cell

white blood cell

plasma

b. Lymphocyte

c. Eosinophil

d. Basophil

e. Monocyte

5.4 Muscular Tissue

Muscular (contractile) tissue is composed of cells called muscle fibers. Muscular tissue has the ability to contract, and contraction usually results in movement. The body contains skeletal, cardiac, and smooth muscle.

Observation: Skeletal Muscle

Skeletal muscle occurs in the muscles attached to the bones of the skeleton. The contraction of skeletal muscle is said to be **voluntary** because it is under conscious control. Skeletal muscle is striated; it contains light and dark bands. The striations are caused by the arrangement of contractile filaments (actin and myosin filaments) in muscle fibers. Each fiber contains many nuclei, all peripherally located.

1. Study a model or diagram of skeletal muscle (Fig. 5.12). Striations are present. You should see several muscle fibers, each marked with striations.
2. Examine a prepared slide of skeletal muscle. The striations may be difficult to make out, but bringing the slide in and out of focus may help.

Observation: Cardiac Muscle

Cardiac muscle is found only in the heart. It is called **involuntary** because its contraction does not require conscious effort. Cardiac muscle is striated in the same way as skeletal muscle. However, the fibers are branched and bound together at **intercalated disks,** where their folded plasma membranes touch. This arrangement aids communication between fibers.

1. Study a model or diagram of cardiac muscle (Fig. 5.13). Striations are present.
2. Examine a prepared slide of cardiac muscle. Find an intercalated disk. What is the function of

    cardiac muscle? _____

    _____

Figure 5.12   Skeletal muscle.
Skeletal muscle is striated and voluntary. Its cells are tubular and contain many nuclei.

Figure 5.13   Cardiac muscle.
Cardiac muscle is striated and involuntary. Its branched cells join at intercalated disks.

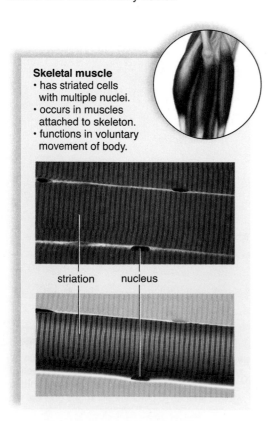

Skeletal muscle
• has striated cells with multiple nuclei.
• occurs in muscles attached to skeleton.
• functions in voluntary movement of body.

striation   nucleus

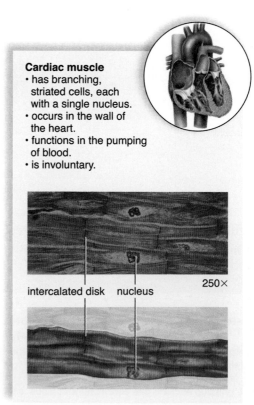

Cardiac muscle
• has branching, striated cells, each with a single nucleus.
• occurs in the wall of the heart.
• functions in the pumping of blood.
• is involuntary.

intercalated disk   nucleus   250×

Smooth muscle is sometimes called **visceral muscle** because it makes up the walls of the internal organs, such as the intestines and the blood vessels. Smooth muscle is involuntary because its contraction does not require conscious effort.

1. Study a model or diagram of smooth muscle (Fig. 5.14), and note the shape of the cells and the centrally placed nucleus. Smooth muscle has spindle-shaped cells. What does *spindle-shaped*

   mean? _____

   _____

2. Examine a prepared slide of smooth muscle. Distinguishing the boundaries between the different cells may require you to bring the slide in and out of focus.

Figure 5.14 Smooth muscle.
Smooth muscle is nonstriated and involuntary. This type of muscle is composed of spindle-shaped cells.

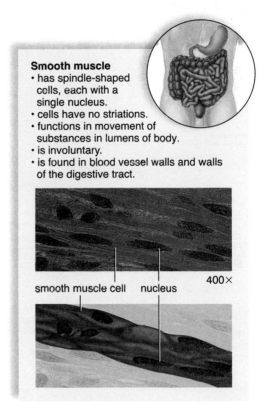

Smooth muscle
- has spindle-shaped cells, each with a single nucleus.
- cells have no striations.
- functions in movement of substances in lumens of body.
- is involuntary.
- is found in blood vessel walls and walls of the digestive tract.

smooth muscle cell   nucleus   400×

5.5 Nervous Tissue

Nervous tissue is found in the brain, spinal cord, and nerves. Nervous tissue is composed of two types of cells: **neurons** that transmit messages and **neuroglia** that largely service the neurons (see Fig. 5.1). Motor neurons, which take messages from the spinal cord to the muscles, are often used to exemplify typical neurons (Fig. 5.15). Motor neurons have several **dendrites,** processes that take signals to a **cell body,** where the nucleus is located, and an **axon** that takes nerve impulses away from the cell body.

1. Study a model or diagram of a neuron, and then examine a prepared slide. You will not be able to see neuroglial cells because they are small and cannot be seen at this magnification.
2. Identify the dendrites, cell body, and axon in Figure 5.15 and label the micrograph. Long axons are called nerve fibers.
3. Explain the appearance and function of the parts of a motor neuron:

   a. Dendrites _____

   b. Cell body _____

   c. Axon _____

Figure 5.15   Motor neuron anatomy.

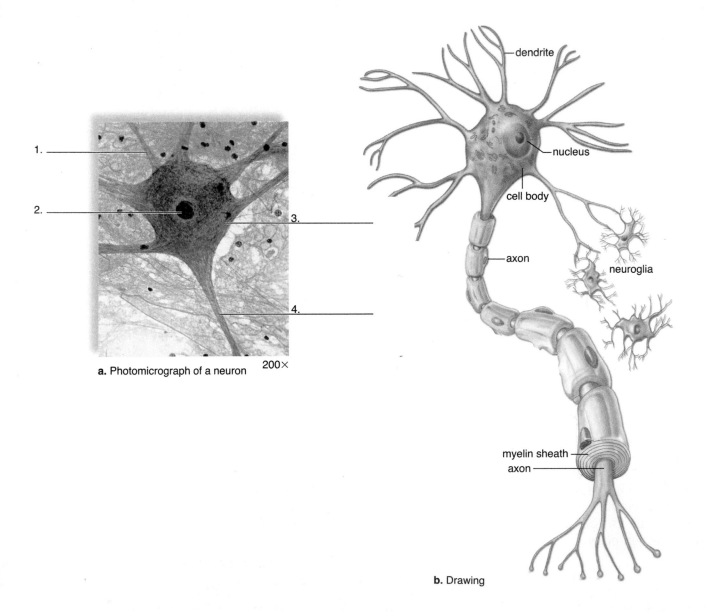

a. Photomicrograph of a neuron   200×

b. Drawing

Tissue Engineering

Just a few years ago, scientists believed that transplant tissues and organs had to come from humans. Now, however, tissue engineering is demonstrating that it is possible to make replacement tissues and organs in the lab. For example, two skin products have now been approved for use in humans. One is composed of dermal cells growing on a degradable polymer, which can be used to temporarily cover the wounds of burn patients while their own skin regenerates (Fig. 5.16). The other uses only live human skin cells to treat diabetic leg and foot ulcers. Similarly, the damaged cartilage of a knee can be replaced with a tissue produced after chondrocytes are harvested from a patient. Soon to come are a host of other products, including replacement corneas, heart valves, bladder valves, and breast tissue.

After nine years, researchers were able to produce a working urinary bladder in the laboratory. This bladder can be implanted in humans whose bladders have been damaged by accident or disease. Another group of scientists have been able to grow arterial blood vessels in the lab using a pig's small intestine as the mold. Tissue engineers also hope to one day produce larger internal organs, such as a liver or a kidney.

Figure 5.16   Burn victim.
Burn victim who received skin, produced in the laboratory, as a transplant.

Laboratory Review 5

_____ 1. What is the name for a group of cells that has the same structural characteristics and performs the same functions?

_____ 2. Which type of epithelium has flattened cells?

_____ 3. Name a body location for pseudostratified ciliated columnar epithelium.

_____ 4. What is the function of goblet cells?

_____ 5. What type of tissue occurs in the epidermis of the skin?

_____ 6. Name a body location for hyaline cartilage.

_____ 7. The cells of which tissue have a large, central, fat-filled vacuole?

_____ 8. What type of muscular tissue is involuntary and striated?

_____ 9. Name a body location for smooth muscle.

_____ 10. What types of muscular tissue are striated?

_____ 11. Name a body location for nervous tissue.

_____ 12. Where is the nucleus located in a nerve cell?

_____ 13. What type of tissue accounts for the movement of food along the digestive tract?

_____ 14. Which skin layer contains blood vessels?

_____ 15. What portion of a nerve cell transmits information away from the cell body?

Thought Questions

16. List the four major types of human body tissues and the distinguishing characteristics of each. Why does the human body contain all four types rather than a single type?

17. List the five types of epithelial tissue and the distinguishing characteristics of each.

18. Your lab instructor gives you a slide containing prepared muscle tissue. How would you identify the type of muscle tissue located on the slide?

19. Why might an injury to a bone have a faster recovery/healing time when compared to a muscle or nerve cell?

Human Biology Website

The companion website for *Human Biology* provides a wealth of information organized and integrated by chapter. You will find practice tests, animations, and much more that will complement your learning and understanding of general biology.

www.mhhe.com/maderhuman11

McGraw-Hill Access Science Website

An online encyclopedia of science and technology that provides information, including videos, that can enhance the laboratory experience.

www.accessscience.com

6

Organization of the Body

Learning Outcomes

6.1 Human Torso Model
- State and give a function for organs in the mouth, thoracic cavity, neck region, and abdominal cavity.
Question: State the path of food from the mouth to the anus.

6.2 External Anatomy
- State four directive terms used when dissecting.
- Describe the external anatomy of a fetal pig.
- Tell how you would identify the gender of a fetal pig.
Question: Aside from the mouth, name two orifices of the mammalian body.

6.3 Oral Cavity and Pharynx
- Describe the general anatomy of the oral cavity and pharynx.
Question: Explain why food does not enter the trachea.

6.4 Thoracic and Abdominal Incisions
- For those doing fetal pig dissections, describe the proper procedure for making incisions.
Question: Why is it important to point scissors up and not down?

6.5 Neck Region
- Describe and state a function for the thymus gland, the larynx, the trachea, and the thyroid gland.
Question: When might a physician be sure to check the size of the thyroid gland if a patient complains of feeling tired?

6.6 Thoracic Cavity
- Describe the position of the diaphragm.
- Describe the anatomy of the thoracic cavity, paying particular attention to the path of air.
Question: Which is more posterior, the lungs or the liver? Explain.

6.7 Abdominal Cavity
- Describe the organs of the abdominal cavity, paying particular attention to the organs of the digestive system, the liver, and the gallbladder.
Question: What attribute accounts for the small intestine being called the *small* intestine?

Application for Daily Living: The Systems Work Together

Introduction

This laboratory and Laboratory 7 will give you an opportunity to observe the organs of the fetal pig, a mammal, just as you are a mammal. You will be interested to know that investigators are in the process of genetically modifying pigs so that fetal pig organs can be used as transplant organs in humans.

Your instructor will decide whether you are to follow the directions for dissecting the fetal pig yourself or whether you are to observe the organs in pigs that have already been dissected. Also, virtual dissection of a human cadaver is possible using *Anatomy and Physiology Revealed*, a CD-ROM, available from McGraw-Hill Higher Education.

We begin this laboratory by observing the organs to be dissected or observed in a pig by identifying the organs in a human torso model.

6.1 Human Torso Model

Identify these organs in a human torso model (Fig. 6.1). Either now or later after you have studied the material in the manual, state to which human system each belongs (see key) and give a function for each.

1. Oral cavity (mouth)

Organ	**System**	**Function**
Hard palate and soft palate	_____	_____
Teeth and tongue	_____	_____

2. Pharynx

Nasopharynx	_____	_____
Glottis and epiglottis	_____	_____

Figure 6.1 Human internal organs.
The dotted lines indicate the full shape of an organ that is partially covered by another organ.

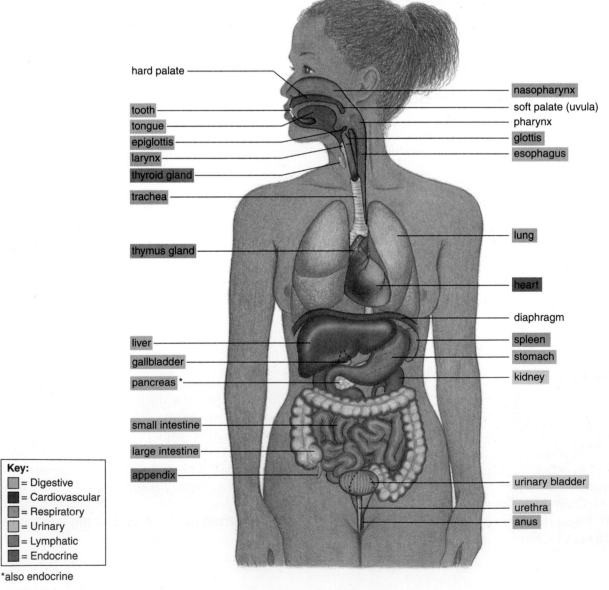

hard palate
tooth
tongue
epiglottis
larynx
thyroid gland
trachea
thymus gland
liver
gallbladder
pancreas *
small intestine
large intestine
appendix

nasopharynx
soft palate (uvula)
pharynx
glottis
esophagus
lung
heart
diaphragm
spleen
stomach
kidney
urinary bladder
urethra
anus

Key:
▢ = Digestive
▢ = Cardiovascular
▢ = Respiratory
▢ = Urinary
▢ = Lymphatic
▢ = Endocrine

*also endocrine

3. Neck region

   Trachea and larynx _____ _____

   Esophagus _____ _____

   Thyroid gland _____ _____

4. Thoracic Cavity (above the diaphragm)

   Lungs _____ _____

   Heart _____ _____

   Thymus gland _____ _____

5. Abdominal Cavity (below the diaphragm)

   Liver _____ _____

   Gallbladder _____ _____

   Stomach _____ _____

   Pancreas _____ _____

   Small intestine _____ _____

   Large intestine _____ _____

   Anus _____ _____

   Appendix _____ _____

   Spleen _____ _____

   Kidney _____ _____

   Urinary bladder _____ _____

   Urethra _____ _____

6.2 External Anatomy

Perspective is important in dissections. If an animal is lying facedown, *top* and *bottom* mean something different than when the animal is lying on its back. For this reason, this manual uses the following terms, which are identified in Figure 6.2*a*:

   Dorsal: a body part located toward the back
   Ventral: a body part located toward the front
   Anterior: a body part located toward the head
   Posterior: a body part located toward the rear

If you are dissecting or observing the organs only, notice that there is a slash in the right neck region of preserved pigs, indicating the site of blood drainage. A red latex solution was injected into the **arterial system,** and a blue latex solution was injected into the **venous system** of the pig. Therefore, when a vessel appears red, it is an artery; and when a vessel appears blue, it is a vein. Do not confuse this color pattern with circulatory diagrams that differentiate O_2-rich blood flow and O_2-poor blood flow by using red- and blue-colored vessels, respectively.

> ⚠ **Latex gloves** Wear protective latex gloves when handling preserved animal organs. Use protective eyewear and exercise caution when using sharp instruments during this laboratory. Wash hands thoroughly upon completion of this laboratory.

Figure 6.2 External anatomy of the fetal pig.

a. Directional terms and body regions. **b, c.** The sexes can be distinguished by the external genitals.

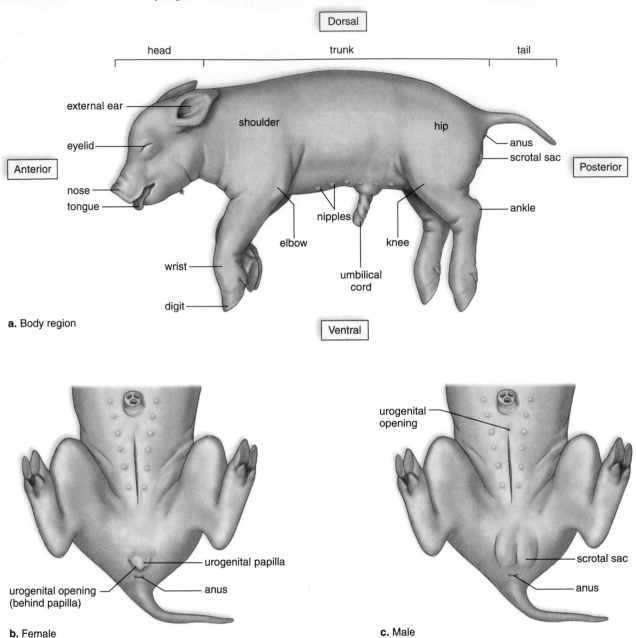

Dorsal

head   trunk   tail

external ear
shoulder   hip
eyelid   anus
scrotal sac
Anterior   Posterior
nose   ankle
tongue
nipples
elbow   knee
wrist
umbilical
cord
digit
a. Body region   Ventral

urogenital
opening

urogenital papilla
scrotal sac
urogenital opening   anus   anus
(behind papilla)

b. Female   **c.** Male

Observation: External Anatomy

These observations can be done by all students.

Body Regions

1. Externally, observe the following body regions: the rather large head; the short, thick neck; the cylindrical trunk with two pairs of appendages (forelimbs and hindlimbs); and the short tail (Fig. 6.2*a*).

Umbilical Cord

1. Fetal pigs have an umbilical cord arising from the ventral portion of the abdomen. Fetal pigs have not been born yet, and this is why they have a prominent umbilical cord. The function of the umbilical cord is to bring oxygen and nutrients from the mother's circulation to the fetus and return oxygen and waste to the mother's circulation.

Nipples and Hair

1. Nipples, the external openings of the **mammary glands,** are *not* an indication of sex, because both males and females possess them.
2. Pigs have a few whiskers, the only indication of hair.

Anus and External Genitals

1. The anus, an opening under the tail, is a part of what system in the body? _____
2. Females have a **urogenital opening,** just anterior to the anus, and a small, fleshy **urogenital papilla** projecting from the urogenital opening (Fig. 6.2*b*).
3. Males have a urogenital opening just posterior to the umbilical cord. The duct leading to it runs forward from between the legs in a long, thick tube, the **penis,** which can be felt under the skin. In males, the urinary system and the genital system are always joined (Fig. 6.2*c*).

6.3 Oral Cavity and Pharynx

All students will use Figure 6.3 to make these observations:

The **oral cavity** is the space in the mouth that contains the tongue and the teeth. What system of the body includes the tongue and teeth? _____

The tongue manipulates the food chewed by the teeth for swallowing. The **hard palate** is the ridged roof of the mouth that separates the oral cavity from the nasal passages. The **soft palate** is a smooth region posterior to the hard palate. An extension of the soft palate—the **uvula**—hangs down into the throat in humans. (A pig does not have an uvula.)

Observation: Oral Cavity and Pharynx

If you are doing a pig dissection, follow these directions. If you are observing a pig that has already been dissected or are doing a virtual dissection, answer the questions and proceed to Section 6.5.

Oral Cavity

1. Insert a sturdy pair of scissors into one corner of the specimen's mouth, and cut posteriorly (toward the hind end) for approximately 4 cm. Repeat on the opposite side.
2. Place your thumb on the tongue at the front of the mouth, and gently push downward on the lower jaw. This will tear some of the tissue in the angles of the jaws so that the mouth will remain partly open (Fig. 6.3).
3. Note small, underdeveloped teeth in both the upper and lower jaws. Other embryonic, nonerupted teeth may also be found within the gums. The teeth are used to chew food.
4. Examine the tongue, partly attached to the lower jaw region but extending posteriorly and attached to a bony structure at the back of the oral cavity (Fig. 6.3).
5. Locate the hard and soft palates (Fig. 6.3).

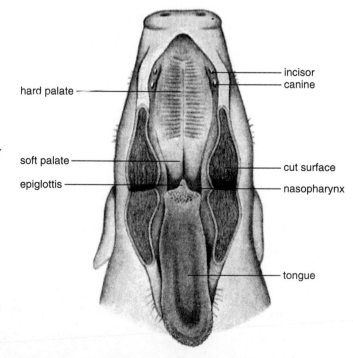

Figure 6.3   Oral cavity of the fetal pig.
The roof of the oral cavity contains the hard and soft palates. The tongue lies above the floor of the oral cavity.

Organization of the Body   Laboratory 6   **67**

Pharynx

1. Push down on the tongue until you open the jaws far enough to see a slightly pointed flap of tissue pointing dorsally (toward the back) (Fig. 6.3). This flap is the **epiglottis,** which covers the glottis. The glottis leads to the trachea (Fig. 6.4*a*).
2. Posterior and dorsal to the glottis, find the opening into the esophagus. Note the proximity of the glottis and the opening to the esophagus. Each time the pig—or a human—swallows, the epiglottis shifts position, closing the glottis to keep food and fluids from going into the lungs via the trachea.
3. Insert a blunt probe into the glottis, and it enters the trachea. Remove the probe, insert it into the esophagus, and note the position of the esophagus beneath, or dorsal to, the trachea.
4. Make a midline cut in the soft palate from the epiglottis to the hard palate. Then make two lateral cuts at the edge of the hard palate.
5. Posterior to the soft palate, locate the openings to the nasal passages.
6. Explain why it is correct to say that the air and food passages cross in the pharynx.

_____

_____

_____

Figure 6.4 Air and food passages in the fetal pig.
The air and food passages cross in the pharynx.
a. Drawing. **b.** Dissection of specimen.

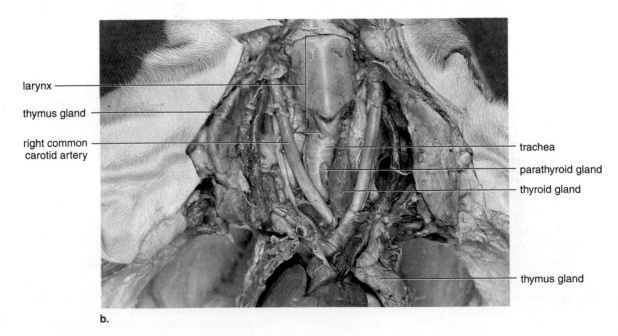

6.4 Thoracic and Abdominal Incisions

If you are doing a pig dissection, follow these directions. If you are observing a pig that has been dissected or doing a virtual dissection, proceed to Section 6.5.

First, prepare your pig according to the following directions, and then make thoracic and abdominal incisions so that you will be able to study the internal anatomy of your pig.

Preparation of Pig for Dissection

1. Place the fetal pig on its back in the dissecting pan.
2. Tie a cord around one forelimb, and then bring the cord around underneath the pan to fasten back the other forelimb.
3. Spread the hindlimbs in the same way.
4. With scissors always pointing up (never down), make the following incisions to expose the thoracic and abdominal cavities. The incisions are numbered on Figure 6.5 to correspond with the following steps.

Thoracic Incisions

1. Cut anteriorly up from the **diaphragm,** a structure that separates the thoracic cavity from the abdominal cavity, until you reach the hairs in the throat region.
2. Make two lateral cuts, one on each side of the midline incision anterior to the forelimbs, taking extra care not to damage the blood vessels around the heart.
3. Make two lateral cuts, one on each side of the midline just posterior to the forelimbs and anterior to the diaphragm, following the ends of the ribs. Pull back the flaps created by these cuts to expose the **thoracic cavity.** List the organs you find in the thoracic cavity.

_____

Abdominal Incisions

4. With scissors pointing up, cut posteriorly from the diaphragm to the umbilical cord.
5. Make a flap containing the umbilical cord by cutting a semicircle around the cord and by cutting posteriorly to the left and right of the cord.
6. Make two cuts, one on each side of the midline incision posterior to the diaphragm. Examine the diaphragm, attached to the chest wall by radially arranged muscles. The central region of the diaphragm, called the **central tendon,** is a membranous area.
7. Make two more cuts, one on each side of the flap containing the umbilical cord and just anterior to the hindlimbs. Pull back the side flaps created by these cuts to expose the **abdominal cavity.**

Exposing the Abdominal Cavity

1. Lifting the flap with the umbilical cord requires cutting the **umbilical vein.** Before cutting the umbilical vein, tie a thread on each side of where you will cut to mark the vein for future reference.
2. Rinse out your pig as soon as you have opened the abdominal cavity. If you have a problem with excess fluid, obtain a disposable plastic pipette to suction off the liquid.
3. Anatomically, the diaphragm separates what two cavities? _____

Figure 6.5 Ventral view of the fetal pig indicating incisions.

These incisions are to be made preparatory to dissecting the internal organs. They are numbered here in the order they should be done.

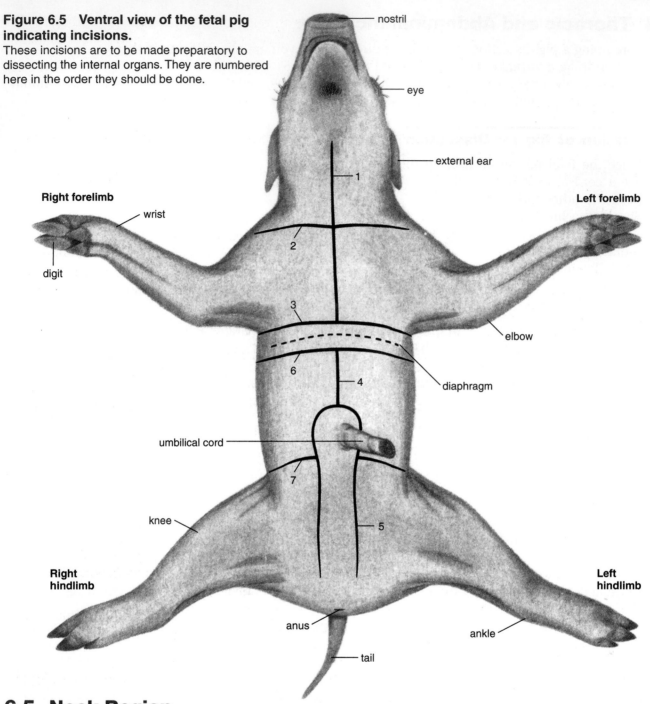

6.5 Neck Region

All students will use Figure 6.4b to make these observations:

1. Unlike humans, the **thymus gland** is located in the neck region of a fetal pig. The thymus gland is a part of the lymphatic system. Certain white blood cells called T (for thymus) lymphocytes mature in the thymus gland and help fight disease.
2. The **larynx,** or voice box, is part of the **trachea,** or windpipe, which leads to the lungs. The glottis is the opening to the trachea in the pharynx. The trachea is held open by cartilaginous rings. Why is that advantageous? _____
3. The **thyroid gland** is ventral to the trachea. It secretes hormones that travel in the blood and act upon other body cells, causing their metabolism to speed up. These hormones (e.g., thyroxine) regulate the rate at which metabolism occurs in cells. The thyroid gland is a part of which body system? _____

4. The **esophagus** opens into the pharynx but it travels through the neck region and through the diaphragm to reach the stomach. Is the esophagus located ventral to or dorsal to the trachea? _____ What holds the esophagus open? _____

Observation: Neck Region

If you are doing a pig dissection or are observing a pig that has been dissected, follow these directions. If you are not dissecting the pig, proceed to Section 6.6.

Use Figure 6.4b as a guide, but *keep all the flaps on your pig* so you can close the thoracic and abdominal cavities at the end of the laboratory session.

Thymus Gland

1. Move the skin apart in the neck region just below the hairs mentioned earlier. If necessary, laterally cut the body wall to make flaps. You will most likely be viewing exposed muscles.
2. *Cut through and clear away muscle* to expose the *thymus gland,* a diffuse gland that lies among the muscles. The thymus is particularly large in fetal pigs, because their immune systems are still developing.

Trachea and Esophagus

1. Probe down into the deeper layers of the neck. Medially (toward the center), beneath several strips of muscle, you will find the hard-walled larynx, the upper part of the trachea. Dorsal to the trachea, find the esophagus.
2. Open the mouth and insert a probe into the glottis and esophagus from the pharynx to better understand the orientation of these two organs.

Thyroid Gland

Locate the thyroid gland just posterior to the larynx, lying ventral to the trachea.

6.6 Thoracic Cavity

All students will use Figure 6.6 to make these observations:

The body cavity of mammals, including humans, is divided by the diaphragm (horizontal sheet of muscle and connective tissue) into the thoracic cavity (above) and the abdominal cavity (below). These organs are easily observable in the thoracic cavity:

1. The heart pumps the blood into attached arteries, blood vessels that take blood away from the heart. The heart is surrounded by the pericardial membrane, which keeps the heart moist. The heart is a part of which system in the body? _____

2. The trachea divides into the **bronchi,** which enter the lungs. The lungs are enclosed by pleural membrane. Trace the path of air from the nose to the lungs. _____

_____

3. The lungs carry on gas exchange with the external environment and with the blood. The right lung has four lobes and the left lung has three lobes.

Observation: Thoracic Cavity

If you are doing a pig dissection or are observing a pig that has been dissected, follow these directions. If you are doing a virtual dissection, proceed to Section 6.7.

Heart and Lungs

1. If you have not yet done so, fold back the chest wall flaps. To do this, you will need to tear the thin membranes that divide the thoracic cavity into three compartments: the left **pleural cavity** containing

Figure 6.6 Internal anatomy of the fetal pig.
Most of the major organs are shown in this photograph. The stomach has been removed. The spleen, gallbladder, and pancreas are not visible. *Do not* remove any organs or flaps from your pig.

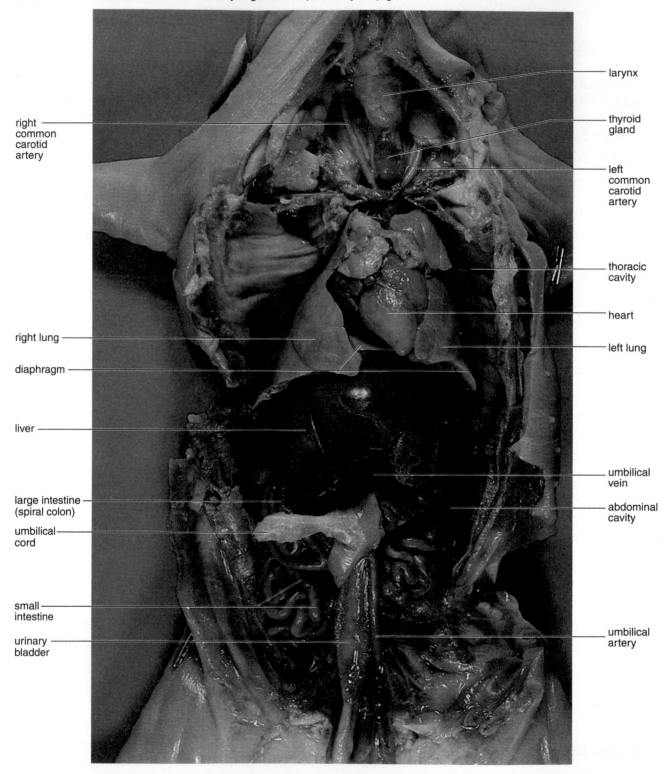

right common carotid artery

right lung

diaphragm

liver

large intestine (spiral colon)

umbilical cord

small intestine

urinary bladder

larynx

thyroid gland

left common carotid artery

thoracic cavity

heart

left lung

umbilical vein

abdominal cavity

umbilical artery

the left lung, the right pleural cavity containing the right lung, and the **pericardial cavity** containing the heart.

2. Examine the lungs. Locate the four lobes of the right lung and the three lobes of the left lung. The trachea, dorsal to the heart, divides into the bronchi, which enter the lungs. Later, when the heart is removed, you will be able to see the trachea and bronchi.

6.7 Abdominal Cavity

All students will use Figure 6.6 to make these observations:

The abdominal wall and organs are lined by a connective tissue membrane called **peritoneum.** Double-layered sheets of peritoneum, called **mesenteries,** project from the body wall and support the organs.

1.   The abdominal cavity also contains organs of the digestive tract, including the stomach, small intestine, and large intestine. The **stomach** stores food and has numerous gastric glands that secrete gastric juice, which digests protein. The **small intestine** is the part of the digestive tract that receives secretions from the pancreas and gallbladder. Ducts from these organs enter the **duodenum,** the first part of the small intestine. Besides being an organ for the digestion of all components of food—carbohydrate, protein, and fat—the small intestine absorbs the products of digestion: glucose, amino acids, glycerol, and fatty acids. The **large intestine** is the part of the digestive tract that absorbs water and prepares feces for defecation at the anus. The main portion of the large intestine is the **colon,** which first runs anteriorly and then horizontally before turning posteriorly again. In the pelvic region, the **rectum** is the last portion of the large intestine. The rectum leads to the **anus.**

2.   The **liver,** the largest organ in the abdomen (Fig. 6.6), performs numerous vital functions, including disposing of worn-out red blood cells, producing bile, storing glycogen, maintaining the blood glucose level, and producing blood proteins.

3.   The **gallbladder** stores and releases bile, which aids the digestion of fat. A duct from the gallbladder takes bile to the small intestine. Bile is an emulsifier, that breaks up fat-to-fat droplets so digestion can take place.

4.   The **pancreas** is both an exocrine and an endocrine gland. As an exocrine gland, it produces and secretes pancreatic juice, which digests all the components of food in the small intestine. Both bile and pancreatic juice enter the duodenum by way of ducts. As an endocrine gland, the pancreas secretes the hormones insulin and glucagon into the bloodstream. Insulin and glucagon regulate blood glucose levels.
     Place the terms insulin and glucagon over or under one of these arrows:

$$glucose \rightleftharpoons glycogen$$

5.   The **spleen** is a lymphatic organ in the lymphatic system that contains both white and red blood cells. It purifies blood and disposes of worn-out red blood cells.

Observation: Abdominal Cavity

If you are doing a pig dissection or observing a pig that has already been dissected, follow these directions. If you are doing a virtual dissection, answer the questions and proceed to the review, page 75.

Liver

1.   If your particular pig is partially filled with dark, brownish material, take your animal to the sink and rinse it out. This material is clotted blood. Consult your instructor before removing any red or blue latex masses, because they may enclose organs you will need to study.

2.   Locate the liver, a large, brown organ. Its anterior surface is smoothly convex and fits snugly into the concavity of the diaphragm.

3.   Name several functions of the liver. _____

_____

Stomach and Spleen

1. Push aside and identify the stomach, a large sac dorsal to the liver on the left side.
2. Locate the point near the midline of the body where the **esophagus** penetrates the diaphragm and joins the stomach.
3. Find the spleen, a long, flat, reddish organ attached to the stomach by mesentery.
4. The spleen is a part of what system? _____

    What is its function? _____

Small Intestine

1. Look posteriorly where the stomach makes a curve to the right and narrows to join the anterior end of the small intestine called the **duodenum.**
2. From the duodenum, the small intestine runs posteriorly for a short distance and is then thrown into an irregular mass of bends and coils held together by a common mesentery.
3. The small intestine is a part of what system? _____

    What is its function? _____

Gallbladder and Pancreas

1. Locate the **bile duct,** which runs in the mesentery stretching between the liver and the duodenum. Find the gallbladder, embedded in the liver on the underside of the right lobe. It is a small, greenish sac.
2. Lift the stomach and locate the pancreas, the light-colored, diffuse gland lying in the mesentery between the stomach and the small intestine. The pancreas has a duct that empties into the duodenum of the small intestine.
3. What is the function of the gallbladder? _____
4. What is the function of the pancreas? _____

Large Intestine

1. Locate the distal (far) end of the small intestine, which joins the large intestine posteriorly, in the left side of the abdominal cavity (right side in humans). At this junction, note the **cecum,** a blind pouch.
2. Follow the main portion of the large intestine, known as the **colon,** as it runs from the point of-juncture with the small intestine into a tight coil (spiral colon), out of the coil anteriorly, and then posteriorly again along the midline of the dorsal wall of the abdominal cavity. In the pelvic region, the **rectum** is the last portion of the large intestine. The rectum leads to the **anus.**
3. The large intestine is a part of what system? _____
4. What is the function of the large intestine? _____
5. Trace the path of food from the mouth to the anus*. _____

    _____

Storage of Pigs

1. Before leaving the laboratory, place your pig in the plastic bag provided.
2. Expel excess air from the bag, and tie it shut.
3. Write your *name* and *section* on the tag provided, and attach it to the bag. Your instructor will indicate where the bags are to be stored until the next laboratory period.
4. Clean the dissecting tray and tools, and return them to their proper location.
5. Wipe off your goggles. Wash your hands.

Anatomy and Physiology Revealed, a CD-ROM, available from McGraw-Hill Higher Education, has animations that trace the path of air, food, etc.

The Systems Work Together

This laboratory has involved a number of different systems, including the respiratory system, the cardiovascular system, and the digestive system. Can one of these systems malfunction without negatively affecting the other systems? Likely not. For example, if you climb a high mountain and can't breathe adequately, the cardiovascular system will not be able to deliver oxygen to your cells (Fig. 6.7). Or, if you go on a hunger strike, the cardiovascular system will not be able to deliver glucose to your cells. Without oxygen and glucose, even your heart will not be able to continue beating. Blood vessels not only deliver oxygen and glucose to the heart, they also take these molecules to the lungs and the walls of the digestive tract.

In the body as in the environment, everything is connected to everything else. The systems work together under the direction of the nervous and endocrine systems as a harmonious whole so that your cells and you can continue to function as you should.

Figure 6.7 The systems work together.
The cardiovascular system receives nutrients from the digestive tract and oxygen from the respiratory system which it delivers to the cells. It also delivers CO_2 and other wastes from the cells to the respiratory system and urinary system respectively.

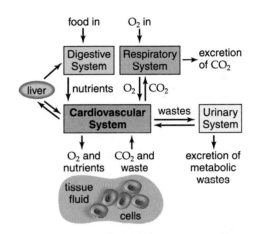

Laboratory Review 6

_____ 1. In the fetal pig, what sex has a urogenital opening beneath the papilla just superior to the anus?

_____ 2. What two characteristics do all mammals have?

_____ 3. The esophagus connects the pharynx with which organ?

_____ 4. What is the hard portion of the roof of the mouth called?

_____ 5. What is the opening to the trachea called?

_____ 6. Name the largest organ in the abdominal cavity.

_____ 7. What structure separates the thoracic cavity from the abdominal cavity?

_____ 8. Name the structure just dorsal to the thyroid gland.

_____ 9. What structure covers the glottis?

_____ 10. If a probe is placed through the glottis, it will enter what structure?

_____ 11. The heart is located in what major cavity?

_____ 12. What other major organs are in the same cavity?

_____ 13. The stomach connects to what part of the small intestine?

_____ **14.** The pancreas belongs to what system of the body?

_____ **15.** Where do air and food passages cross one another?

_____ **16.** What organ releases bile?

Thought Questions

17. What difficulty would probably arise if a person were born without an epiglottis?

18. A large portion of the abdominal cavity is taken up by digestive organs. Which organs are these?

19. The small intestine exists as a series of folds and coils. What might be the advantage of such a configuration?

20. Difficulties maintaining blood glucose level, bile production, and the production of blood proteins might be associated with problems in what organ?

Human Biology Website

The companion website for _Human Biology_ provides a wealth of information organized and integrated by chapter. You will find practice tests, animations, and much more that will complement your learning and understanding of general biology.

www.mhhe.com/maderhuman11

Anatomy & Physiology Revealed

A program that includes cadaver photos that allow you to peel away layers of the human body to reveal structures beneath the surface. This program also includes animations. radiological pronunciations, audio pronunciations and practice quizzing. Check out _www.aprevealed.com_. APR has been proven to help improve student grades!

7

Cardiovascular System

Learning Outcomes

7.1 The Heart
- Name the four chambers of the heart and the blood vessels attached to these chambers.
- Trace the path of blood through the heart, naming the chambers and the valves in proper order.
- Describe the conduction system of the heart, including the nodes that control the heartbeat.

Question: Which side of the heart pumps O_2-poor blood and which side pumps O_2-rich blood?

7.2 Heartbeat and Blood Pressure
- Describe the heartbeat, including the sounds that occur when the heart beats.
- Relate blood pressure to the beat of the heart.
- Show blood pressure rises with exercise and offer an explanation.

Question: Relate normal blood pressure (120/80) to the beat of the heart.

7.3 The Blood and Blood Flow
- Distinguish between red blood cells and the various types of white blood cells.
- Describe the structure and function of arteries, veins, and capillaries.
- Name the major blood vessels and trace the path of blood in both the pulmonary and systemic circuits.

Question: Relate the axiom "structure suits function" to the function of the different types of blood cells.

Application for Daily Living: High Blood Pressure

Introduction

The heart and blood vessels form the cardiovascular system. The heart is a double pump that (1) keeps the blood flowing in one direction—blood flows away from and then back to the heart; (2) keeps O_2-poor blood separate from O_2-rich blood; and (3) creates blood pressure, which moves the blood through the blood vessels. The blood vessels, on the other hand, (1) transport blood and its contents; (2) serve the needs of the body's cells by carrying out exchanges with them; and (3) direct blood flow to those systemic tissues that most require it at the moment.

We will make note of these functions again as we first study the structure and function of the heart and then the blood vessels.

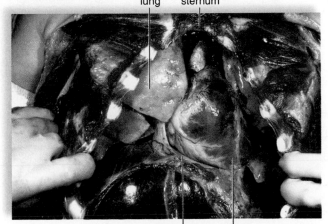

lung   sternum

pericardium   heart

7.1 The Heart

The heart has right and left sides divided by the **septum.** To tell the right from the left side, position Figure 7.1 so it corresponds to your body. There are four **chambers:** two upper, thin-walled atria and two lower, thick-walled ventricles. The heart has valves that keep the blood flowing in one direction; special muscles and tendons secure the valves to prevent backflow from the ventricles to the atria. The right side of the heart sends blood through the lungs, and the left side sends blood into the body. Therefore, the heart is called a double pump.

Anatomy of the Heart

The heart model or preserved sheep heart will be used to study the anatomy of the heart (Fig. 7.1).

> ⚠ **Latex gloves** Wear protective latex gloves when handling preserved animal organs. Use protective eyewear and exercise caution when using sharp instruments during this laboratory. Wash hands thoroughly upon completion of this laboratory.

Figure 7.1 External view of heart.
Externally, notice the coronary arteries and cardiac veins that serve the heart.

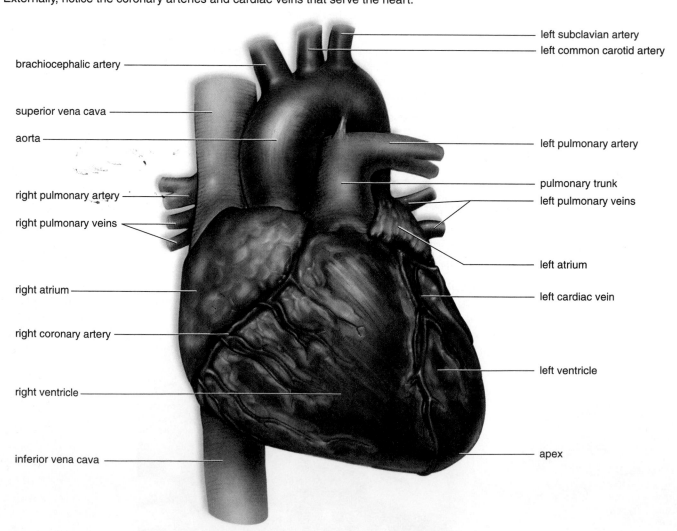

Names of Blood Vessels

1. Use Figure 7.7 to complete Table 7.3 by stating the name of the artery that takes blood to the body part and the name of the vein that takes blood away from the body part.

Table 7.3 Major Blood Vessels in the Systemic Circuit		
Body part	**Artery**	**Vein**
Heart		
Head		
Arms		
Kidney		
Legs		
Intestines		

2. When tracing the path of blood in the systemic system, always mention in the order listed:
    a. What chamber of the heart? _____
    b. What major artery? _____
    c. Name of the artery to an organ, such as _____
    d. Name of vein from this organ, which is _____
    e. One of what two major veins? _____
    f. What chamber of the heart? _____

Application for Daily Living

High Blood Pressure

Blood pressure is an indication of cardiovascular health because high blood pressure at rest is associated with clogged arteries that impede blood flow. Blood should flow freely to all parts of the body and especially to the heart because it has to pump the blood to keep it moving about the body. Unfortunately, the carotid arteries, which serve the heart, are the ones most apt to become clogged with fatty deposits called plaque.

Optimal blood pressure at rest is at or below 120/80. (These numbers are in mm Hg, a way to measure pressure, and systolic blood pressure is given first.) Prehypertension occurs when systolic pressures are between 120 and 139 and diastolic pressures are between 80 and 89 mm Hg. Hypertension, or high blood pressure, occurs when systolic pressure exceeds 140 and diastolic pressure exceeds 90, as in 150/95.

Age (over 55), male gender, and African American ethnicity are all risk factors for developing plaque in the arteries. However, blood pressure can be improved through adequate exercise, good diet, loss of weight, not smoking, and reduced stress.

_____ 1. What type of blood cells are lymphocytes and monocytes?

_____ 2. Nutrients exit and wastes enter which type of blood vessel?

_____ 3. Which blood cells contain a respiratory pigment?

_____ 4. Which chamber of the heart receives venous blood from the systemic circuit?

_____ 5. Identify the vessel that conducts blood from the left ventricle.

_____ 6. The pulmonary trunk leaves which chamber?

_____ 7. Identify the artery that nourishes the heart tissue.

_____ 8. Which heart chamber pumps blood throughout the body?

_____ 9. Which is higher—systolic or diastolic pressure?

_____ 10. Identify the pacemaker region of the heart.

_____ 11. Does the pulmonary artery in adults carry O_2-rich or O_2-poor blood?

_____ 12. Identify the artery that serves the kidney.

_____ 13. Identify the arteries that take blood from the aorta to the legs.

_____ 14. What part of the human body is served by the subclavian vessels?

_____ 15. Identify the large abdominal vein that runs alongside the aorta and enters the right atrium.

_____ 16. Which type of blood vessel (artery or vein) has valves?

Thought Questions

17. Why is it important to maintain an adequate blood pressure?

18. What might be the significance of nonfunctional or defective chordae tendineae?

19. During a heart attack, cardiac muscle cells are deprived of their blood supply, yet the atria are still receiving blood. Explain.

20. Evaluate the following statement: All arteries carry oxygenated blood and all veins carry deoxygenated blood. Based on what you have learned in this laboratory, is this statement correct? Explain your answer.

Human Biology Website

The companion website for _Human Biology_ provides a wealth of information organized and integrated by chapter. You will find practice tests, animations, and much more that will complement your learning and understanding of general biology.

www.mhhe.com/maderhuman11

Anatomy & Physiology Revealed

A program that includes cadaver photos that allow you to peel away layers of the human body to reveal structures beneath the surface. This program also includes animations. radiological pronunciations, audio pronunciations and practice quizzing. Check out _www.aprevealed.com_. APR has been proven to help improve student grades!

8

Chemical Aspects of Digestion

Learning Outcomes

8.1 Protein Digestion by Pepsin
- Associate the enzyme pepsin with the ability of the stomach to digest protein.
- Explain why stomach contents are acid and how a warm body temperature aids digestion.
Question: An acid pH plays what role in digestion by pepsin?

8.2 Fat Digestion by Pancreatic Lipase
- Associate the enzyme lipase with the ability of the small intestine to digest fat.
- Explain why the emulsification process assists the action of lipase.
- Explain why a change in pH indicates that fat digestion had occurred.
- Explain the relationship between time and enzyme activity.
Question: Sufficient time plays what role in digestion by any enzyme?

8.3 Starch Digestion by Pancreatic Amylase
- Associate the enzyme amylase with the ability of the small intestine to digest starch.
- Explain the effect of boiling on the digestive action of amylase.
Question: A denatured enzyme cannot carry out digestion. Explain.

8.4 Requirements for Digestion
- Assuming a specific enzyme, list six factors that can affect the activity of an enzyme.
- Explain why the operative procedure called duodenal switch causes an individual to lose weight.
Question: Of the six factors that can affect enzymatic action, which cause an enzyme to be unable to function to any degree?

Application for Daily Living: Acid Reflux and Heartburn

Introduction

In Laboratory 3, we studied how the enzymes of digestion break down the organic molecules classified as protein, carbohydrate, and fat. Then in Laboratory 6, we examined the organs of digestion in the fetal pig. Now we wish to further our knowledge of the digestive process by associating certain digestive enzymes with particular organs. This will also give us an opportunity to study the action of enzymes, much as William Beaumont did when he took samples through a hole in the stomach wall of his patient, Alexis St. Martin. Every few hours, Beaumont would remove a sample and observe how well the food had been digested. Today, we know that enzymes are very specific and usually participate in only one type of reaction. The active site of an enzyme has a shape that accommodates its substrate, and if an environmental factor such as boiling or the wrong pH disturb this shape, the enzyme loses its ability to function well, if at all. We will have an opportunity to make these observations with controlled experiments. The control sample lacks the enzyme being tested and, therefore, the results should be negative. If it is not negative, then the experiment is invalid.

8.1 Protein Digestion by Pepsin

Certain foods, such as meat and egg whites, are rich in protein. Egg whites contain albumin, the protein used in this exercise. Protein is digested by **pepsin** in the stomach (Fig. 8.1), a process described by the following reaction:

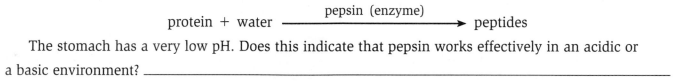

$$\text{protein + water} \xrightarrow{\text{pepsin (enzyme)}} \text{peptides}$$

The stomach has a very low pH. Does this indicate that pepsin works effectively in an acidic or a basic environment? _____

The acidity of the stomach can be troublesome to humans who often have to take antacids or even prescription medications to treat heartburn.

Figure 8.1 Digestion of protein.
Pepsin, produced by the gastric glands of the stomach, helps digest protein.

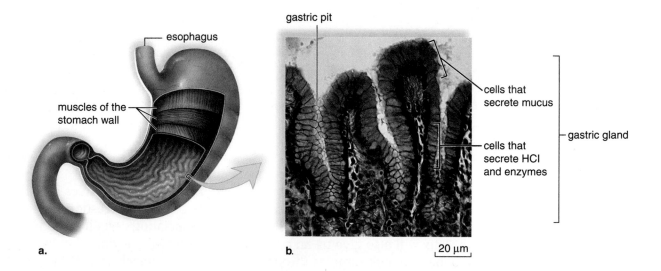

Test for Protein Digestion

Biuret reagent is used to test for protein digestion. If digestion has not occurred, Biuret reagent turns purple, indicating that protein is present. If digestion has occurred, Biuret reagent turns pinkish-purple, indicating that peptides are present.

 Biuret reagent Biuret reagent is highly corrosive. Exercise care in using this chemical. If any should spill on your skin, wash the area with mild soap and water. Use protective eyewear when performing this experiment. Follow your instructor's directions for disposal of this chemical.

With a wax pencil, number four test tubes, and mark at the 2 cm, 4 cm, 6 cm, and 8 cm levels. Fill all tubes to the 2 cm mark with *albumin solution.*

Tube 1 Fill to the 4 cm mark with *pepsin solution* and to the 6 cm mark with *0.2% HCl.* Swirl to mix, and incubate at 37°C. After 1 ½ hours, fill to the 8 cm mark with *Biuret reagent.* Record your results in Table 8.1.

Tube 2 Fill to the 4 cm mark with *pepsin solution* and to the 6 cm mark with *0.2% HCl.* Swirl to mix, and keep at room temperature. After 1 ½ hours, fill to the 8 cm mark with *Biuret reagent.* Record your results in Table 8.1.

Tube 3 Fill to the 4 cm mark with *pepsin solution* and to the 6 cm mark with *water.* Swirl to mix, and incubate at 37°C. After 1 ½ hours, fill to the 8 cm mark with *Biuret reagent.* Record your results in Table 8.1.

Tube 4 Fill to the 6 cm mark with *water.* Swirl to mix, and incubate at 37°C. After 1 ½ hours, fill to the 8 cm mark with *Biuret reagent.* Record your results in Table 8.1.

Table 8.1 Protein Digestion by Pepsin

Tube	Contents	Temperature	Results of Test	Explanation
1	Albumin Pepsin HCl Biuret reagent			
2	Albumin Pepsin HCl Biuret reagent			
3	Albumin Pepsin Water Biuret reagent			
4	Albumin Water Biuret reagent			

Conclusions: Protein Digestion

- Explain your results in Table 8.1 by giving a reason digestion did or did not occur.

- Which tube was the control? _____

  Explain. _____

- If this control tube had given a positive result for protein digestion, what could you conclude about this experiment? _____

8.2 Fat Digestion by Pancreatic Lipase

Lipids include fats (e.g., butterfat) and oils (e.g., sunflower, corn, olive, and canola). Lipids are digested by **pancreatic lipase** in the small intestine, a process described by the following two reactions:

(1) fat $\xrightarrow{\text{bile (emulsifier)}}$ fat droplets

(2) fat droplets + water $\xrightarrow{\text{lipase (enzyme)}}$ glycerol + fatty acids

Both of these steps occur in the small intestine, where bile enters from the gallbladder and lipase enters from the pancreas (Fig. 8.2).

With regard to the first step, consider that fat is not soluble in water; yet, lipase makes use of water when it digests fat. Therefore, bile is needed to emulsify fat—cause it to break up into fat droplets that disperse in water. The reason for disperal is that bile contains molecules with two ends. One end is soluble in fat, and the other end is soluble in water. Bile can emulsify fat because of this.

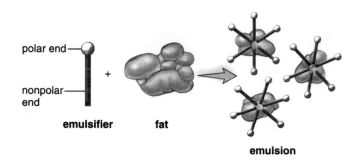

With regard to the second step, would the pH of the solution be lower before or after the enzymatic reaction? (*Hint:* Remember that an acid decreases pH and a base increases pH.) _____

_____

Figure 8.2 Emulsification and digestion of fat.
Bile from the liver (stored in the gallbladder) enters the small intestine, where lipase in pancreatic juice from the pancreas digests fat.

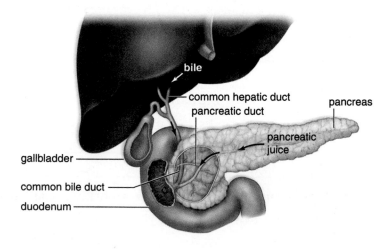

Test for Fat Digestion

In the test for fat digestion you will be using a pH indicator that changes color as the solution in the test tube goes from basic conditions to acidic conditions. Phenol red is a pH indicator that is red in basic solutions and yellow in acidic solutions. Bile salts will be used as an emulsifier.

Experimental Procedure: Fat Digestion

With a wax pencil, number three clean test tubes, and mark at the 1 cm, 3 cm, and 5 cm levels. Fill all the tubes to the 1 cm mark with *vegetable oil* and to the 3 cm mark with *phenol red*.

Tube 1   Fill to the 5 cm mark with *pancreatin solution* (pancreatic lipase). Add a pinch of *bile salts*. Invert gently to mix, and record the initial color in Table 8.2. Incubate at 37°C, and check every 20 minutes. Record the length of time for any color change.

Tube 2   Fill to the 5 cm mark with *pancreatin solution*. Invert gently to mix, and record the initial color in Table 8.2. Incubate at 37°C, and check every 20 minutes. Record the length of time for any color change.

Tube 3   Fill to the 5 cm mark with *water*. Invert gently to mix, and record the initial color in Table 8.2. Incubate at 37°C, and check every 20 minutes. Record the length of time for any color change.

Table 8.2 Fat Digestion by Pancreatic Lipase

Tube	Contents	Time	Color Change		Explanation
			Initial	*Final*	
1	Vegetable oil Phenol red Pancreatin Bile salts				
2	Vegetable oil Phenol red Pancreatin				
3	Vegetable oil Phenol red Water				

Conclusions: Fat Digestion

- Explain your results in Table 8.2 by giving a reason why digestion did or did not occur.

- What role did bile salts play in this experiment? _____

_____

- What role did phenol red play in this experiment? _____

- Which test tube in this experiment could be considered a control? _____

_____

8.3 Starch Digestion by Pancreatic Amylase

Starch is present in bakery products and in potatoes, rice, and corn. Starch is digested by **pancreatic amylase** in the small intestine, a process described by the following reaction:

$$\text{starch} + \text{water} \xrightarrow{\text{amylase (enzyme)}} \text{maltose}$$

1. If digestion does *not* occur, which will be present—starch or maltose? _____

2. If digestion *does* occur, which will be present—starch or maltose? _____

3. To which category of organic compounds (carbohydrate, fat, or protein) do enzymes such as amylase

   belong? _____ What happens to enzymes when

   they are boiled? _____ Will disgestion occur?_____

   Explain._____

Tests for Starch Digestion

You will be using two tests for starch digestion:

1. If digestion has not taken place, the iodine test for starch will be positive. If starch is present, a blue-black color immediately appears after a few drops of iodine are added to the test tube.

2. If digestion has taken place, a test for sugar (maltose) will be positive. To test for sugar, add an equal amount of Benedict's reagent to the test tube. Place the tube in a boiling water bath for two to five minutes, and note any color changes. A color change of blue $\longrightarrow$ green $\longrightarrow$ yellow $\longrightarrow$ orange $\longrightarrow$ red indicates the presence of maltose. Red shows the highest concentration of maltose and green shows the lowest (see Table 8.4, page 99). Boiling the test tube is necessary for the Benedict's reagent to react.

 Benedict's reagent Use protective eyewear when performing this experiment. Benedict's reagent is highly corrosive. Exercise care in using this chemical. If any should spill on your skin, wash area with mild soap and water. Follow your instructor's directions for disposal of this chemical.

Preparation

1. With a wax pencil, number eight clean test tubes above the level of the boiling water bath, and mark at the 1 cm and 2 cm levels.
2. Fill tubes 1 through 6 to the 1 cm mark with *pancreatic amylase solution.* Fill tubes 7 and 8 to the 1 cm mark with *water.*
3. Shake the starch suspension well each time before dispensing.
4. Fill tubes 3 and 4 to the 2 cm mark with *starch suspension,* and allow them to stand at room temperature for 30 minutes.
5. Place tubes 5 and 6 in a boiling water bath for 10 minutes. After boiling, fill to the 2 cm mark with *starch suspension,* and allow the tubes to stand for 20 minutes.
6. Fill tubes 7 and 8 to the 2 cm mark with *starch suspension.* Allow the tubes to stand for 30 minutes.

Testing

Tube 1	Fill to the 2 cm mark with *starch suspension,* and test for starch *immediately,* using the iodine test described previously. Record your results in Table 8.3.
Tube 2	Fill to the 2 cm mark with *starch suspension,* and test for sugar *immediately,* using *Benedict's reagent,* described earlier, which requires boiling. Record your results in Table 8.3.

Why do you expect tube 1 to have a positive test for starch and tube 2 to have a negative test for

sugar? _____

Record your explanation in Table 8.3.

Tubes 3, 5, and 7	After 30 minutes, test for starch using the iodine test. Record your results in Table 8.3.
Tubes 4, 6, and 8	After 30 minutes, test for sugar using the Benedict's test. Record your results in Table 8.3.

Why do you expect tube 3 to have a negative test for starch and tube 4 to have a positive test for

sugar? _____

Why do you expect tube 5 to have a positive test for starch and tube 6 to have a negative test for

sugar? _____

Why do you expect tube 7 to have a positive test for starch and tube 8 to have a negative test for

sugar? _____

Record your explanations for your results in Table 8.3.

Table 8.3 Starch Digestion by Amylase

Tube	Contents	Time	Type of Test	Results	Explanation
1	Pancreatic amylase Starch				
2	Pancreatic amylase Starch				
3	Pancreatic amylase Starch				
4	Pancreatic amylase Starch				
5	Pancreatic amylase boiled Starch				
6	Pancreatic amylase boiled Starch				
7	Water Starch				
8	Water Starch				

Conclusions: Starch Digestion

- This experiment demonstrated that, for an enzymatic reaction to occur, an active

  _____ must be present, and _____ must pass to allow the reaction to occur.

- Which test tubes served as a control in this experiment? _____

  Explain. _____

Absorption of Sugars and Other Nutrients

Figure 8.3 shows that the folded lining of the small intestine has many fingerlike projections called villi. The small intestine not only digests food, it also absorbs the products of digestion, such as sugars from carbohydrate digestion, amino acids from protein digestion, and glycerol and fatty acids from fat digestion at the villi.

Figure 8.3 Anatomy of the small intestine.
Nutrients enter the bloodstream across the much convoluted walls of the small intestine.

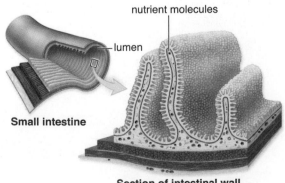

nutrient molecules

lumen

Small intestine

Section of intestinal wall

8.4 Requirements for Digestion

Explain in Table 8.4 how each of the requirements listed influences effective digestion.

Table 8.4 Requirements for Digestion	
Requirement	**Explanation**
Specific enzyme	
Specific substrate	
Warm temperature	
Time	
Specific pH	
Fat emulsifier	

To lose weight, some obese individuals undergo an operation in which the stomach is reduced to the size of a golf ball, and food bypasses the duodenum (first two feet) of the intestine. To explain how this operation would affect the requirements for digestion, answer these questions:

1. Why is the amount of substrate reduced? _____

2. Why is the amount of digestive enzymes reduced? _____

3. Why is time reduced? _____

4. Why is the pH of the small intestine higher than before? _____

5. Why is fat emulsification reduced? _____

6. Why does surgery to reduce obesity sometimes result in malnutrition?

_____

Application for Daily Living

Acid Reflux and Heartburn

In the absence of other symptoms, that burning sensation in your chest may have nothing to do with your heart. Instead, it is likely due to acid reflux. The stomach contents are more acidic than those of the esophagus. When the stomach contents pass upward into the esophagus, the acidity begins to erode the lining of the esophagus, producing the burning sensation associated with heartburn.

These measures can help avoid acid reflux and heartburn:

- Avoid high-fat meals, such as those served by fast-food chains.
- Eat several small meals instead of three large meals; don't overeat at any particular meal.
- Exercise at a slow pace. Riding a bike, walking, yoga, and light weight lifting are helpful.
- Keep your weight down to avoid pressure being placed on the stomach by excess abdominal weight.

_____ 1. When iodine (IKI) solution turns blue-black, what substance is present?

_____ 2. What color is Benedict's reagent originally?

_____ 3. What happens to an enzyme when it is boiled?

_____ 4. Saliva and pancreatic juice contains what enzyme to digest starch?

_____ 5. As oil is digested, why does the solution turn from red to yellow, indicating an acid pH?

_____ 6. What temperature promotes enzymatic action?

_____ 7. What do you call a sample that goes through all the steps of an experiment but lacks the factor being tested?

_____ 8. What role do bile salts play in the digestion of fat?

_____ 9. What color does Biuret reagent turn when peptides are present?

_____ 10. Is the optimal pH for pepsin acidic or basic?

_____ 11. Why would you predict that pepsin would not digest starch?

_____ 12. In addition to pepsin and water, what is needed to digest protein?

_____ 13. Name the enzyme responsible for the hydrolysis of starch.

Thought Questions

14. Which of the following two combinations is most likely to result in digestion?

    a. Pepsin, protein, water, body temperature

    b. Pepsin, protein, hydrochloric acid (HCl), body temperature

    Explain.

15. Which of the following two combinations is most likely to result in digestion?

    a. Amylase, starch, water, body temperature, testing immediately

    b. Amylase, starch, water, body temperature, waiting 30 minutes

    Explain.

Human Biology Website

The companion website for _Human Biology_ provides a wealth of information organized and integrated by chapter. You will find practice tests, animations, and much more that will complement your learning and understanding of general biology.

www.mhhe.com/maderhuman11

McGraw-Hill Access Science Website

An online encyclopedia of science and technology that provides information, including videos, that can enhance the laboratory experience.

www.accessscience.com

9

Energy Requirements and Ideal Weight

Learning Outcomes

9.1 Average Daily Energy Intake
- Keep a food diary and use it to calculate your average daily energy intake.
Question: What unit of measurement is used for daily energy intake?

9.2 Average Daily Energy Requirement
- Keep a physical activity diary and use it to calculate average daily energy required for physical activity.
- Calculate the daily energy required for your basal metabolism.
- Calculate the daily energy required for your specific dynamic action.
- Calculate your total average daily energy requirement.
Question: Daily energy requirement has what three components?

9.3 Comparison of Average Daily Energy Intake and Average Daily Energy Requirement
- Predict whether weight gain or weight loss will occur after energy intake is compared to energy required.
Question: What two energy measurements determine whether you gain weight or lose weight?

9.4 Ideal Weight
- Calculate ideal weight based on body mass index (BMI).
- Calculate ideal weight based on body composition.
- Make a recommendation regarding daily energy intake and daily energy required for achieving or maintaining ideal weight.
Question: What are two methods for calculating ideal weight?

Introduction

This laboratory helps you determine your average daily energy (Kcal) requirements, your average daily energy (Kcal) intake, and your ideal weight. In addition to the energy content of food, other nutritional aspects are also important. Minerals and vitamins, along with specific types of biological molecules, contribute to a healthy diet. So, while the focus of this lab is on energy in our food, there is more to diet than just calories.

Before you come to the laboratory, it is necessary for you to keep two daily diaries for three days. The physical activity diary is a record of the energy you expend for physical activity. Physical activity is only a portion of your daily energy requirement. You also need energy for **basal metabolism** (energy needed when the body is resting) and **specific dynamic action** (energy needed to process food), also known as thermal effect of food.

The food diary is a record of the energy you take in as food. If the energy you expend and the energy you take in are in balance, you will neither gain nor lose weight. If your ideal weight is different from your present weight, you will be able to determine whether to increase or decrease your physical activity and food intake to attain an ideal weight.

9.1 Average Daily Energy Intake

To complete this laboratory, you must calculate an average daily energy intake. The first method given is preferred because it makes use of your actual intake. However, when appropriate, a hypothetical method is also provided.

Personal Diet

Follow these directions.

1. Keep a written food diary of your own design for three days. Your diary should list all food and beverages consumed throughout an entire three-day period, including snacks and alcoholic beverages.
2. Make sure your food diary contains a column for recording the energy in Kcal (K calories)* of the food you eat. Table 9.1 may be helpful to you in this regard. Also, food packages often contain Kcal information, as do various calorie books and computer programs. For example, after eating two slices of bread, your diary might look like this:

Day of Week _____

Type of Food	Portion Size	Kcal	Total Kcal
Bread	Two slices	70/one slice	140

Continue in this manner until you have listed all the foods you eat in one day. Do the same for two more days.

3. Add up your total Kcal intake for each day, and record the information here:

   Day 1 energy intake _____ Kcal

   Day 2 energy intake _____ Kcal

   Day 3 energy intake _____ Kcal

   Total _____ Kcal

4. Divide the total by 3 to calculate the average daily energy intake.

   Av. energy intake/day = _____ Kcal

*The amount of heat required to raise 1 kg (kilogram) of water 1°C.

Table 9.1 Nutrient and Energy Content of Foods*

Breads

1 slice of bread or any of the following:

3/4 cup ready-to-eat cereal

1/3 cup corn

1 small potato

(1 bread = 15 g carbohydrate, 20 g protein, and 70 Kcal)

Milk

1 cup skim milk or: (2% milk—add 5 g fat)

1 cup skim-milk yogurt, plain   (Whole milk—add 8 g fat)

1 cup buttermilk

1/2 cup evaporated skim milk or milk dessert

(1 milk = 12 g carbohydrate, 8 g protein, and 80 Kcal)

Vegetables

1/2 cup greens

1/2 cup carrots

1/2 cup beets

(1 vegetable = 5 g carbohydrate, 1 g protein, and 25 Kcal)

Fruits

1/2 small banana or

1 small apple

1/2 cup orange juice or 1/2 grapefruit

(1 fruit = 10 g carbohydrate and 40 Kcal)

Meats (lean)

1 oz. lean meat or:

1 oz. chicken meat without the skin

1 oz. any fish

1/4 cup canned tuna or 1 oz. low-fat cheese

(1 oz. low-fat meat = 7 g protein, 3 g fat, and 55 Kcal)

Meats (medium fat)

1 oz. pork loin

1 egg

1/4 cup creamed cottage cheese

(1 medium-fat meat = 7 g protein,

5 1/2 g fat, and about 80 Kcal)

Meats (high fat)

1 oz. high-fat meat is like:

1 oz. country-style ham

1 oz. cheddar cheese

A small hot dog (frankfurter)

(1 high-fat meat = 7 g protein, 8 g fat, and 100 Kcal)

Peanut butter

Peanut butter is like a meat in terms of its protein content but is very high in fat. It is estimated as (2 Tbsp. peanut butter = 7 g protein, 15 1/2 g fat, and about 170 Kcal)

Fats

1 tsp. butter or margarine

1 tsp. any oil

1 Tbsp. salad dressing

1 strip crisp bacon

5 small olives

10 whole Virginia peanuts

(1 fat = 5 g fat and 45 Kcal)

Legumes (beans and peas)

Legumes are like meats because they are rich in protein and iron, but are lower in fat than meat. They contain much starch. They can be treated as (1/2 cup legumes = 15 g carbohydrate, 9 g protein, 3 g fat, and 125 Kcal)

Miscellaneous Foods								
	g (grams)			Kcal		g (grams)		Kcal
	Protein	Fat	Carbohydrate			Protein	Fat	Carbohydrate	

	Protein	Fat	Carbohydrate	Kcal		Protein	Fat	Carbohydrate	Kcal
Ice cream (1 cup)	5	14	32	274	Beer (1 can)	1	0	14	60
Cake (1 piece)	3	1	32	149	Soft drink	0	0	37	148
Doughnuts (1)	3	11	22	199	Soup (1 cup)	2	3	15	95
Pie	3	15	51	351	Coffee and tea	0	0	0	0
Caramel candy (1 oz.)	1	3	22	119					

From B. L. Frye and R. L. Neill, "A Laboratory Exercise in Nutrition" in *American Biology Teacher* 9:372, 1987. Copyright © 1987 National Association of Biology Teachers, Reston, VA.

*Use this table for the Food Diary mentioned on p. 102.

Hypothetical Diet

Suppose you have decided to eat your meals at the fast-food restaurants listed on this page.

1. Circle the restaurant and the items you have chosen for breakfast, lunch, and dinner. Choose a different restaurant for each meal.
2. Record the number of Kcal for the items chosen.
3. Add the number of Kcal.
4. This will be your average energy intake/day.

Fast-Food Menus and Calories

Restaurant/Menu	Calories	Restaurant/Menu	Calories
Taco Bell (www.tacobell.com)		**McDonald's (www.mcdonalds.com)**	
Steak Baja chalupa	390	Egg McMuffin®	300
Soft beef taco supreme	240	Sausage McMuffin® w/egg	450
Chicken Baja gordita	320	Ham and egg cheese bagel	550
Spicy chicken soft taco	170	Hash browns	130
Nachos Bellgrande®	760	Hotcakes (w/margarine & syrup)	350
Soft drink (small)	150	Breakfast burrito	290
Subway (www.subway.com)		6 pc. chicken nugget	280
Meatball marinara	560	Barbeque sauce	50
6" roasted chicken breast	310	Hamburger	250
6" roast beef	290	Quarter pounder w/cheese	510
Soft drink (small)	150	Big Mac	540
Burger King (www.burgerking.com)		Filet-O-Fish	380
Croissan'wich® w/sausage, egg & cheese	520	Chicken McGrill w/mayo	420
Croissan'wich® w/egg & cheese	320	Med. french fries	380
Egg'wich™ w/Canadian bacon & egg	380	Large french fries	500
French toast sticks	390	Hot fudge sundae	340
Lg. hash brown rounds	390	Vanilla milk shake	570
Double Whopper w/Cheese and mayo	1150	Soft drink (small)	150
Whopper w/cheese and mayo	760	**Papa John's (www.papajohns.com)**	
BK big fish	710	Cheese pizza	283
King-sized fries w/salt	600	All-meat pizza	390
Med.-sized fries w/salt	360	Garden special pizza	280
King-sized onion rings	550	The works pizza	342
Med.-sized onion rings	320	Cheese sticks	180
Dutch apple pie	340	Breadsticks	140
Hershey's sundae pie	310	Garlic sauce	235
Soft drink (small)	150	Pizza sauce	25
Vanilla milk shake (medium)	720	Nacho cheese sauce	60
		Soft drink (small)	150

Av. energy intake/day = _____ Kcal

9.2 Average Daily Energy Requirement

As stated at the beginning of this laboratory, the body needs energy for three purposes: (1) energy for physical activity, (2) energy to support basal metabolism, and (3) energy for the specific dynamic action of processing food. We will calculate the daily energy requirement for each of these.

Calculating Average Daily Energy Required for Physical Activity

You will need to know your average daily energy requirement for physical activity before coming to this laboratory.

1. Keep a physical activity diary for three days. Make three copies of Table 9.2, one for each day.
2. See the nomogram in Figure 9.1 (Scale 3), p. 107, to convert your body weight to kg (kilograms). Place this value on the appropriate line in your physical activity diary (Table 9.2).
3. Consult Table 9.3 and fill in column 4 of your physical activity diary.
4. Fill in column 5 of your physical activity diary by using a calculator and this formula:

$$\underset{\text{(min.)}}{\text{time spent}} \times \text{energy cost} \times \underset{\text{(kg)}}{\text{body weight}} = \underset{\text{Kcal}}{\text{total energy expended}}$$

Therefore, if 100 minutes were spent doing typing, and the body weight is 77.3 kg, the Kcal expended for typing would be

$$100 \text{ min} \times 0.01 \text{ Kcal/kg min.} \times 77.3 \text{ kg} = 77.3 \text{ Kcal}$$

5. Total the number of Kcal expended for each of the three days, and divide this total by 3 to get the average (av.) daily energy required for physical activity:

Energy for physical activity (day 1)   _____ Kcal (see p. 106)

Energy for physical activity (day 2)   _____ Kcal

Energy for physical activity (day 3)   _____ Kcal

Total energy for physical activity/three days   _____ Kcal

Av. energy required for physical activity/day   _____ Kcal

A completed food diary and physical activity diary are necessary before you begin the laboratory.

Table 9.2 Physical Activity Diary for One Day

Time of Day	Activity	Time Spent (min.)	Factor (Kcal/kg min.)	Total Energy Expended (Kcal)

Body weight _____ kg   Total energy expended _____

Table 9.3 Energy Cost for Activities (exclusive of basal metabolism and specific dynamic action)

Type of Activity	Energy Cost (Kcal/kg min.)	Type of Activity	Energy Cost (Kcal/kg min.)
Sitting or standing still	0.010	Heavy exercise	0.070
Studying		Fast dancing	
Writing		Walking uphill	
Typing		Jogging	
TV watching		Fast swimming	
Eating		Severe exercise	0.110
Very light activity	0.020	Tennis	
Driving car		Racquetball	
Walking slowly		Running	
Light exercise	0.025	Aerobic dancing	
Light housework		Soccer	
Walking at moderate speed		Very severe exercise	0.140
Carrying books or packages		Wrestling	
Moderate exercise	0.040	Boxing	
Fast walking		Racing	
Slow dancing		Rowing	
Slow bicycling		Full-court basketball	
Golf			

Calculating Daily Energy Required for BMR

Basal metabolism is the minimum amount of energy the body needs at rest in the fasting state. The beating of the heart, breathing, maintaining body temperature, and sending nerve impulses are some of the activities that maintain life. The **basal metabolic rate (BMR)** is the rate at which Kcal are spent for basal metabolism—these maintenance activities. BMR varies according to a person's sex, age, and amount of body surface area. For example, a tall, thin person has a higher BMR than a short, stout person. Also, the younger the person, the more likely it is that cell division is occurring; therefore, BMR is higher for younger persons than for older persons. Males have a higher BMR than females because males have a greater percentage of muscle tissue. The Experimental Procedure for calculating BMR takes all these factors into consideration.

Figure 9.1 Nomogram to estimate body surface area from height and weight.

A straight line is drawn from the subject's height (Scale 1) to the subject's weight (Scale 3). The point at which the line intersects Scale 2 is the subject's body surface area in m^2 (meters squared).

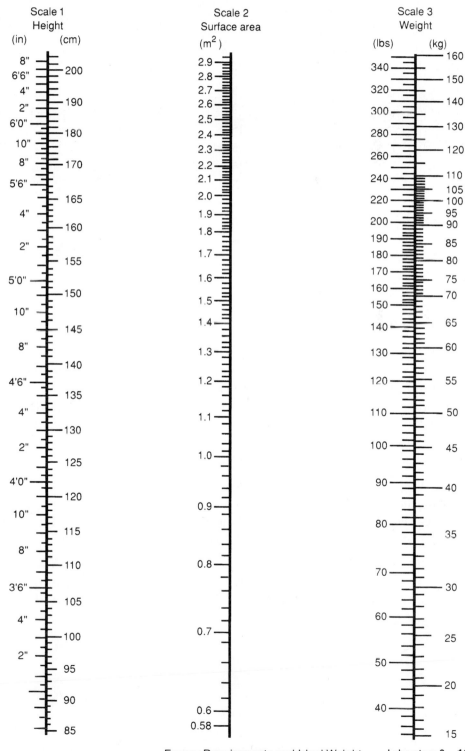

Table 9.4 Basal Metabolic Rate Constants

	BMR (Kcal/m^2 hr)				BMR (Kcal/m^2 hr)	
Age	Males	Females	Age	Males	Females
10	47.7	44.9	29	37.7	35.0
11	46.5	43.5	30	37.6	35.0
12	45.3	42.0	31	37.4	35.0
13	44.5	40.5	32	37.2	34.9
14	43.8	39.2	33	37.1	34.9
15	42.9	38.3	34	37.0	34.9
16	42.0	37.2	35	36.9	34.8
17	41.5	36.4	36	36.8	34.7
18	40.8	35.8	37	36.7	34.6
19	40.5	35.4	38	36.7	34.5
20	39.9	35.3	39	36.6	34.4
21	39.5	35.2	40–44	36.4	34.1
22	39.2	35.2	45–49	36.2	33.8
23	39.0	35.2	50–54	35.8	33.1
24	38.7	35.1	55–59	35.1	32.8
25	38.4	35.1	60–64	34.5	32.0
26	38.2	35.0	65–69	33.5	31.6
27	38.0	35.0	70–74	32.7	31.1
28	37.8	35.0	75+	31.8	

W. M. Boothby in *Handbook of Biological Data*, edited by W. S. Spector. Copyright © 1956 W. B. Saunders, Orlando, FL.

Experimental Procedure

1. Use the scale and measuring device available to determine your weight and height. It is assumed that you are fully clothed and wearing shoes with a 1-inch heel. **Be honest about your weight.** There is no need to tell anyone else.

2. Body surface area. Use the data you have just collected and Figure 9.1 to determine your body surface area. Using a ruler, draw a straight line from your height to your weight. The point where that line crosses the middle column shows your surface area in m^2 (squared meters). For example, a person who is 6 ft tall and weighs 170 lbs has a body surface area of 1.99 m^2.

   What is your body surface area? _____

3. Hourly BMR. Use Table 9.4 to find the BMR constant for your age and sex. Multiply your surface area by this factor to calculate your BMR/hr. For example, a 17-year-old male has a BMR constant of 41.5 Kcal/m^2 hr. If his surface area is 1.99 m^2, his BMR is 82.6 Kcal/hr.

   What is your BMR/hr? _____

4. Daily BMR. Multiply your hourly rate by 24 to obtain the total number of Kcal you need for BMR/day. For example, if the BMR is 82.6 Kcal/hr, then the daily BMR rate is 1,982 Kcal/day.

   What is your **BMR/day?** _____

Calculating Energy Required for SDA

The **specific dynamic action (SDA)** refers to the amount of energy needed to process food. For example, muscles that move food along the digestive tract and glands that make digestive juices use up energy. To calculate the amount of average energy you require for daily SDA, add the energy for daily BMR and the average energy required for daily physical activity. Multiply the total by 10% to obtain an estimated daily SDA. For example, if 1,882 Kcal/day are required for BMR and 1,044 Kcal/day are required for physical activity, then an average SDA = 293 Kcal/day.

What is your **average SDA/day?** _____ Kcal

Calculating Average Daily Energy Requirement

Total the amounts you have calculated for average daily physical activity, daily BMR, and average daily SDA. This is your average (av.) energy requirement/day.

Av. physical activity/day   _____ Kcal (see p. 105)

BMR/day   _____ Kcal (see p. 108)

Av. SDA/day   _____ Kcal (see p. 109, above)

Av. energy requirement/day = _____ Kcal

9.3 Comparison of Average Daily Energy Intake and Average Daily Energy Requirement

Figure 9.2 illustrates that if the average daily energy intake is the same as the average daily energy requirement, weight is likely to remain the same.

1. Compare your average daily energy intake (p. 102 or p. 104) to your average daily energy requirement: _____

2. Our methods of calculation are only approximate. If your two figures are within 20% of each other, you will most likely neither lose nor gain weight. If the two figures are not within 20% of each other, are you apt to lose weight or gain weight? _____

Explain. _____

_____

Figure 9.2   **Comparison between average daily energy intake and average daily energy requirement.**
If average daily energy intake is the same as the average daily energy requirement, the person's weight stays the same.

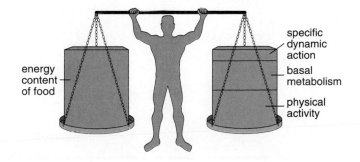

9.4 Ideal Weight

Three methods of determining your ideal weight are explained next. Your instructor will choose which one you are to use.

Ideal Weight Based on Height and Weight Tables

Tables 9.5 and 9.6 are constructed by life insurance companies from data on thousands of people, at an age when bone and muscle growth is complete. Such tables are not highly accurate. Determine your

Table 9.5 Weight and Height Table for Males

Height (ft)	Height (in)	Small Frame (lb)	Medium Frame (lb)	Large Frame (lb)
5	2	128–134	131–141	138–150
5	3	130–136	133–143	140–153
5	4	132–138	135–145	142–156
5	5	134–140	137–148	144–160
5	6	136–142	139–151	146–164
5	7	138–145	142–154	149–168
5	8	140–148	145–157	152–172
5	9	142–151	148–160	155–176
5	10	144–154	151–163	158–180
5	11	146–157	154–166	161–184
6	0	149–160	157–170	164–188
6	1	152–164	160–174	168–192
6	2	155–168	164–178	172–197
6	3	158–172	167–182	176–202
6	4	162–176	171–187	181–207

Table 9.6 Weight and Height Table for Females

Height (ft)	Height (in)	Small Frame (lb)	Medium Frame (lb)	Large Frame (lb)
4	10	102–111	109–121	118–131
4	11	103–113	111–123	120–134
5	0	104–115	113–126	122–137
5	1	106–118	115–129	125–140
5	2	108–121	118–132	128–143
5	3	111–124	121–135	131–147
5	4	114–127	124–138	134–151
5	5	117–130	127–141	137–155
5	6	120–133	130–144	140–159
5	7	123–136	133–147	143–163
5	8	126–139	136–150	146–167
5	9	129–142	139–153	149–170
5	10	132–145	142–156	152–173
5	11	135–148	145–159	155–176
6	0	138–151	148–162	158–179

Weight at ages 25–59 based on lowest mortality. Weight according to frame (indoor clothing weighing 3 lb is allowed for women; 5 lb for men), shoes with 1-inch heels. Courtesy of Metropolitan Life Insurance Co.

ideal weight range. A person more than 10% over the weight in the tables is overweight; a person 20% over is obese. Similarly, a person 10% below the weight in the table is underweight. What is your ideal weight based on these height and weight tables?

Ideal weight _____ lb

Ideal Weight Based on Body Mass Index (BMI)

Your BMI is a measure of your weight relative to your height. The formula to calculate your BMI is: $BMI = Kg/m^2$. Table 9.7, based on pounds and inches, has done the math for you. To use the table, find the row with your height in inches. Go across that row to the column corresponding to your weight. Read up the column to the top where it lists your BMI (numbered 19–35). A BMI of 18.5–24.9 is considered ideal. Below a BMI of 18.5, a person is considered underweight, and above a BMI of 25, a person is considered overweight. A person is considered obese with a BMI of 30 or greater.

Table 9.7   Body Mass Index

	19	20	21	22	23	24	25	26	27	28	29	30	31	32	33	34	35
Height (inches)								Body weight (pounds)									
58	91	96	100	105	110	115	119	124	129	134	138	143	148	153	158	162	167
59	94	99	104	109	114	119	124	128	133	138	143	148	153	158	163	168	173
60	97	102	107	112	118	123	128	133	138	143	148	153	158	163	168	174	179
61	100	106	111	116	122	127	132	137	143	148	153	158	164	169	174	180	185
62	104	109	115	120	126	131	136	142	147	153	158	164	169	175	180	186	191
63	107	113	118	124	130	135	141	146	152	158	163	169	175	180	186	191	197
64	110	116	122	128	134	140	145	151	157	163	169	174	180	186	192	197	204
65	114	120	126	132	138	144	150	156	162	168	174	180	186	192	198	204	210
66	118	124	130	136	142	148	155	161	167	173	179	186	192	198	204	210	216
67	121	127	134	140	146	153	159	166	172	178	185	191	198	204	211	217	223
68	125	131	138	144	151	158	164	171	177	184	190	197	203	210	216	223	230
69	128	135	142	149	155	162	169	176	182	189	196	203	209	216	223	230	236
70	132	139	146	153	160	167	174	181	188	195	202	209	216	222	229	236	243
71	136	143	150	157	165	172	179	186	193	200	208	215	222	229	236	243	250
72	140	147	154	162	169	177	184	191	199	206	213	221	228	235	242	250	258
73	144	151	159	166	174	182	189	197	204	212	219	227	235	242	250	257	265
74	148	155	163	171	179	186	194	202	210	218	225	233	241	249	256	264	272
75	152	160	168	176	184	192	200	208	216	224	232	240	248	256	264	272	279
76	156	164	172	180	189	197	205	213	221	230	238	246	254	263	271	279	287

National Heart, Lung, and Blood Institute

Experimental Procedure: Ideal Weight

1. Use Table 9.7 as directed, and determine your BMI. _____
2. Is your BMI within the normal range (18.5–24.9)? _____ If not, do you need to gain or lose weight? _____

Comparison

How does your ideal weight range based on BMI compare to your ideal weight based on the height and weight tables? _____

Ideal Weight Based on Body Composition

Body composition refers to the lean body weight plus the body fat. In adult males, lean body weight should equal about 84% of weight, and body fat should be only 16% of weight. In adult females, lean body weight should equal about 77% of weight, and body fat should be only 23% of weight. Well-conditioned male athletes, such as marathon runners and swimmers, usually have 10–12% body fat, whereas football players can have as high as 19–20% body fat. At no time should the percent of body fat drop below 5% in males and 10% in females.

To calculate **lean body weight (LBW)**, it is necessary to subtract your present amount of body fat from your present weight. The amount of body fat is to be determined by taking skin-fold measurements, because the fat attached to the skin is roughly proportional to total body fat. The more areas of the body measured, the more accurate the estimate of body fat will be. In this laboratory, we will take only those measurements that permit you to remain fully clothed.

Experimental Procedure: Lean Body Weight

1. Work in pairs. Obtain calipers designed to measure skin folds. All measurements should be done on the right side in mm (millimeters). Firmly grasp the fold of skin between the left thumb and the other four fingers and lift. Pinch and lift the fold several times to make sure no musculature is grasped. Hold the skin fold firmly, and place the contact side of the calipers 1/2 inch below the thumb and fingers; do not let go of the fold. Close the calipers on the skin fold, and do the measurements noted in items 2–6 following. Take the reading to the nearest 1/2 mm. Release the grip on the caliper and release the fold. To make sure the reading is accurate, repeat the measurement a few times. If the second measurement is within 1–2 mm of the first, it is reliable.

2. **Triceps (females only).** The triceps skin fold is measured on the back of the upper arm, halfway between the elbow and the tip of the shoulder, while the arm is hanging loosely at the subject's side. Grasp the skin fold parallel to the long axis of the arm and measure as described in step 1. Record in #7 below.

3. **Ilium—hip (males and females).** Fold the skin diagonally just above the top of the hip bone on an imaginary line that would divide the body into front and back halves. Measure and record as before.

4. **Abdomen (males and females).** Fold the skin vertically 1 inch to the right of the navel. Measure and record as before.

5. **Chest (males only).** Fold the skin diagonally, midway between the nipple and the armpit. Measure and record as before.

6. **Axilla—side (males only).** Fold the skin vertically at the level of nipple on an imaginary line that would divide the body into front and back halves. Measure and record as before.

7. Total your skin-fold measurements.

	Females	Males
Triceps	_____ mm	
Ilium	_____ mm	_____ mm
Abdomen	_____ mm	_____ mm
Chest		_____ mm
Axilla		_____ mm
Total skin-fold measurements	_____ mm	_____ mm

8. Consult Table 9.8 (males) and Table 9.9 (females) to determine percent (%) body fat from the sum of your skin-fold measurements.

What is your % body fat? _____ %

Table 9.8 Percent Fat Estimates for Males

Sum of 4 Skin Folds (mm)	Age to Last Year								
	18–22	23–27	28–32	33–37	38–42	43–47	48–52	53–57	58–older
8–12	1.9	2.5	3.2	3.8	4.4	5.0	5.7	6.3	6.9
13–17	3.3	3.9	4.5	5.1	5.7	6.4	7.0	7.6	8.2
18–22	4.5	5.2	5.8	6.4	7.0	7.7	8.3	8.9	9.5
23–27	5.8	6.4	7.1	7.7	8.3	8.9	9.5	10.2	10.8
28–32	7.1	7.7	8.3	8.9	9.5	10.2	10.8	11.4	12.0
33–37	8.3	8.9	9.5	10.1	10.8	11.4	12.0	12.6	13.2
38–42	9.5	10.1	10.7	11.3	11.9	12.6	13.2	13.8	14.4
43–47	10.6	11.6	11.9	12.5	13.1	13.7	14.4	15.0	15.6
48–52	11.8	12.4	13.0	13.6	14.2	14.9	15.5	16.1	16.7
53–57	12.9	13.5	14.1	14.7	15.4	16.0	16.6	17.2	17.9
58–62	14.0	14.6	15.2	15.8	16.4	17.1	17.7	18.3	18.9
63–67	15.0	15.6	16.3	16.9	17.5	18.1	18.8	19.4	20.0
68–72	16.1	16.7	17.3	17.9	18.5	19.2	19.8	20.4	21.0
73–77	17.1	17.7	18.3	18.9	19.5	20.2	20.8	21.4	22.0
78–82	18.0	18.7	19.3	19.9	20.5	21.0	21.8	22.4	23.0
83–87	19.0	19.6	20.2	20.8	21.5	22.1	22.7	23.3	24.0
88–92	19.9	20.5	21.2	21.8	22.4	23.0	23.6	24.3	24.9
93–97	20.8	21.4	22.1	22.7	23.3	23.9	24.8	25.2	25.8
98–102	21.7	22.6	22.9	23.5	24.2	24.8	25.4	26.0	26.7
103–107	22.5	23.2	23.8	24.4	25.0	25.6	26.3	26.9	27.5
108–112	23.4	24.0	24.6	25.2	25.8	26.5	27.1	27.7	28.3
113–117	24.1	24.8	25.4	26.0	26.6	27.3	27.9	28.5	29.1
118–122	24.9	25.5	26.2	26.8	27.4	28.0	28.6	29.3	29.9
123–127	25.7	26.3	26.9	27.5	28.1	28.8	29.4	30.0	30.6
128–132	26.4	27.0	27.6	28.2	28.8	29.5	30.1	30.7	31.3
133–137	27.1	27.7	28.3	28.9	29.5	30.2	30.8	31.4	32.0
138–142	27.7	28.3	29.0	29.6	30.2	30.8	31.4	32.1	32.7
143–147	28.3	29.0	29.6	30.2	30.8	31.5	32.1	32.7	33.3
148–152	29.0	29.6	30.2	30.8	31.4	32.7	32.7	33.3	33.9
153–157	29.5	30.2	30.8	31.4	32.0	32.7	33.3	33.9	34.5
158–162	30.1	30.7	31.3	31.9	32.6	33.2	33.8	34.4	35.1
163–167	30.6	31.2	31.9	32.5	33.1	33.7	34.3	35.0	35.6
168–172	31.1	31.7	32.4	33.0	33.6	34.2	34.8	35.5	36.1
173–177	31.6	32.2	32.8	33.5	34.1	34.7	35.3	35.9	36.6
178–182	32.0	32.7	33.3	33.9	34.5	35.2	35.8	36.4	37.0
183–187	32.5	33.1	33.7	34.3	34.9	35.6	36.2	36.8	37.4
188–192	32.9	33.5	34.1	34.7	35.3	36.0	36.6	37.2	37.8
193–197	33.2	33.8	34.5	35.1	35.7	36.3	37.0	37.8	38.2
198–202	33.6	34.2	34.8	35.4	36.1	36.7	37.3	37.9	38.5
203–207	33.9	34.5	35.1	35.7	36.4	37.0	37.6	38.2	38.9

Reprinted from *The Y's Way to Physical Fitness*, 3rd edition, 1989, with permission of the YMCA of the USA, 101 N. Wacker Drive, Chicago, IL 60606.

Table 9.9 Percent Fat Estimates for Females

Sum of 4 Skin Folds (mm)	Age to Last Year								
	18–22	23–27	28–32	33–37	38–42	43–47	48–52	53–57	58–older
8–12	8.8	9.0	9.2	9.4	9.5	9.7	9.9	10.1	10.3
13–17	10.8	10.9	11.1	11.3	11.5	11.7	11.8	12.0	12.2
18–22	12.6	12.8	13.0	13.2	13.4	13.5	13.7	13.9	14.1
23–27	14.5	14.6	14.8	15.0	15.2	15.4	15.6	15.7	15.9
28–32	16.2	16.4	16.6	16.8	17.0	17.1	17.3	17.5	17.7
33–37	17.9	18.1	18.3	18.5	18.7	18.9	19.0	19.2	19.4
38–42	19.6	19.8	20.0	20.2	20.3	20.5	20.7	20.9	21.1
43–47	21.2	21.4	21.6	21.8	21.9	22.1	22.3	22.5	22.7
48–52	22.8	22.9	23.1	23.3	23.5	23.7	23.8	24.0	24.2
53–57	24.2	24.4	24.6	24.8	25.0	25.2	25.3	25.5	25.7
58–62	25.7	25.9	26.0	26.2	26.4	26.6	26.8	27.0	27.1
63–67	27.1	27.2	27.4	27.6	27.8	28.0	28.2	28.3	28.5
68–72	28.4	28.6	28.7	28.9	29.1	29.3	29.5	29.7	29.8
73–77	29.6	29.8	30.0	30.2	30.4	30.6	30.7	30.9	31.1
78–82	30.9	31.0	31.2	31.4	31.6	31.8	31.9	32.1	32.3
83–87	32.0	32.2	32.4	32.6	32.7	32.9	33.1	33.3	33.5
88–92	33.1	33.3	33.5	33.7	33.8	34.0	34.2	34.4	34.6
93–97	34.1	34.3	34.5	34.7	34.9	35.1	35.2	35.4	35.6
98–102	35.1	35.3	35.5	35.7	35.9	36.0	36.2	36.4	36.6
103–107	36.1	36.2	36.4	36.6	36.8	37.0	37.2	37.3	37.5
108–112	36.9	37.1	37.3	37.5	37.7	37.9	38.0	38.2	38.4
113–117	37.8	37.9	38.1	38.3	39.2	39.4	39.6	39.8	40.0
118–122	38.5	38.7	38.9	39.1	39.4	39.6	39.8	40.0	40.5
123–127	39.2	39.4	39.6	39.8	40.0	40.1	40.3	40.5	40.7
128–132	39.9	40.1	40.2	40.4	40.6	40.8	41.0	41.2	41.3
133–137	40.5	40.7	40.8	41.0	41.2	41.4	41.6	41.7	41.9
138–142	41.0	41.2	41.4	41.6	41.7	41.9	42.1	42.3	42.5
143–147	41.5	41.7	41.9	42.0	42.2	42.4	42.6	42.8	43.0
148–152	41.9	42.1	42.3	42.8	42.6	42.8	43.0	43.2	43.4
153–157	42.3	42.5	42.6	42.8	43.0	43.2	43.4	43.6	43.7
158–162	42.6	42.8	43.0	43.1	43.3	43.5	43.7	43.9	44.1
163–167	42.9	43.0	43.2	43.4	43.6	43.8	44.0	44.1	44.3
168–172	43.1	43.2	43.4	43.6	43.8	44.0	44.2	44.3	44.5
173–177	43.2	43.4	43.6	43.8	43.9	44.1	44.3	44.5	44.7
178–182	43.3	43.5	43.7	43.8	44.0	44.2	44.4	44.6	44.8

Reprinted from *The Y's Way to Physical Fitness*, 3rd edition, 1989, with permission of the YMCA of the USA, 101 N. Wacker Drive, Chicago, IL 60606.

9. Multiply your present body weight in pounds by your present % body fat to determine how much of your body weight is fat.

   How much of your body weight is fat? _____ lb

10. Subtract the weight of fat from your present body weight. This is lean body weight (LBW).

    What is your **LBW?** _____ lb

Ideal weight based on body composition is preferred because then you know how much of your weight is due to fat.

11. To calculate ideal weight based on body composition, choose either the male or female procedure. For males, 84% of ideal weight should be LBW. Therefore, ideal weight = LBW/0.84. What is your ideal weight based on body composition?

   ┌───┐
   │ Male ideal weight = _____ lb │
   └───┘

(At this weight, your body will contain 16% fat, the amount generally recommended for males.) For females, 77% of ideal weight should be LBW. Therefore, ideal weight = LBW/0.77. What is your ideal weight based on body composition?

   ┌───┐
   │ Female ideal weight = _____ lb │
   └───┘

(At this weight, your body will contain 23% fat, the amount generally recommended for females.)

Comparison

How does your ideal weight based on body composition compare to your ideal weight based on BMI? _____

_____

Conclusions: Lean Body Weight

- What is your average daily energy requirement? _____ Kcal (p. 109)
- What is your average daily energy intake? _____ Kcal (p. 102)
- What is your ideal weight (take an average of any you have calculated)? _____ lb

  For your information, 1 lb of fat represents 3,500 Kcal. Therefore, if you want to lose 1 lb of fat, you must either reduce your intake by 3,500 Kcal or increase your activity by 3,500 Kcal. Assuming the same amount of physical activity, you could lose 1 lb per week by reducing your Kcal intake by 500 Kcal per day or gain 1 lb per week by increasing your Kcal intake by 500 Kcal per day.

- What is your recommendation for maintaining or achieving your ideal weight? _____

  _____

_____ 1. What is a listing of all foods eaten for a day?

_____ 2. What does Kcal mean?

_____ 3. Daily energy requirement includes energy for physical activity, SDA, and what else?

_____ 4. Give an example of a basal metabolism activity.

_____ 5. SDA refers to energy needed for what activity?

_____ 6. With age, the BMR decreases. What is the implication for daily energy intake?

_____ 7. Why does a tall, thin person have a higher BMR than a short, stout person?

_____ 8. Daily energy requirement must be in balance with what to not gain weight?

_____ 9. If you find that the average energy intake/day equals the average energy requirement/day, the person will not _____.

_____ 10. Ideal weight includes lean body weight and what else?

_____ 11. Generally speaking, a male should have no more than what percentage body fat?

_____ 12. Calculation of ideal weight is considered to be the most accurate if it is based on your _____.

_____ 13. How many Kcal are equal to a pound of fat?

_____ 14. In which sex is it natural to have a higher percentage of body fat?

Thought Questions

15. Why do males typically have a higher basal metabolic rate than females?

16. Why is energy needed when the body is at rest?

17. Why is energy needed to process food?

18. Why should someone monitor his or her average daily energy intake when attempting to maintain average body weight?

Human Biology Website

The companion website for _Human Biology_ provides a wealth of information organized and integrated by chapter. You will find practice tests, animations, and much more that will complement your learning and understanding of general biology.

www.mhhe.com/maderhuman11

McGraw-Hill Access Science Website

An online encyclopedia of science and technology that provides information, including videos, that can enhance the laboratory experience.

www.accessscience.com

10

Urinary and Reproductive Systems

Learning Outcomes

10.1 Urinary System
- Trace the path of urine in the male and female.
- State a function for each of the major organs of the urinary system.

Question: Explain the term urogenital system with reference to male anatomy.

10.2 Male Reproductive System
- Trace the path of sperm in the male from the testes to the exterior.
- State a function for each of the major organs of the male reproductive system.
- Describe the composition of semen.
- Compare the male reproductive system of the pig with that of the human male.

Question: How does male reproductive anatomy relate to the contribution of males to the human life cycle?

10.3 Female Reproductive System
- Trace the path of an egg in the female, and name the other organs of the female reproductive system.
- State a function for each of the major organs of the female reproductive system.
- Compare the female reproductive system of the pig with that of the human female.

Question: How does female reproductive anatomy relate to the contribution of females to the human life cycle?

10.4 Anatomy of Testis and Ovary
- Identify the major regions and structures in a cross-section slide of the testis and seminiferous tubules.
- Describe the specialization of a sperm for its function.
- Identify the major regions and structures in a slide of the ovary and the follicles.
- Describe the specialization of the egg for its function.

Question: How does the anatomy of the sperm differ from the anatomy of the egg?

Application for Daily Living: Infertility and Multiple Births

Introduction

In today's laboratory, we will be examining the urinary and reproductive systems of males and females in models and the fetal pig. Your instructor will decide if you are to observe the organs in a pig that has already been dissected and/or if you are to do a virtual dissection. A virtual dissection of a human cadaver is possible by using *Anatomy and Physiology Revealed,* a CD-ROM, available from McGraw-Hill Higher Education.

We will see that the male reproductive system delivers sperm specialized to carry chromosomes to the female egg. We will also see that the female reproductive system produces an egg with a full complement of cytoplasm as well as chromosomes.

We also want to emphasize the contribution of the primary sex organs—the testes in males and the ovaries in females—to the masculinization of males and the feminization of females. The testes produce the male sex hormone, testosterone, which maintains the primary sex organs of males and brings about the characteristics we associate with the male external anatomy. The ovaries produce the female sex hormones, estrogen and progesterone, that maintain the primary sex organs of females and bring about the external characteristics we associate with the female anatomy.

10.1 Urinary System

The urinary system consists of the kidneys, which produce urine; the ureters, which transport urine to the urinary bladder, where urine is stored; and the urethra, which transports urine to the outside. As we shall see, the urethra in males also transports sperm at the time of ejaculation. There is no connection between the urinary system and the reproductive system in females.

Observation: Urinary System

In Figure 10.1, state the function beside each label for an organ that belongs to the urinary system.

Urinary System Model

1. Examine a urinary system model and identify the organs noted:

   a. **Kidneys** are (1) bean-shaped and reddish-brown in color and (2) about the size of a bar of bath soap (12 cm long, 5 cm wide and 2.5 cm thick). The kidneys produce urine whose composition is regulated according to the needs of the body. As we shall study in

Figure 10.1 The urinary system.
Urine is found only with the kidneys, the ureters, the urinary bladder, and the urethra.

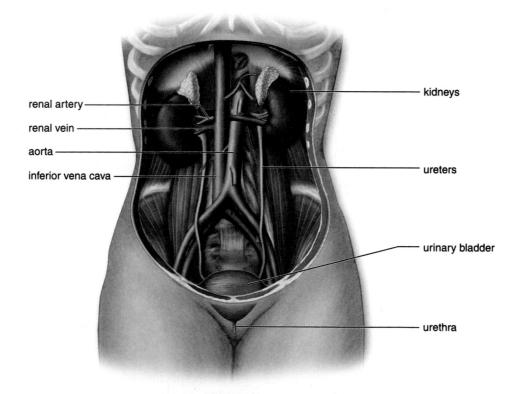

Laboratory 11, the kidneys are the most important organs of homeostasis in the body, and it is impossible to live without at least one functional kidney. Note the following:

- The hilum is a depression on the concave side of the kidney where the ureters and renal vein exit and where the renal artery enters. What blood vessel gives rise to the renal arteries? _____ What blood vessel receives the renal veins?

  _____

- The right kidney is slightly lower than the left because of space occupied by the liver above it.
- The adrenal glands, which sit atop the kidneys, are a part of the endocrine system, and they have no function in either the urinary or the reproductive systems. What color is the adrenal gland in your model? _____

b. **Ureters** are muscular tubes (about 25 cm long and 5 mm in diameter) that extend from the kidneys to the bladder. Their sole function is to transport urine to the bladder. Rhythmical contractions of the ureters causes urine to enter the bladder, even if a person is lying down. Blockage of a ureter would cause urine to collect in which organ? _____

c. **Urinary bladder,** which expands to store urine, has three openings: two ureters and one urethra. Two sphincters, circular muscles that can close a tube, are found where the urethra exits the bladder. These sphincters are under nervous control and relax when urination (release of urine) occurs. The average adult bladder can hold about 1/2 liter (a pint) for about 2–5 hours.

d. **Urethra** is a small tube that extends from the urinary bladder to an external opening. As we shall see in the fetal pig, the urethra is much longer in the male than the female.

2. Defecation, the expulsion of feces from the anus, and urination, the expulsion of urine from the bladder, has two separate functions. Urine is only found in which human organs?

_____

Observation: Urinary System in Pigs

Your instructor will decide whether you are to observe the urinary system in a fetal pig on display or whether you are to do a virtual dissection.

1. In a fetal pig, as in a human, the kidneys (Fig. 10.2) are reddish-brown organs covered by **peritoneum,** a membrane that anchors them to the dorsal wall of the abdominal cavity. Considering the location of the kidneys, how would you recognize when a prize fighter has landed a kidney punch, which is against the rules of boxing?

> ⚠ **Latex gloves** Wear protective latex gloves when handling preserved animal organs. Use protective eyewear and exercise caution when using sharp instruments during this laboratory. Wash hands thoroughly upon completion of this laboratory.

_____

2. Locate the **ureters,** which leave the kidneys and run posteriorly under the peritoneum.
3. On one side the peritoneum has been cleaned away. It will be possible to follow a ureter to the **urinary bladder,** which normally lies in the posterior ventral portion of the abdominal cavity. The urinary bladder is on the inner-surface of a flap of tissue to which the umbilical cord was attached.
4. The **urethra,** which arises from the bladder posteriorly, runs parallel to the rectum. Follow the urethra until it passes from view into the ring formed by the pelvic girdle.
5. Compare the length of the urethra in the male and female pig. Offer an explanation for why human females are more apt than males to have a urinary infection. _____

_____

Figure 10.2 Urinary system of the fetal pig.

In **(a)** females and **(b)** males, urine is made by the kidneys, transported to the bladder by the ureters, stored in the bladder, and then excreted from the body through the urethra.

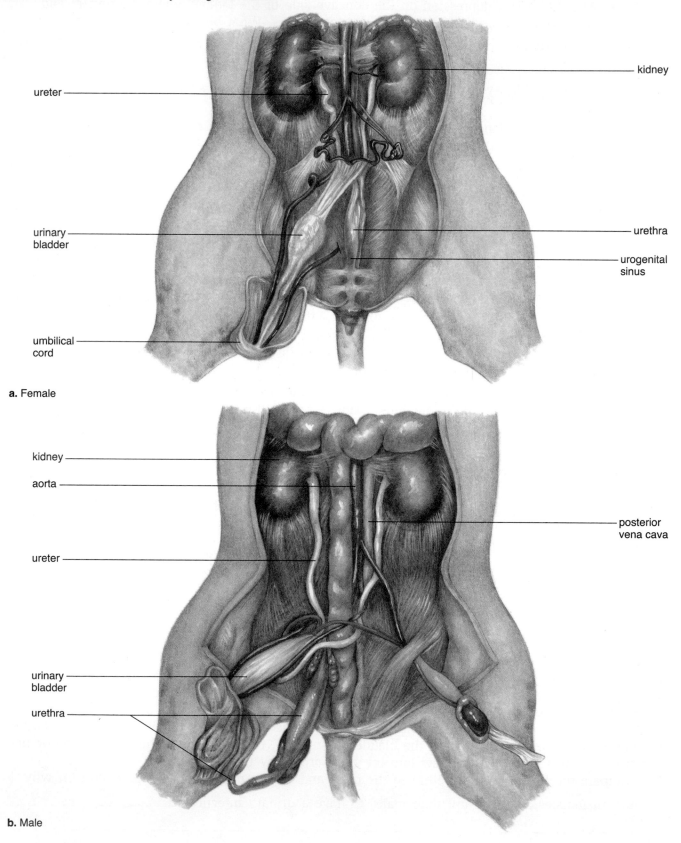

ureter

kidney

urinary
bladder

urethra

urogenital
sinus

umbilical
cord

a. Female

kidney

aorta

posterior
vena cava

ureter

urinary
bladder

urethra

b. Male

10.2 Male Reproductive System

The functions of the male reproductive system are to (1) produce sperm and the male sex hormones within the testes; (2) transport the sperm in ducts until they exit through the penis; (3) nourish and provide a medium for sperm in which they can survive, and (4) deliver sperm to the vagina of the female.

Observation: Male Reproductive System Model

Review Figure 10.3, and state a function beside each label for an organ that belongs to the male reproductive system. Identify the following organs in a model:

1. **Testes.** The primary sex organs of males where the sperm and male sex hormones (e.g., testosterone) are produced. Each testis is oval, about 4 cm long and 2.5 cm in diameter. The testes are suspended within the sacs of the **scrotum**, where the temperature is cooler than the body temperature. Sperm production is hampered by the warmer temperature of the body. Tight clothing or sitting for long hours is detrimental to sperm production because it keeps the testes at body temperature.

    The testes fulfill the first function noted previously for the male reproductive system.

2. **Epididymis.** A tightly coiled, threadlike tube that would stretch about 6 m if uncoiled. Runs posteriorly down along a testis and becomes a vas deferens. Sperm are stored in the epididymides until they are mature and capable of fertilizing an egg. Peristaltic contractions move the sperm along as they mature.

3. **Vas deferens.** A muscular tube about 45 cm long and 2.5 mm in diameter that conducts sperm. The vas deferens enters the pelvic cavity where it turns and joins with a duct from the seminal vesicle, a gland mentioned later.

Figure 10.3   The male reproductive system.
The testes produce sperm. The seminal vesicles, the prostate gland, and the bulbourethral glands provide a fluid medium for the sperm, which move from the vas deferens through the ejaculatory duct to the urethra in the penis. The foreskin (prepuce) is removed when the penis is circumcised.

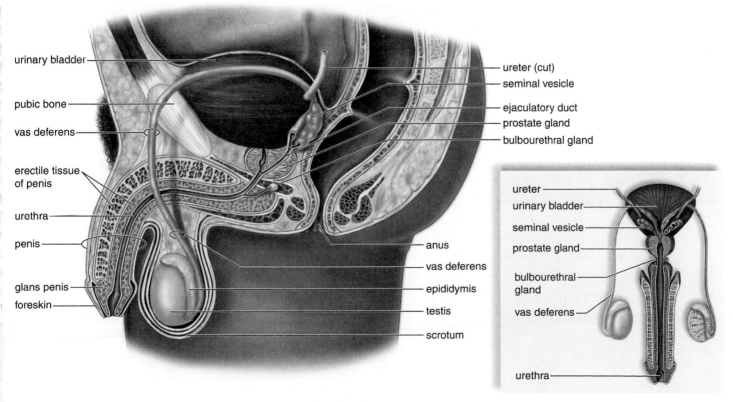

4. **Ejaculatory duct.** When the vas deferens and the duct from the seminal vesicle meet, they form a short (2 cm) ejaculatory duct, which passes through the prostate gland and empties into the urethra.

5. **Urethra.** The male urethra is shared by the reproductive and urinary systems. For this reason, the term urogenital system can be applied to males. The urethra either conducts semen or it conducts urine to the exterior and does not pass them both at the same time. What function of the male reproductive system previously listed is fulfilled by the ducts (2–5) just described?

_____

6. **Seminal vesicles,** the **prostate gland,** and the **bulbourethral glands.** These glands do not produce hormones, but they do produce secretions that account for why semen (the substance that exits the penis during ejaculation) is a thick fluid. The secretions of these glands are favorable to the health of the sperm. What function noted previously for the male reproductive

system is fulfilled by these glands? _____

The prostate gland surrounds one end of the urethra. Is the prostate gland part of the urinary

system or the reproductive system? _____ The prostate gland frequently

enlarges in older men and blocks the urethra. Under these conditions, a male is apt to have

difficulty urinating. Explain. _____

Observation: Male Reproductive System in Pigs

Your instructor will decide whether you are to observe the reproductive system in a fetal pig on display or whether you are to do a virtual dissection.

Inguinal Canal, Testis, Epididymis, and Vas Deferens

1. Locate the opening of the left inguinal canal, which leads to the left scrotal sac (Fig. 10.4).
2. Observe the testis in the opened sac. Note the much-coiled tubule—the epididymis—that lies alongside the testis. This is continuous with the vas deferens, which passes back toward the abdominal cavity.
3. Trace a vas deferens as it loops over an umbilical artery and ureter until it apparently unites with the urethra dorsally at the posterior end of the urinary bladder.

Penis, Urethra, and Accessory Glands

1. The skin has been opened just posterior to the umbilical cord. This exposes the rather undeveloped penis, which extends from this point posteriorly toward the anus. The central duct of the penis is the urethra.
2. If possible, view the urethra passing ventrally above the rectum. It is somewhat heavier in the male due to certain accessory glands:
   a. Bulbourethral glands, about 1 cm in diameter, lie laterally and well back toward the anal opening.
   b. The prostate gland, about 4 mm across and 3 mm thick, is located on the dorsal surface of the urethra, just posterior to the juncture of the bladder with the urethra. It is often difficult to locate and is not shown in Figures 10.3 and 10.4. Therefore, it is doubtful that you will find an ejaculatory duct.
   c. Small, paired seminal vesicles may be seen on either side of the prostate gland.
3. Trace the urethra as it leaves the bladder. It proceeds posteriorly, but when it nears the posterior end of the body, it turns rather abruptly anterioventrally and runs forward just under the skin of the midventral body wall, where you may have observed it. As stated, the urethra lies within the penis.
4. Trace the path of sperm in the male.

_____

Figure 10.4 Male reproductive system of the fetal pig.

a. This drawing shows that the urinary system and the reproductive system are joined. The vasa deferentia (sing., vas deferens) enter the urethra, which also carries urine. **b.** Compare the diagram in (**a**) with this photograph to help identify the structures of the male urogenital system.

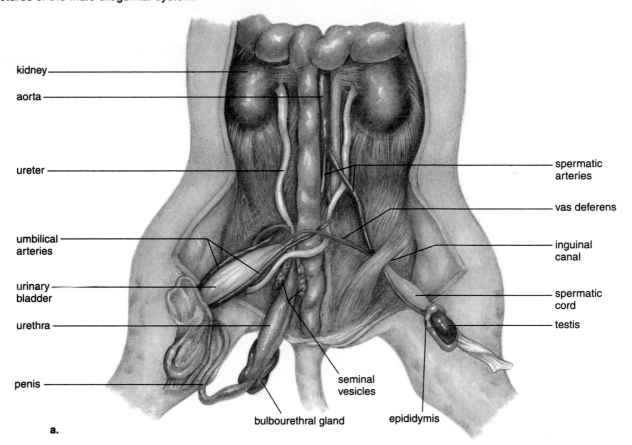

kidney

aorta

ureter

umbilical arteries

urinary bladder

urethra

penis

spermatic arteries

vas deferens

inguinal canal

spermatic cord

testis

seminal vesicles

bulbourethral gland

epididymis

a.

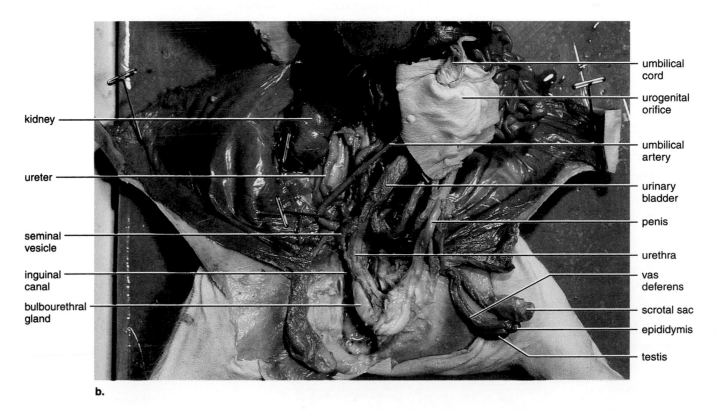

kidney

ureter

seminal vesicle

inguinal canal

bulbourethral gland

umbilical cord

urogenital orifice

umbilical artery

urinary bladder

penis

urethra

vas deferens

scrotal sac

epididymis

testis

b.

Urinary and Reproductive Systems   Laboratory 10

Comparison of Male Fetal Pig and Human Male

Use Figures 10.3 and 10.4 to help you compare the male fetal pig reproductive system with the human male reproductive system. Complete Table 10.1, which compares the location of the penis in these two mammals.

Table 10.1 Location of Penis in Male Fetal Pig and Human Male

	Fetal Pig	Human
Penis		

10.3 Female Reproductive System

The function of the female reproductive system is to (1) produce eggs and sex hormones within the ovaries; (2) transport eggs from the oviducts to the uterus; (3) receive the sperm in the vagina, also the birth canal; and (4) protect the fertilized egg (zygote) until it matures and is born.

Observation: Female Reproductive System Model

Review Figure 10.5 and state a function beside each label for an organ that belongs to the female reproductive system. Identify the following organs in a model:

1. **Ovaries.** The primary sex organs of females where eggs and female sex hormones (e.g., estrogen and progesterone) are produced. Each ovary is about 3 cm in length by 1 cm in width and less than 1 cm thick. They lie to either side of the uterus on the lateral walls of the pelvic cavity. Several ligaments hold the ovaries in place.

Figure 10.5   The female reproductive system.
The ovaries usually release one egg a month; fertilization occurs in the oviduct, and development occurs in the uterus. The vagina is the birth canal, as well as the organ of sexual intercourse and outlet for menstrual flow.

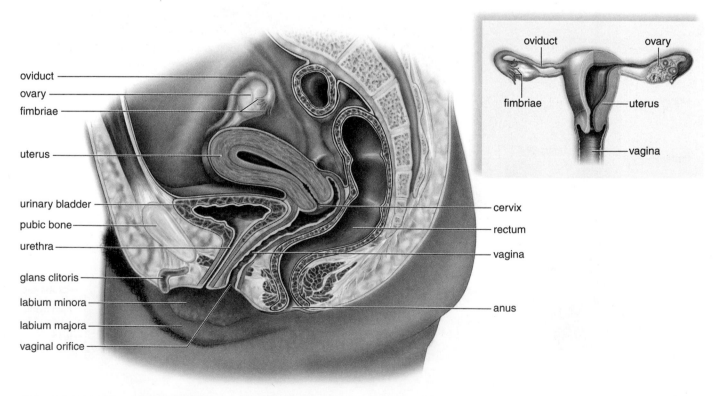

2. **Oviducts.** Extend from the uterus to the ovaries. At the end nearest the ovaries, the oviducts have fimbriae that sweep over an ovary so that a released egg enters the oviduct. Cilia that line the oviduct and muscular contraction of its walls propel the egg toward the uterus. Fertilization, if it occurs, happens in an oviduct.
3. **Uterus.** A thick-walled, muscular organ about the size and shape of an inverted pear, where development of the embryo and fetus occur. If fertilization does not occur, the uterine lining is shed and menstruation occurs. The cervix surrounds the opening to the uterus.
4. **Vagina.** The uterus empties into the vagina, which makes a 45° angle with the small of the back. Its fibromuscular wall can stretch to receive the penis and to serve as the birth canal.

<hr>

Observation: Female Reproductive System in Pigs

Your instructor will decide whether you are to observe the reproductive system in a fetal pig on display or whether you are to do a virtual dissection.

Ovaries and Oviducts

1. Locate the paired ovaries, small bodies suspended from the peritoneal wall in mesenteries, posterior to the kidneys (Fig. 10.6).
2. Closely examine one ovary. Note the small, short, coiled oviduct, sometimes called the fallopian tube. The oviduct does not attach directly to the ovary but ends in a funnel-shaped structure with fingerlike processes (fimbriae) that partially enclose the ovary.

Uterine Horns

1. Locate the **uterine horns.** (Do not confuse the uterine horns with the oviducts; the latter are much smaller and are found close to the ovaries.)
2. Find the median body of the uterus located at the joined posterior ends of the uterine horns.

Vagina

1. Separate the hindlimbs of your specimen, which has been cut down along the midventral line. The cut passes through muscle and the cartilaginous pelvic girdle. With your fingers, spread the cut edges apart, and use blunt dissecting instruments to separate connective tissue, if necessary.
2. Note three ducts passing from the body cavity to the animal's posterior surface. One of these is the urethra, which leaves the bladder and passes into the **urogenital sinus.** The urethra is a part of the urinary system. The most dorsal of the three ducts is the **rectum,** which passes to its own opening, the **anus.** The rectum and anus are part of the digestive system, not the reproductive system.
3. Find the vagina, located dorsally to the urethra. The vagina is the organ of copulation and is the birth canal. Anteriorly, it connects to the uterus, and posteriorly it enters the urogenital sinus. This sinus is absent in adult humans and several other female mammals.

Figure 10.6 Female reproductive system of the fetal pig.

a. This drawing shows that in the adult female, the urinary system and the reproductive system are separate. In the fetus, the vagina joins the urethra just before the urogenital sinus. **b.** Compare the drawing in (a) with this photograph to help identify the structures of the female urinary and reproductive systems.

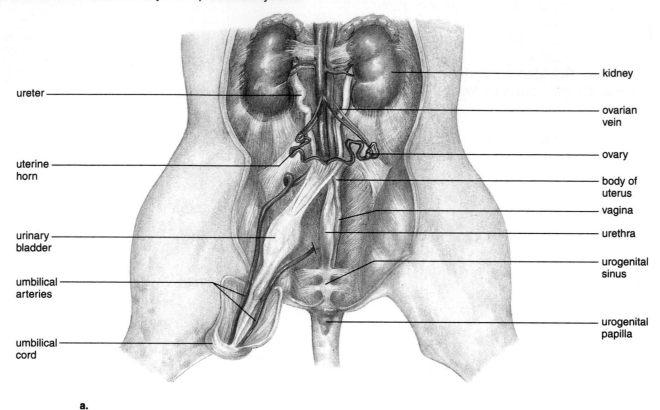

kidney
ureter
ovarian vein
uterine horn
ovary
body of uterus
vagina
urinary bladder
urethra
umbilical arteries
urogenital sinus
umbilical cord
urogenital papilla

a.

large intestine
kidney
umbilical artery
ureter
umbilical cord
ovaries
urinary bladder
uterine horn
urethra
body of uterus
urogenital sinus
vagina
urogenital papilla

b.

Comparison of Female Fetal Pig with Human Female

Use Figures 10.5 and 10.6 to compare the female pig reproductive system with the human female reproductive system. Complete Table 10.2, which compares the appearance of the oviducts and the uterus, as well as the presence or absence of a urogenital sinus in these two mammals.

Table 10.2 Comparison of Female Fetal Pig with Human Female		
	Fetal Pig	**Human**
Oviducts		
Uterus		
Urogenital sinus		

10.4 Anatomy of Testis and Ovary

Recall that the testes produce sperm (the male gametes) and that the ovaries produce oocytes (the female gametes). A testis contains **seminiferous tubules,** where sperm formation takes place, and **interstitial cells** scattered in the spaces between seminiferous tubules. Interstitial cells produce the male sex hormone **testosterone,** which brings about and maintains the internal and external characteristics of males. An ovary contains **follicles** in various stages of maturation. Ovarian follicles produce the female sex hormones estrogen and progesterone, which help bring about and maintain the internal and external characteristics of females. One or more follicles complete maturation during each cycle and produce an oocyte.

Observation: Microscopic Examination of the Testis, Sperm, and Penis

Testes

1. Obtain a slide of the testis. As shown in Figure 10.7a and b, a testis (sing.) contains many seminiferous tubules where spermatogenesis (production of sperm) is occurring. Note under low power the circular nature of a tubule.
2. Switch to high power, and observe one tubule in particular. Between the tubules, try to identify interstitial cells which produce testosterone. Testosterone enters the body by way of the blood and not by way of ducts. Explain why a vasectomy, a cutting of the vas deferens, causes a male to be sterile but has no effect on his masculinity. _____

    _____
3. **Spermatogenesis** occurs in the seminiferous tubules (Fig. 10.7c). Identify:
    Sertoli cells nuclei. The cytoplasm of a Sertoli cell surrounds a cell undergoing spermatogenesis.
    Germ cells. First spermatogonia, next spermatocytes, and finally spermatids occur, but they are hard to identify. Males produce four viable spermatids for each spermatogenesis. Each spermatid becomes a sperm.
    Sperm. Sperm look like thin, fine, dark lines in the lumen of the tubule. Why is it important for sperm cells to have a tail? _____

    _____

Sperm

Obtain a prepared slide of sperm and compare what you see to Figure 10.7*d* and *e*. An acrosome contains enzymes that digest a path through cells that surround an egg and the outer covering of an egg so that one sperm can enter. How are sperm specialized? _____

The ejaculated semen of a normal male contains several hundred million sperm, each a product of spermatogenesis, but only one sperm normally enters an egg. Speculate why so many sperm are needed for fertilization to occur. _____

Figure 10.7   Testis and sperm.

a. The lobules of a testis contain seminiferous tubules. **b.** Electron micrograph of a cross section of the seminiferous tubules, where spermatogenesis occurs. Note the location of interstitial cells in clumps among the seminiferous tubules.
c. Diagrammatic representation of spermatogenesis, which occurs in wall of tubules. During spermatogenesis the chromosome number is reduced from 46 to 23. **d.** Micrograph of sperm. **e.** A sperm has a head, a middle piece, and a tail. The nucleus is in the head, capped by an acrosome.

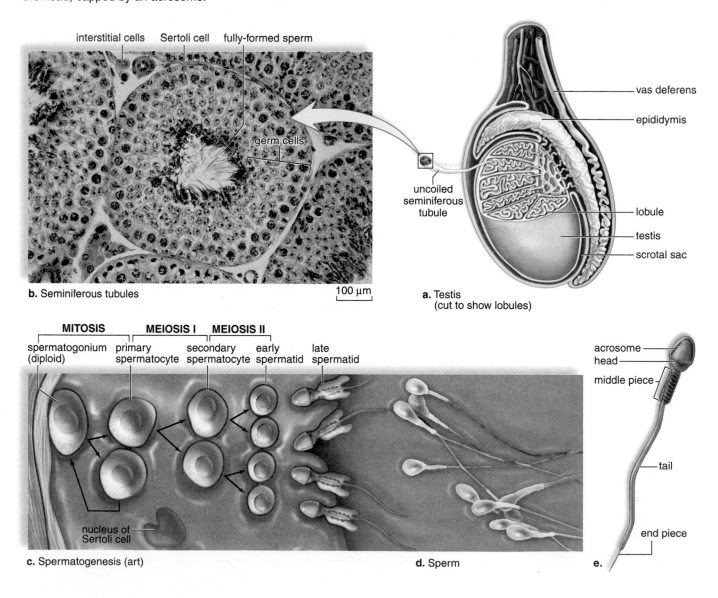

b. Seminiferous tubules   100 µm

a. Testis
   (cut to show lobules)

c. Spermatogenesis (art)   d. Sperm   e.

Penis

1. Obtain a prepared slide of a penis cross section (Fig. 10.8b) and examine it with low-power magnification. Spongy erectile tissue, containing distensible blood spaces, extends through the shaft of the penis. When these spaces fill with blood, the penis becomes erect and able to enter the vagina of the female. Erectile dysfunction occurs when erectile tissue doesn't expand enough. The medications available for the treatment of erectile dysfunction bring about full distention of these spaces.

Figure 10.8   Penis anatomy.
a. Penis shaft. The shaft of the penis ends in an enlarged tip called the glans penis, which, in uncircumsized males, is partially covered by a foreskin (prepuce). The penis contains columns of erectile tissue. **b.** Micrograph of shaft in cross section showing location of erectile tissue. One column surrounds the urethra.

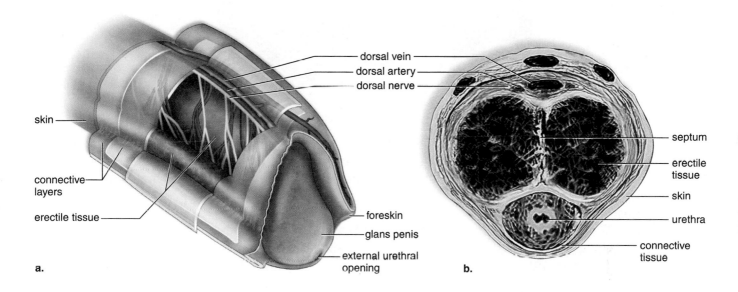

Observation: Microscopic Examination of the Ovary

Ovary

1. Examine a prepared slide of an ovary, and refer to Figure 10.9 for help in identifying the structures. The female gonad contains an inner core of loose, fibrous tissue. The outer part contains the follicles that produce eggs.
2. Locate a **primary follicle,** which appears as a circle of small cells surrounding a somewhat larger cell, the primary oocyte.
3. Find a **secondary follicle,** and switch to high power. Note the **secondary oocyte** (egg), surrounded by numerous cells, to one side of the liquid-filled follicle. Why is it important for females to produce an egg that has plentiful cytoplasm? _____
4. Look for a large, fluid-filled vesicular (Graafian) follicle, which contains a mature secondary oocyte to one side. This follicle will be next to the outer surface of the ovary because it is the type of follicle that releases the egg during ovulation.

Figure 10.9 Photomicrograph of ovarian tissue.
An ovary contains follicles in different stages of maturity. A secondary follicle contains a secondary oocyte, which will burst from the ovary during ovulation. A follicle also produces the female sex hormones.

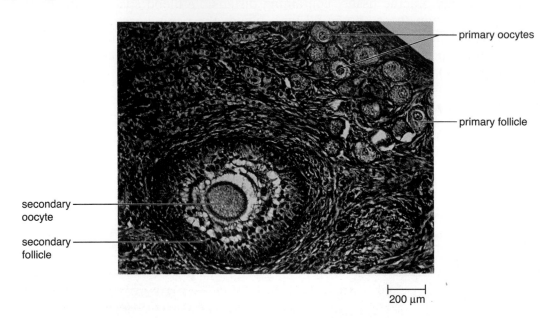

primary oocytes

primary follicle

secondary oocyte

secondary follicle

200 μm

5. Look for the remains of the corpus luteum, which will look like scar tissue. The corpus luteum develops after the vesicular follicle has released its egg, and then later it deteriorates. Not all slides will contain a corpus luteum and a vesicular follicle because they may not have been present when the slide was made.

6. **Oogenesis**
   Germ cells. The primary follicle and the secondary follicle are a part of oogenesis.
   Egg. Each oogenesis event in females produces a single egg. In contrast to males, females produce one egg a month.

Summary of Reproductive Systems

- Complete Table 10.3 to describe the differences between the male and female mammalian reproductive systems. A **gonad** is an organ that produces gametes, the sperm and egg.

Table 10.3 Comparison of Human Male and Female Reproductive Systems		
	Male	**Female**
Gonad		
Duct from gonad		
Structure connected to gonad by duct		
Copulatory organ		

- The most important contribution of the male and female reproductive systems is the production of gametes. With this in mind, state the function of the male organs, aside from the testes.

  _____

  With this in mind, state the function of the female organs, aside from the ovaries. _____

  _____

- Consider the external differences in the male and female form. Considering these differences referred to as secondary sex characteristics, what is another function of the hormones produced by the testes and ovaries?

  _____

Application for Daily Living

Infertility and Multiple Births

People who find it difficult to reproduce are said to be infertile. If the male has a low sperm count, one choice is in vitro fertilization, during which eggs are fertilized in laboratory glassware before they are transferred to a uterus. Today, ultrasound machines can spot ovarian follicles that hold immature eggs, and a needle can be used to retrieve the eggs; therefore, the administration of fertility drugs is no longer needed. The immature eggs are brought to maturity in glassware, then the sperm are added. Several embryos are transferred to the uterus where more than one may implant at a time. If multiple embryos implant and space per fetus is limited, premature delivery of several babies is expected. This manner of treating infertility can put a strain on the woman who must carry the babies, the hospital that cares for premies, and the couple who have to raise several children at once.

Storage of Pigs

1. Before leaving the laboratory, place your pig in the plastic bag provided.
2. Expel excess air from the bag, and tie it shut.
3. Write your *name* and *section* on the tag provided, and attach it to the bag. Your instructor will indicate where the bags are to be stored until the next laboratory period.
4. Clean the dissecting tray and tools, and return them to their proper location.
5. Wipe off your goggles.
6. Wash your hands.

_____ 1. Which structure in the urinary system carries urine to the bladder?

_____ 2. Which structure in the urinary system receives urine from the bladder?

_____ 3. What portion of the urinary system carries sperm?

_____ 4. Where are the testes located in human males?

_____ 5. What is the function of the vas deferens?

_____ 6. What is the function of the prostate gland?

_____ 7. Where are the ovaries located?

_____ 8. What is the function of the uterus?

_____ 9. What is the function of the ovaries?

_____ 10. The vas deferens in males compares with which structure in females?

_____ 11. What organ in males is analogous to the vagina?

_____ 12. Where are sperm produced in the testes?

_____ 13. What structure in the ovary contains the developing oocyte?

_____ 14. Name two glands that add fluid to semen after sperm reach the urethra.

Thought Questions

15. On the basis of anatomy, explain why the urethra is part of both the urinary and reproductive systems in males.

16. A vasectomy is a procedure in which both of the vas deferens are severed. Why would such a procedure cause sterility?

Human Biology Website

The companion website for _Human Biology_ provides a wealth of information organized and integrated by chapter. You will find practice tests, animations, and much more that will complement your learning and understanding of general biology.

www.mhhe.com/maderhuman11

Anatomy & Physiology Revealed

A program that includes cadaver photos that allow you to peel away layers of the human body to reveal structures beneath the surface. This program also includes animations. radiological pronunciations, audio pronunciations and practice quizzing. Check out _www.aprevealed.com_. APR has been proven to help improve student grades!

11
Homeostasis

Learning Outcomes

11.1 The Cardiovascular System and Capillary Exchange in Tissues
- Describe the exchange of molecules across a capillary wall and the mechanisms involved in this exchange.
Question: In general, what is the function of the systemic circuit?

11.2 Lungs
- Describe the role of the lungs in helping maintain homeostasis.
- Describe the anatomy and the role of the alveoli in gas exchange.
Question: When CO_2 exits blood at the alveoli, how does the pH of blood change?

11.3 Liver
- Describe the anatomy of the liver, including the path of blood from the intestines, through the liver, and to the heart.
- Compare the glucose level in the mesenteric artery, the hepatic portal vein, and the hepatic vein before and after eating.
- Describe two contributions of the liver to homeostasis.
Question: What hormone causes the liver to store glucose as glycogen?

11.4 Kidneys
- Describe the anatomy of the kidneys and a nephron, including circulation of the blood about a nephron.
- State the three steps in urine formation and how they relate to the parts of a nephron.
- Predict whether substances will normally be in the filtrate and/or urine, and explain.
- State several ways that the kidneys contribute to homeostasis.
Question: Reabsorption plays what role in urine formation?

Application for Daily Living: The Liver Is a Vital Organ

Introduction

Homeostasis refers to the dynamic equilibrium of the body's internal environment. The internal environment of humans consists of blood and tissue fluid. To meet their needs, cells take nutrients (e.g., glucose) and O_2 from the blood, and return waste products, including CO_2, to the blood. These wastes are eventually excreted from the blood. Homeostasis also involves adjusting blood pH, ionic concentrations, and blood volume. All internal organs contribute to homeostasis, but this laboratory specifically examines the contributions of the lungs, liver, and kidneys (Fig. 11.1).

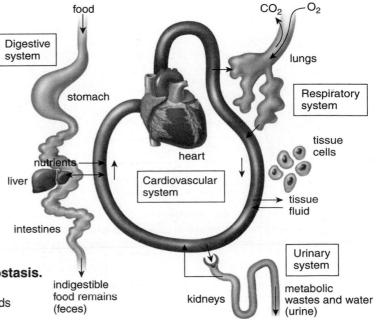

Figure 11.1 Contributions of organs to homeostasis.
The lungs, the liver, and the kidneys are involved in the exchange of materials with blood. All the organs and fluids of the body are connected by the blood stream.

11.1 The Cardiovascular System and Capillary Exchange in Tissues

As shown in Figure 7.6, the cardiovascular system consists of the heart, blood vessels, and blood. Arteries carry blood away from the heart, while veins transport blood toward the heart. Arteries branch into smaller vessels called arterioles; veins branch into venules. The arterioles and venules are connected by capillary beds, tiny branching vessels that extend throughout the organs and tissues of the body.

The exchange of materials between the tissue fluid and the blood takes place across the thin walls of the capillaries. Tissue fluid is continually created and refreshed at the capillaries when certain molecules leave the blood and others are picked up by the blood. This allows metabolically active cells a continuous supply of glucose and oxygen and permits the removal of carbon dioxide and other wastes (Fig. 11.2). In Figure 11.2, write *oxygen* and *glucose* next to an appropriate arrow. Write *wastes* and *carbon dioxide* next to an appropriate arrow.

1. The beating of the heart creates blood pressure which moves blood in arteries. What type of pressure causes water to exit from the arterial side of the capillary? _____

2. By the time blood reaches the venous side of a capillary blood pressure has decreased and osmotic pressure is higher than blood pressure. **Osmotic pressure** is due to osmosis; in this case due to presence of plasma proteins which are too big to cross a capillary wall. The higher the osmotic pressure, the more likely water will diffuse in that direction. What type of pressure causes water to enter the venous side of the capillary? _____

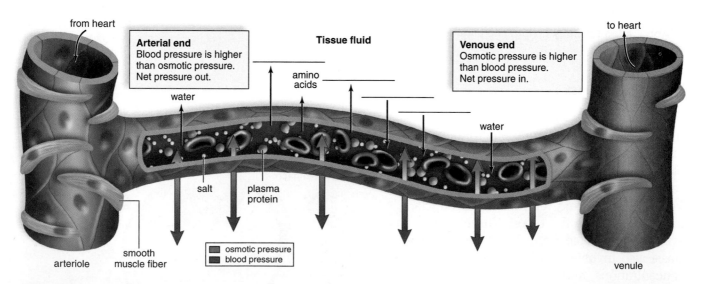

Figure 11.2   Capillary exchange.
A capillary, illustrating the exchange that takes place across a capillary wall. Blood pressure causes water to exit a capillary at the arterial end and osmotic pressure causes water to enter a capilary at the venous end. In between, nutrients are exchanged for waste molecules.

Conclusions: Capillary Exchange

- What generates blood pressure? _____
  _____

- How is osmotic pressure created? _____
  _____

- Why are cells always in need of glucose and oxygen? _____
  _____

- Why are cells always producing carbon dioxide? _____
  _____

11.2 Lungs

Air moves from the nasal passages to the trachea, bronchi, bronchioles, and finally, lungs. The right and left lungs lie in the thoracic cavity on either side of the heart.

Lung Structure

A **lung** is a spongy organ consisting of irregularly shaped air spaces called **alveoli** (sing., *alveolus*). The alveoli are lined with a single layer of squamous epithelium and are supported by a mesh of fine, elastic fibers. The alveoli are surrounded by a rich network of tiny blood vessels called **pulmonary capillaries.**

Observation: Lung Structure

1. Observe a prepared slide of a stained section of a lung. In stained slides, the nuclei of the cells forming the thin alveolar walls appear purple or dark blue (Fig. 11.3a).
2. Look for areas with groups of red- or orange-colored, disc-shaped **erythrocytes** (red blood cells). When these appear in strings, you are looking at capillary vessels in side view.
3. In some part of the slide, you may even observe an artery. Thicker, circular or oval structures with a lumen (cavity) are cross sections of **bronchioles,** tubular pathways through which air reaches the air spaces.

Lung Function

Oxygen concentration in the air in alveoli is *greater* than in the blood in pulmonary capillaries. By the same token, carbon dioxide concentration in the air in alveoli is *less* than in the blood in pulmonary capillaries. Gas exchange in the lungs takes place by diffusion as gases move along a **concentration gradient** from greater to lesser concentration.

During gas exchange in the lungs, carbon dioxide (CO_2) leaves the blood and enters the alveoli, and oxygen (O_2) leaves the alveoli and enters the blood. Show gas exchange in Figure 11.3b by writing O_2 or CO_2 by the appropriate arrows.

Oxygen and Carbon Dioxide Transport

1. Oxygen is transported by hemoglobin inside red blood cells as HbO_2. Hemoglobin binds and releases O_2 in response to changes in blood O_2 concentration. Why do cells require oxygen?
   _____

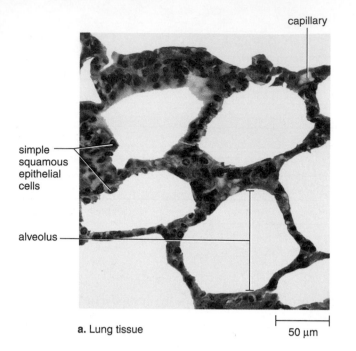

a. Lung tissue

50 μm

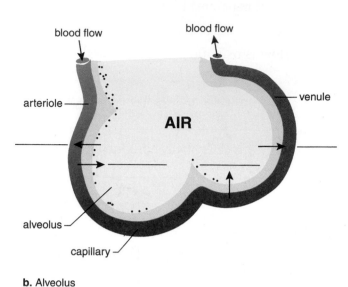

b. Alveolus

Figure 11.3   Gas exchange in the lungs.
a. A photomicrograph shows that the lungs contain many air sacs called alveoli. The alveoli are surrounded by blood capillaries. **b.** During gas exchange, carbon dioxide leaves the blood and enters the alveoli; oxygen leaves the alveoli and enters the blood. Label the arrows with O_2 and CO_2 to show gas exchange in the lungs.

2. Carbon dioxide is carried in the blood as bicarbonate ions (Fig. 11.4):

$$CO_2 \; + \; H_2O \; \rightarrow \; \underset{\text{carbonic acid}}{H_2CO_3} \; \rightarrow \; \underset{\text{bicarbonate ion}}{HCO_3^-} \; + \; \underset{\text{hydrogen ions}}{H^+}$$

Hydrogen ions increase the acidity of blood. Is blood more acidic when it is carrying carbon dioxide? _____ Explain. _____
_____

3. As CO_2 leaves the blood, the following reaction is driven to the right:

$$HCO_3^- \; + \; H^+ \; \rightarrow \; H_2CO_3 \; \rightarrow \; CO_2 \; + \; H_2O$$

Is blood less acidic when the carbon dioxide exits? _____ Explain. _____
_____

Ventilation can be regulated to maintain normal blood values of oxygen and pH. Chemoreceptors of the nervous system located in the aorta and carotid arteries detect changes in the blood's acidity and oxygen content. Nerve impulses trigger contractions in the diaphragm and thoracic muscles, causing alterations in the rate and depth of breathing. Interestingly, during breathing cessation, it is the increase in acidity rather than the depletion of oxygen that first stimulates the urge to breathe.

Lung Function and Homeostasis

Explain how the lungs help maintain homeostasis of blood. _____
_____
_____
_____

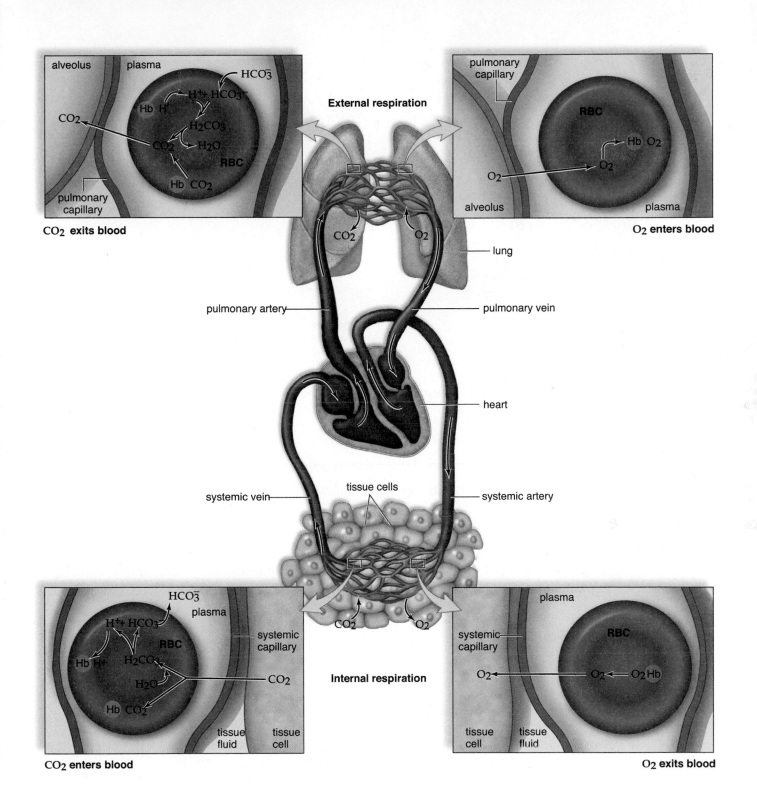

Figure 11.4 External and internal respiration.
Red blood cells play an important role in the transport and release of O_2 and CO_2.

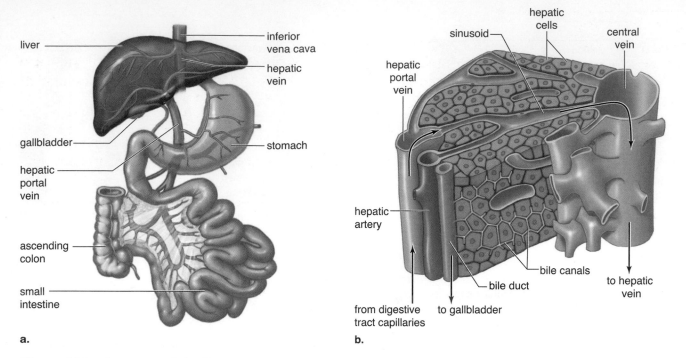

Figure 11.5 Anatomy of the liver.
a. The liver, a large organ in the abdominal cavity, plays a primary role in homeostasis. The hepatic portal system consists of the hepatic portal and hepatic vein. **b.** One lobule.

11.3 Liver

The **liver,** which is the largest organ in the body, lies mainly in the upper-right quadrant of the abdominal cavity under the diaphragm.

Liver Structure

The liver has two main **lobes** and the lobes are further divided into **lobules,** which contain the cells of the liver, called **hepatic cells** (Fig. 11.5*a*).

Observation: Liver Structure

Study a model of the liver, and identify the following:

1. **Right and left lobes:** The liver has two lobes. The right lobe is larger than the left lobe.
2. **Lobules:** Each lobe has many lobules.
3. **Hepatic cells:** Each lobule has many cells.
4. **Hepatic vein:** The blood vessel that transports O_2-poor blood out of the liver to the inferior vena cava.
5. **Hepatic artery:** The blood vessel that transports O_2-rich blood to the liver.
6. **Hepatic portal vein:** The blood vessel that transports blood containing nutrients from the intestine to the liver.
7. **Bile duct:** The passageway for bile going to the gallbladder.

Liver Function

The liver has many functions in homeostasis. It produces **urea,** the primary nitrogenous end product of humans. In general, the liver is the gatekeeper of the blood—it regulates blood composition. For example, it stores glucose as glycogen and then releases glucose to keep the blood glucose concentration at about 0.1%.

Urea Formation

The liver removes amino groups ($-NH_2$) from amino acids and converts them to urea, a relatively nontoxic nitrogenous end product.

1. In the chemical formula for urea that follows, circle the portions that would have come from amino groups:

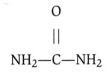

$$NH_2-C-NH_2$$

2. State one way the liver contributes to homeostasis. _____

_____

Regulation of Blood Glucose Level

After you eat, blood glucose levels rise. This increase is detected by the pancreas, which in response secretes the hormone insulin. Insulin binds to the plasma membrane receptors of the cells and promotes the uptake of glucose by the liver. The liver stores excess glucose as glycogen. Before your next meal, the drop in blood sugar causes the release of glucagon, a hormone that promotes the breakdown of glycogen and the release of glucose.

1. Complete the following equation by writing *glucose* and *glycogen* on the appropriate sides of the arrows.

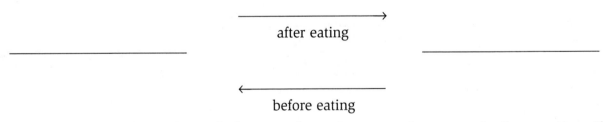

2. Now add the words *insulin* and *glucagon* above the appropriate arrow in the equation. If glucose is excreted in the urine, instead of being stored, the individual has the medical condition called **diabetes mellitus,** commonly known as diabetes. In diabetes type 1, the pancreas is no longer making insulin; in diabetes type 2, the plasma membrane receptors are unable to bind properly to insulin. In diabetes type 1, but not type 2, ketones (strong organic acids), a breakdown product of fat metabolism, also appear in the urine.

3. State another way in which the liver contributes to homeostasis. _____

Study the diagram of the human cardiovascular system in Figure 7.6, and trace the path of blood from the aorta to the vena cava via the intestine and liver. Simulated serum samples have been prepared to correspond to these blood vessels in a person who ate a short time ago:

A_1: Serum from a mesenteric artery. The mesenteric arteries take blood from the aorta to the intestine.

B_1: Serum from the hepatic portal vein, which lies between the intestine and the liver.

C_1: Serum from the hepatic vein, which takes blood from the liver to the inferior vena cava.

> **⚠ Benedict's reagent** Use protective eyeware when performing this experiment. Benedict's reagent is highly corrosive. Exercise care in using this chemical. If any should spill on your skin, wash the area with mild soap and water. Follow your instructor's directions for disposal of this chemical.

1. With a wax pencil, label three test tubes A_1, B_1, and C_1, and mark them at 1 cm and 2 cm.
2. Fill test tube A_1 to the 1 cm mark with *serum A_1* and to the 2 cm mark with *Benedict's reagent*.
3. Fill test tube B_1 to the 1 cm mark with *serum B_1* and to the 2 cm mark with *Benedict's reagent*.
4. Fill test tube C_1 to the 1 cm mark with *serum C_1* and to the 2 cm mark with *Benedict's reagent*.
5. Place all three test tubes in the water bath *at the same time*. Heat the tubes in the same boiling water bath for five minutes.
6. Note any color change in the test tubes, and record the color and your conclusions in Table 11.1. The tube that shows color first has the most glucose, and so forth. Use the following chart to assist you in making your conclusions:

Color change	Amount of glucose
Color is still blue	None
Green	Very low
Yellow-orange	Moderate
Orange	High
Orange-red	Very high

Table 11.1 Blood Glucose Level After Eating

Test Tubes	Color (after heating)	Conclusion
A_1 (mesenteric artery)		
B_1 (hepatic portal vein)		
C_1 (hepatic vein)		

Conclusions: Blood Glucose Level After Eating

- Which blood vessel—a mesenteric artery, the hepatic portal vein, or the hepatic vein—contains the most glucose after eating? _____

- Why do you suppose that the hepatic vein does not contain as much glucose as the hepatic portal vein after eating? _____

_____

Simulated serum samples have been prepared to correspond to these blood vessels in a person who has not eaten for some time:

A_2: Serum from a mesenteric artery
B_2: Serum from the hepatic portal vein
C_2: Serum from the hepatic vein

1. With a wax pencil, label three test tubes A_2, B_2, and C_2, and mark them at 1 cm and 2 cm.
2. Fill test tube A_2 to the 1 cm mark with *serum A_2* and to the 2 cm mark with *Benedict's reagent*.
3. Fill test tube B_2 to the 1 cm mark with *serum B_2* and to the 2 cm mark with *Benedict's reagent*.
4. Fill test tube C_2 to the 1 cm mark with *serum C_2* and to the 2 cm mark with *Benedict's reagent*.
5. Heat the tubes in the same boiling water bath for five minutes.
6. Note any color change in the test tubes, and record the color and your conclusions in Table 11.2. Use the following list to assist you in making your conclusions:

Color change	Amount of glucose
Color is still blue	None
Green	Very low
Yellow-orange	Moderate
Orange	High
Orange-red	Very high

Table 11.2   Blood Glucose Level Before Eating

Test Tubes	Color (after heating)	Conclusion
A_2 (mesenteric artery)		
B_2 (hepatic portal vein)		
C_2 (hepatic vein)		

Conclusions: Blood Glucose Level Before Eating

- Which blood vessel—a mesenteric artery, the hepatic portal vein, or the hepatic vein—contains the most glucose before eating? _____

- Why do you suppose that the hepatic vein now contains more glucose than the hepatic portal vein? _____

11.4 Kidneys

The **kidneys** are bean-shaped organs that lie along the dorsal wall of the abdominal cavity.

Kidney Structure

Figure 11.6 shows the macroscopic and microscopic structure of a kidney. The macroscopic structure of a kidney is due to the placement of over 1 million **nephrons.** Nephrons are tubules that do the work of producing urine.

Figure 11.6   Longitudinal section of a kidney.
a. The kidneys are served by the renal artery and renal vein. **b.** Macroscopically, a kidney has three parts; renal cortex, renal medulla, and renal pelvis. **c.** Microscopically, each kidney contains over a million nephrons.

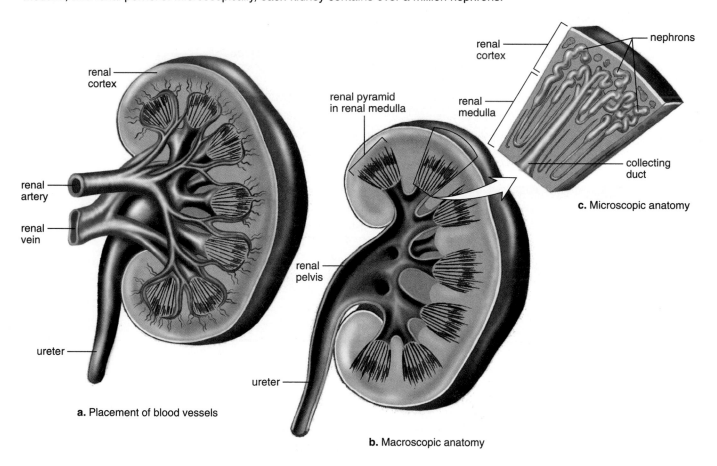

Observation: Kidney Model

Study a model of a kidney, and with the help of Figure 11.6, locate the following:

1. **Renal cortex:** a granular region
2. **Renal medulla:** contains the renal pyramids
3. **Renal pelvis:** where urine collects

Nephron Structure and Circulation

Figure 11.7 shows that the **afferent arteriole** enters the **glomerulus,** situated within the cup-shaped **glomerular capsule** (Bowman's capsule). The **efferent arteriole** leaves the glomerular capsule and enters the **peritubular capillary network** that surrounds the **proximal convoluted tubule,** the **loop of the nephron** (loop of Henle), and the **distal convoluted tubule.** Distal convoluted tubules from several nephrons enter one collecting duct.

Macroscopic and microscopic studies of kidney anatomy show that the glomerular capsule and convoluted tubules are in the renal cortex, while the loop of the nephron and the collecting ducts are in the renal medulla, accounting for the striated appearance of the renal pyramids. The collecting ducts enter the renal pelvis.

Figure 11.7   Structure of a nephron and its blood supply.
As the blood moves through the blood vessels about a nephron, substances exit and/or enter the blood from portions of the nephron. Solid arrows show the movement of blood through the blood vessels; broken arrows show the movement of filtrate through the tubules during urine formation.

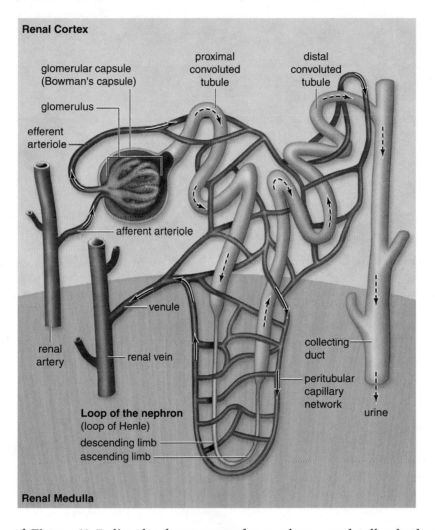

1. With the help of Figure 11.7, list the four parts of a nephron, and tell whether they are located in the renal cortex or the renal medulla (assume that the nephron has a long loop).

_____

_____

_____

_____

2. With the help of Figure 11.7 and Table 11.3, trace the path of blood toward, around, and away from an individual nephron. _____

_____

_____

Table 11.3 Circulation of Blood Around a Nephron	
Name of Structure	**Significance**
Afferent arteriole	Brings arteriolar blood toward glomerular capsule
Glomerulus	Capillary tuft enveloped by glomerular capsule
Efferent arteriole	Takes arteriolar blood away from glomerular capsule
Peritubular capillary network	Capillary bed that envelops the rest of the nephron
Veins	Take venous blood away from the nephron

Kidney Function

The kidneys contribute to homeostasis by (1) excreting nitrogenous wastes, (2) by regulating the salt-water balance, and (3) by regulating the pH balance. Regulating the salt-water balance maintains the blood volume and blood pressure.

Urine Formation

During urine formation, the kidneys perform all three of their functions. Urine formation requires three steps:

1. **Glomerular filtration** requires the movement of molecules outward from the glomerulus to the inside of the glomerular capsule. Blood pressure forces small molecules into the glomerular capsule. Label the arrow in Figure 11.8 that marks the location of glomerular filtration.
2. **Tubular reabsorption** requires the movement of molecules primarily from the proximal convoluted tubule to the peritubular capillary network. Nutrient molecules and water in the nephron filtrate are returned to the blood. Label the arrow in Figure 11.8 that refers to tubular reabsorption.
3. **Tubular secretion** requires the movement of molecules primarily from the peritubular capillary network to the nephron. Waste molecules remaining in the blood after glomerular filtration are moved into the nephron. Label the arrow in Figure 11.8 that refers to tubular secretion.

Figure 11.8   Urine formation.
The three steps in urine formation are glomerular filtration, tubular reabsorption, and tubular secretion. Label the arrows as directed above.

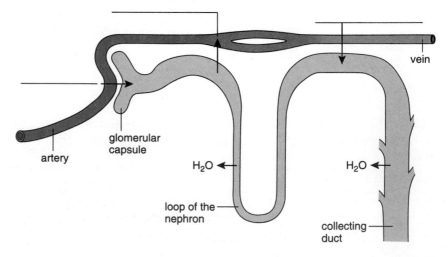

The two parts not considered in this discussion—the loop of the nephron and the collecting duct—are active in water reabsorption. Regulation of water reabsorption maintains blood volume at the proper level.

Glomerular Filtration

Blood entering the glomerulus contains cells, proteins, glucose, amino acids, salts, urea, and water. Blood pressure causes small molecules of glucose, amino acids, salts, urea, and water to exit the blood and enter the glomerular capsule. The fluid in the glomerular capsule is called the **filtrate.**

1. In the list that follows, draw an arrow from left to right for all those molecules that leave the glomerulus and enter the glomerular capsule:

    Glomerulus   **Glomerular Capsule (Filtrate)**
    Cells
    Proteins
    Glucose
    Amino acids
    Salts
    Urea
    Water

2. What substances are too large to leave the glomerulus and enter the glomerular capsule?

    _____

    These substances remain in the blood.

Tubular Reabsorption

When the filtrate enters the proximal convoluted tubule, it contains water, glucose, amino acids, urea, and salts. Enough water and salts are passively reabsorbed to maintain blood volume and pH.

1. What would happen to blood volume and blood pressure if water and salts were not reabsorbed? (Consider what happens to water pressure when the volume of water moving through a hose is reduced.)_____

    _____

2. The cells that line the proximal convoluted tubule are also engaged in active transport and usually completely reabsorb nutrients (glucose and amino acids). What would happen to cells if the body lost all its nutrients by way of the kidneys? _____

    _____

3. In the list that follows, draw an arrow from left to right for all those molecules passively reabsorbed into the blood. Use darker arrows for those actively reabsorbed.

    Proximal Convoluted Tubule   **Peritubular Capillary**
    Water
    Glucose
    Amino acids
    Urea
    Salts

4. What molecule is reabsorbed the least? _____.

Tubular Secretion

During tubular secretion, certain substances—for example, penicillin and histamine—are actively secreted from the peritubular capillary into the fluid of the tubule. Also, hydrogen ions and ammonia are secreted as necessary to maintain blood homeostasis.

Salt-Water Balance

Osmoregulation is the process by which the salt and water balance in the body is controlled. Depending on the inputs and outputs of salt and water, the kidneys may produce very small amounts of concentrated urine or copius amounts of dilute urine. For example, water loss due to sweating would concentrate the blood and decrease its volume and pressure. To compensate and return blood to its normal concentration (osmolarity), antidiuretic hormone (ADH) from the pituitary gland stimulates an increased reabsorbtion of water at the collecting ducts of the kidneys. As a result, a small amount of urine will be produced. Conversely, drinking a large amount of water has the opposite effect—the secretion of ADH is repressed and reabsorbtion of water is decreased to maintain osmolarity. Because less water is reabsorbed, the urine is dilute and in an increased amount.

Complete the following chart by writing *increase* or *decrease* in each empty box.

Event	Change in Blood Concentration	ADH Output	Water Reabsorption	Type of Urine Produced
Dehydration due to insufficient water intake or to water loss				scant, concentrated
Drinking a large amount of water				copious, dilute
Ingesting a large amount of salt				scant, concentrated

Which of the kidneys three functions is illustrated by this chart?_____

When the kidneys maintain the salt-water balance, they maintain blood volume and pressure.

pH Balance

If the blood is more basic than normal, what pH do you suppose the urine will be? _____

If the blood is more acidic than normal, what pH do you suppose the urine will be? _____

Which of the kidney's three functions is illustrated by your answers? _____

When kidneys regulate the salt-water balance, they also regulate the pH. For example, if the blood is acidic, sodium bicarbonate is reabsorbed.

Summary of Kidney Functions

For each substance listed at the left in Table 11.4, place an X in the appropriate column(s) to indicate where you expect the substance to be present.

Table 11.4 Urine Constituents			
Substance	In Blood of Glomerulus	In Filtrate	In Urine
Protein (albumin)			
Glucose			
Urea			
Water and salts			

Answer the following questions.

1. The presence of urea in the urine illustrates which of the kidney's functions? _____

   Do the kidneys make urea? _____ What organ makes urea? _____

   What do the kidneys produce? _____

2. The presence of salts and water in the urine is related to what two functions of the kidneys?

   _____

   _____

   When the kidneys reabsorb water, might the blood become hypertonic or hypotonic?

   _____

   When the kidneys reabsorb sodium bicarbonate, does the blood become more basic or more

   acidic? _____

Urinalysis

Urinalysis can help diagnose a patient's illness. The procedure is easily performed with a Chemstrip test strip, which has indicator spots that produce specific color reactions when certain substances are present in the urine.

Experimental Procedure: Urinalysis

Suppose a patient complains of excessive thirst and urination, loss of weight despite an intake of sweets, and feelings of being tired and run-down. A urinalysis has been ordered, and you are to test the urine. (In this case, you will be testing simulated urine, just as you tested simulated blood sera earlier in this lab.)

1. Review "Regulation of Blood Glucose Level," step 2, on page 139. Obtain a Chemstrip urine test strip (Fig. 11.9) that tests for leukocytes, pH, protein, glucose, ketones, and blood, noted in the "Tests For" column of the figure.
2. The color key on the diagnostic color chart or on the Chemstrip vial label will explain what the color changes mean in terms of the pH level and amount of each substance present in the urine sample. You will use these color blocks to read the results of your test.
3. Obtain a "specimen container of the patient's urine."
4. Briefly (no longer than 1 second) dip the test strip into the urine. Ensure that the chemically treated patches on the test strip are totally immersed.
5. Draw the edge of the strip along the rim of the specimen container to remove excess urine.
6. Turn the test strip on its side, and tap once on a piece of absorbent paper to remove any remaining urine and to prevent the possible mixing of chemicals.
7. After 60 seconds, read the tests as follows: *Hold the strip close to the color blocks on the diagnostic color chart (Figure 11.9) or vial label, and match carefully,* ensuring that the strip is properly oriented to the color chart.
8. Complete the last column of Figure 11.9.

Figure 11.9 Urinalysis test.
A Chemstrip test strip can help determine illness in a patient by detecting substances in the urine.

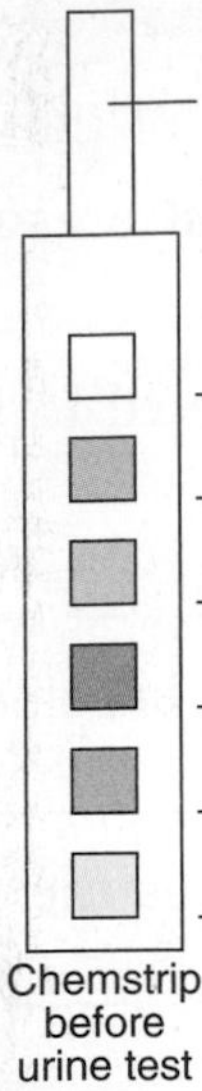

	Normal	Tests For:	Results
☐	negative	leukocytes	_____
▨	pH 5	pH	_____
▨	negative	protein	_____
▨	normal	glucose	_____
▨	negative	ketones	_____
▨	negative	blood	_____

strip handle

Chemstrip before urine test

Conclusions: Urinalysis

- According to your results, what condition might the patient have? _____
  Explain. _____
  _____
  _____

- Given that the patient's blood contains excess glucose, why is the patient suffering from excessive thirst and urination? _____

- Neither the liver nor the body cells are taking up glucose, so why is the patient tired?
  _____
  _____

- The metabolism of fat can explain the low pH of the urine. Why? _____

Summary of Homeostasis

1. As noted at the beginning of this laboratory, homeostasis is the dynamic equilibrium of the body's internal environment, the blood and tissue fluid surrounding tissue cells. The lungs and kidneys have boundaries that interact with the external environment to refresh blood. The liver also regulates blood content. Fill in the following table to show the activities of the lungs, liver, and kidneys.

Processes	Lungs	Liver	Kidneys
Gas exchange	O_2 enters and CO_2 exits the blood	_____	_____
pH maintenance	a.	_____	e.
Glucose level	_____	c.	f.
Waste removal	b.	d.	g.
Blood volume	_____	_____	h.

2. Which of these organs contributes most to homeostasis? _____

3. As described throughout this lab, homeostasis is maintained when a change in the internal environment values triggers a response that restores the normal condition. Complete Table 11.5 to show how the lungs, liver, and kidneys respond to changes in the internal environment. Under "Response," include any hormones involved.

Table 11.5 Changes in Internal Environment		
Change	**Organ (lungs, liver, kidney)**	**Response**
Decrease in blood glucose level.		
Decrease in blood solute concentration and blood volume and pressure.		
Increase in blood CO_2.		

Application for Daily Living

The Liver Is a Vital Organ

The liver is a vital organ because we can't live without one. The liver is the gatekeeper to the blood. After molecules enter the blood at the digestive tract, they go first to the liver, which removes and breaks down poisons, regulates blood glucose, produces blood proteins that have numerous functions, and also produces bile, which is sent to the digestive tract, where it emulsifies fat.

Realize that your behavior can affect your liver. Alcohol is a poison to the liver, and it valiantly breaks it down, but if you keep drinking heavily, the liver can't keep up and develops cirrhosis, characterized by scar tissue instead of working liver cells. Another cause of liver failure is hepatitis, an infection that can be sexually transmitted or acquired by using dirty needles to shoot drugs into the body. The need for a healthy liver provides a good reason for a healthy lifestyle.

_____ 1. What process accounts for gas exchange in the lungs?

_____ 2. What molecule is removed by the lungs?

_____ 3. What are the air spaces in the lungs called?

_____ 4. What blood vessel lies between the intestines and the liver?

_____ 5. In what form is glucose stored in the liver?

_____ 6. The liver removes the amino group from amino acids to form what molecule?

_____ 7. The hepatic vein enters what blood vessel?

_____ 8. When molecules leave the glomerulus, they enter what portion of the nephron?

_____ 9. Name a substance that is in the glomerular filtrate but not in the urine.

_____ 10. Glucose in the urine indicates that a person may have what condition?

_____ 11. Name the process by which molecules move from the proximal convoluted tubule into the blood.

_____ 12. Where does urine collect before exiting the kidney?

_____ 13. Does venous blood in the tissues contain more or less carbon dioxide than arterial blood?

_____ 14. What type of pressure causes water to exit from the arterial side of the capillary?

_____ 15. If a person hyperventilates, does the blood become acidic or basic?

Thought Questions

16. Which systemic blood vessel would you expect to have a high glucose content immediately after eating? Explain.

17. In what ways do the kidneys aid homeostasis?

Human Biology Website

The companion website for _Human Biology_ provides a wealth of information organized and integrated by chapter. You will find practice tests, animations, and much more that will complement your learning and understanding of general biology.

www.mhhe.com/maderhuman11

Anatomy & Physiology Revealed

A program that includes cadaver photos that allow you to peel away layers of the human body to reveal structures beneath the surface. This program also includes animations. radiological pronunciations, audio pronunciations and practice quizzing. Check out _www.aprevealed.com_. APR has been proven to help improve student grades!

12

Musculoskeletal System

Learning Outcomes

12.1 Anatomy of a Long Bone
- Locate and identify the portions of a long bone, and associate particular tissues with each portion.
- Identify significant features of compact bone, spongy bone, and hyaline cartilage.
Question: Which portion of long bone and which type of bone contain osteons?

12.2 The Skeleton
- Locate and identify the bones of the appendicular and axial human skeletons.
Question: To which division of the skeleton should you associate the limbs?

12.3 The Skeletal Muscles
- Locate and identify selected human skeletal muscles.
- Illustrate types of joint movements.
- Give examples of antagonistic pairs of muscles and the actions involved.
- Distinguish between isometric and isotonic contractions.
Question: Why do muscles work in antagonistic pairs?

12.4 Mechanism of Skeletal Muscle Fiber Contraction
- Describe the structure of skeletal muscle.
- Describe an experiment that demonstrates the role of ATP and ions in the contraction of sarcomeres.
Question: In general, what is the role of ATP in muscle contraction?

Application for Daily Living: Bone Marrow Transplants

Introduction

The human skeletal system consists of the bones (206 in adults) and joints, along with the cartilage and ligaments that occur at the joints. The muscular system contains three types of muscles: smooth, cardiac, and skeletal. The term **musculoskeletal system** recognizes that contraction of skeletal muscles causes the bones to move.

In humans, the skeletal muscles are most often attached across a joint (Fig. 12.1). The biceps brachii muscle has two origins, while the triceps brachii has three origins on the humerus and scapula. Find the tendon of insertion of the biceps brachii muscle by feeling on the anterior surface of your elbow while contracting your biceps muscle. Feel for the bone at your posterior elbow. This is the ulna, the site of insertion of the tendon for the triceps brachii muscle.

Muscles work in antagonistic pairs. For example, when the biceps brachii contracts, the bones of the forearm are pulled upward, while the triceps brachii relaxes; and when the triceps brachii contracts, the bones of the forearm are pulled downward, while the biceps brachii relaxes.

Figure 12.1 Muscular action.
Muscles, such as these muscles of the arm (which have their origin on the scapula and their insertion on the bones of the forearm), cause bones to move.

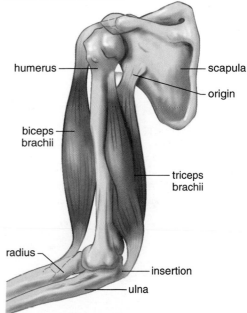

humerus — — scapula
— origin
biceps brachii
triceps brachii
radius
insertion
ulna

12.1 Anatomy of a Long Bone

Although the bones of the skeletal system vary considerably in shape as well as in size, a long bone, such as the human femur, illustrates the general principles of bone anatomy (Fig. 12.2).

Figure 12.2   Anatomy of a bone from the macroscopic to the microscopic level.
A long bone is encased by the periosteum except at the ends, where it is covered by hyaline (articular) cartilage (see micrograph, *top left*). Spongy bone located at the ends may contain red bone marrow. The medullary cavity contains yellow bone marrow and is bordered by compact bone, shown in the enlargement and micrograph (*right*).

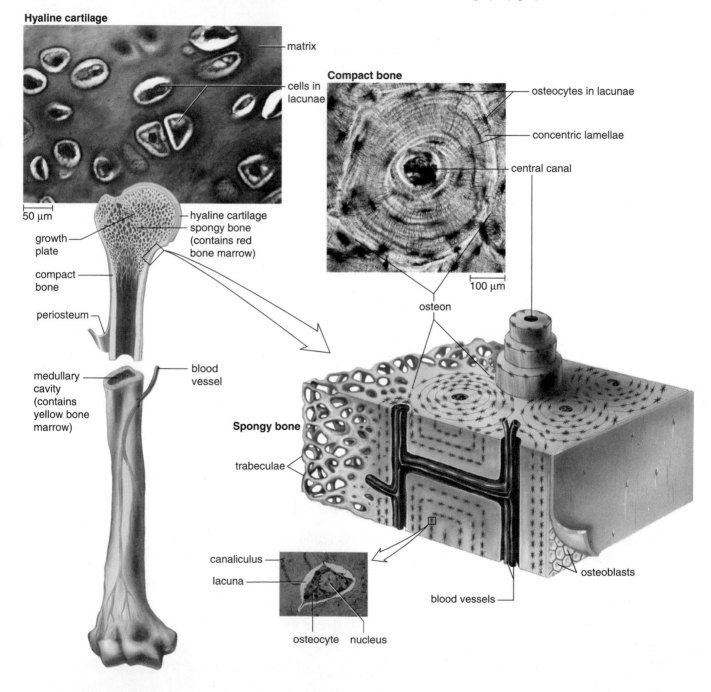

Hyaline cartilage

matrix

cells in lacunae

50 μm

growth plate

hyaline cartilage
spongy bone (contains red bone marrow)

compact bone

periosteum

medullary cavity (contains yellow bone marrow)

blood vessel

Compact bone

osteocytes in lacunae

concentric lamellae

central canal

100 μm

osteon

Spongy bone

trabeculae

canaliculus

lacuna

osteocyte   nucleus

blood vessels

osteoblasts

Observation: Anatomy of a Long Bone

Examine the exterior and a longitudinal section of a long bone or a model of a long bone, and with the help of Figure 12.2, identify the following:

1. **Periosteum:** Tough, fibrous connective tissue covering continuous with the ligament and tendons that anchor bones. The periosteum allows blood vessels to enter the bone and service its cells.
2. Expanded portions at each end of the bone (*epiphysis*) that contain spongy bone.
3. Extended portion, or shaft (*diaphysis*) of a long bone that lies between the epiphyses. Walls of diaphysis are compact bone.
4. **Hyaline (articular) cartilage:** Layer of cartilage where the bone articulates with (meets) another bone; decreases friction between bones during movement.
5. **Medullary cavity:** Cavity located in the diaphysis that stores yellow marrow, which contains a large amount of fat.

Label the diaphysis and the epiphysis (twice) in Figure 12.2. Which of these contains the growth line where a long bone can grow in length? _____

Observation: Tissues of a Long Bone

The medullary cavity is bounded at the sides by **compact bone** and at the ends by **spongy bone.** Beyond a thin shell of compact bone is the layer of articular cartilage. **Red marrow,** a specialized tissue that produces blood cells, occurs in the spongy bone of the skull, ribs, sternum, and vertebrae, and in the ends of the long bones.

1. Examine a prepared slide of compact bone, and with the help of Figure 12.2, identify:
   a. **Osteons:** Cylindrical structural units.
   b. **Lamellae:** Concentric rings of matrix.
   c. **Matrix:** Nonliving material maintained by osteocytes. Contains mineral salts (notably calcium salts) and protein.
   d. **Lacunae:** Cavities between the lamellae that contain osteocytes (bone cells).
   e. **Central canal:** Canal in the center of each osteon. Figure 12.2 shows that there
      are _____ in a central canal.
   f. **Canaliculi:** Tiny channels that contain the processes of cells. These processes allow nutrients to pass between the osteocytes (sing., *canaliculus*).

   Describe how an osteocyte located near a central canal can pass nutrients to osteocytes located far from the central canal. _____
   _____

2. Examine a prepared slide of spongy bone, and with the help of Figure 12.2, identify:
   a. **Trabeculae:** Bony bars and plates made of mineral salts and protein.
   b. **Lacunae:** Cavities scattered throughout the trabeculae that contain osteocytes.
   c. **Red bone marrow:** Within large spaces separated by the trabeculae.

   Where is red bone marrow located, and what activity occurs in red bone marrow?
   _____

3. Examine a prepared slide of hyaline cartilage, and with the help of Figure 12.2, identify:
   a. **Lacunae:** Cavities in twos and threes scattered throughout the matrix, which contain chondrocytes (cells that maintain cartilage).
   b. **Matrix:** Material more flexible than bone because it consists primarily of protein.

   Seniors tend to have joints that creak. What might be the matter? _____

12.2 The Skeleton

The human skeleton is divided into axial and appendicular components. The **axial skeleton** is the main longitudinal portion, and includes the skull, the vertebral column, the sternum, and the ribs. The **appendicular skeleton** includes the bones of the appendages and their supportive pectoral and pelvic (shoulder and hip) girdles.

Observation: Axial Skeleton

Examine a human skeleton, and with the help of Figures 12.3 and 12.4, identify the **foramen magnum,** a large opening through which the spinal cord passes, and the following bones:

1. The **skull** is composed of many small bones fused together. Note the following in the cranium:
   a. **Frontal bone:** Forms forehead.
   b. **Parietal bones:** Extend to sides of skull.
   c. **Occipital bone:** Curves to form base of skull.

Figure 12.3   Skull.
a. Lateral view. **b.** Inferior view. **c.** Facial view.

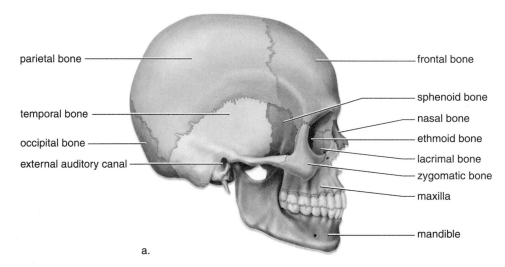

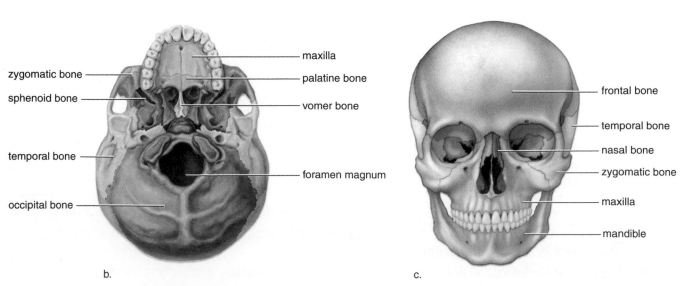

a.

b.

c.

Figure 12.4 Human skeletal system.

a. Anterior view. **b.** Posterior view. The axial skeleton appears in blue, while the appendicular skeleton is shown in tan.

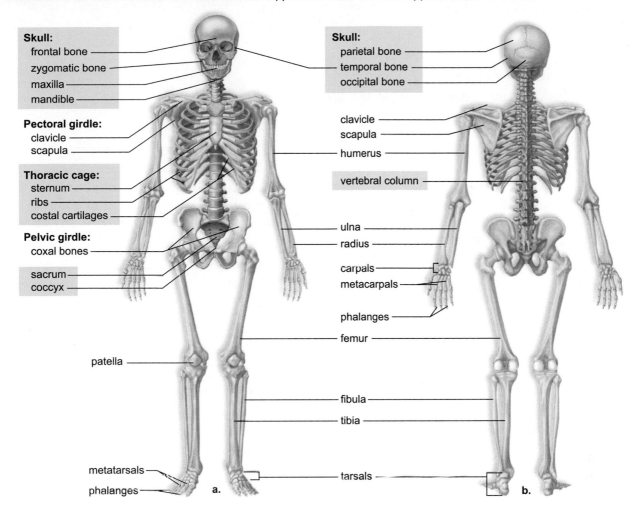

Skull:
frontal bone
zygomatic bone
maxilla
mandible

Pectoral girdle:
clavicle
scapula

Thoracic cage:
sternum
ribs
costal cartilages

Pelvic girdle:
coxal bones

sacrum
coccyx

patella

metatarsals
phalanges

a.

Skull:
parietal bone
temporal bone
occipital bone

clavicle
scapula

humerus

vertebral column

ulna
radius

carpals
metacarpals

phalanges

femur

fibula

tibia

tarsals

b.

NOTE: According to accepted terminology, the upper limb is composed of the humerus in the **arm** and the radius and ulna in the **forearm**. The lower limb is composed of the femur in the **thigh** and the tibia and fibula in the **leg**.

---

d. **Temporal bones:** Located on sides of skull.

e. **Sphenoid bone:** Helps form base and sides of skull, as well as part of the orbits.

Which of these bones contributes to forming the face? _____

Which could best be associated with the wearing of glasses? _____

2. Note the facial bones:

a. **Mandible:** The lower jaw.

b. **Maxillae:** The upper jaw and anterior portion of the hard palate.

c. **Palatine bones:** Posterior portion of hard palate and floor of nasal cavity.

d. **Zygomatic bones:** Cheekbones.

e. **Nasal bones:** Bridge of nose.

Which of these is moveable and allows you to chew your food? _____

3. The **vertebral column** provides support and houses the **spinal cord.** It is composed of many vertebrae separated from one another by intervertebral disks. The vertebral column customarily is divided into five series:

   a. Seven **cervical vertebrae** (forming the neck region)

   b. Twelve **thoracic vertebrae** (with which the ribs articulate)

   c. Five **lumbar vertebrae** (in the abdominal region)

   d. Five fused sacral vertebrae, called the **sacrum**

   e. Four fused caudal vertebrae forming the **coccyx** in humans

   Which of the vertebrae can be associated with the chest? _____

   Which of the vertebrae could be the cause of your aching back? _____

4. The twelve pairs of **ribs** and their associated muscles form a bony case that supports the thoracic cavity wall. The ribs connect posteriorly with the thoracic vertebrae, and some are also attached by cartilage directly or indirectly to the sternum. Those ribs without any anterior attachment are called **floating ribs.**

   Which of the ribs help form the protective part of the rib cage? _____

After studying Figure 12.4, give several reasons why the axial skeleton is critical to life.

Observation: Appendicular Skeleton

Examine a human skeleton, and with the help of Figure 12.4, identify the following bones:

1. The **pectoral girdles,** which support the upper limbs, are composed of the **clavicle** (collarbone) and **scapula** (shoulder bone).

   Why is the shoulder apt to become dislocated? _____

2. The upper limb (arm plus the forearm) is composed of the following:

   a. **Humerus:** The large long bone of the arm.

   b. **Radius:** The long bone of the forearm, with a pivot joint at the elbow that allows rotational motion.

   c. **Ulna:** The other long bone of the forearm, with a hinge joint at the elbow that allows motion in only one plane. Take hold of your elbow, and twist the forearm to show that the radius rotates over the ulna but the ulna doesn't move during this action.

   d. **Carpals:** A group of small bones forming the wrist.

   e. **Metacarpals:** Slender bones forming the palm.

   f. **Phalanges:** The bones of the fingers.

   Which of these bones would you use to pick up a tea cup? _____

3. The **pelvic girdle** forms the basal support for the lower limbs and is composed of two **coxal** (hip) **bones.** The female pelvis is much broader and shallower than that of the male. The angle between the pubic bones looks like a U in females and a V in males.

   How is it advantageous for the female pelvis to be broader and more shallow than that of a

   male? _____

4. The lower limb (the thigh plus the leg) is composed of a series of loosely articulated bones, including the following:

   a. **Femur:** The long bone of the thigh.

   b. **Patella:** Kneecap.

   c. **Tibia:** The larger of the two long bones of the leg. Feel for the bump on the inside of the ankle.

d. **Fibula:** The smaller of the two long bones of the leg. Feel for the bump on the outside of the ankle.

e. **Tarsals:** A group of small bones forming the ankle.

f. **Metatarsals:** Slender anterior bones of the foot.

g. **Phalanges:** The bones of the toes.

Which of these bones would you use to kick a soccer ball? _____

Hip Replacement

Find the hip joint in Figure 12.4. The terminology "hip replacement" is a misnomer because no part of the coxal bone is replaced. Instead, the hip joint is replaced. The head of the femur is replaced with a metal ball attached to a metal stem. The stem is inserted into the femur. The inside of the socket on the coxal bone is bolstered with a plastic (or plastic and metal) cup. After the replacement, no part of the joint is living tissue.

12.3 The Skeletal Muscles

This laboratory is concerned with skeletal muscles—those muscles that make up the bulk of the human body. With the help of Figure 12.5, identify the major muscles of the body. Muscles are named for various characteristics, as shown in the following list:

1. **Size:** The gluteus *maximus* is the largest muscle, and it forms the buttocks.
2. **Shape:** The *deltoid* is shaped like a Greek letter delta, or triangle.
3. **Direction of fibers:** The *rectus* abdominis is a longitudinal muscle of the abdomen (*rectus* means straight).
4. **Location:** The *frontalis* overlies the frontal bone.
5. **Number of attachments:** The *biceps* brachii has two attachments, or origins.
6. **Action:** The extensor *digitorum* extends the fingers, or digits.

Figure 12.5 Human musculature.

Superficial skeletal muscles in **(a)** anterior and **(b)** posterior view.

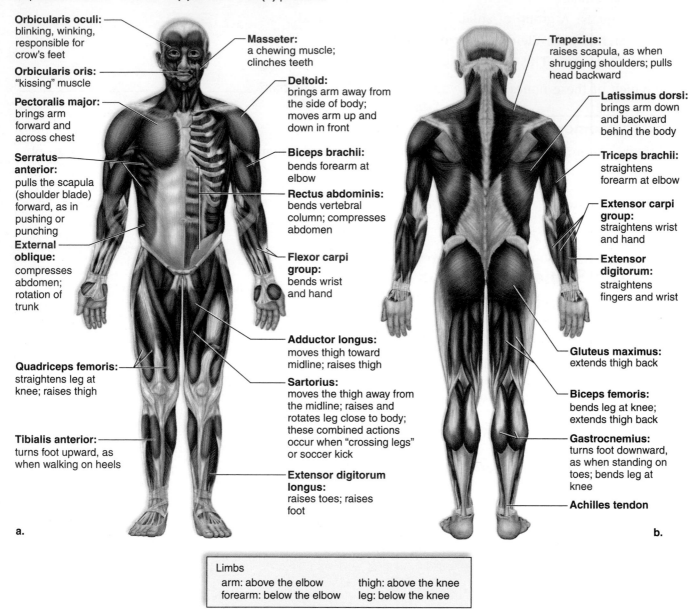

Orbicularis oculi:
blinking, winking, responsible for crow's feet

Orbicularis oris:
"kissing" muscle

Pectoralis major:
brings arm forward and across chest

Serratus anterior:
pulls the scapula (shoulder blade) forward, as in pushing or punching

External oblique:
compresses abdomen; rotation of trunk

Quadriceps femoris:
straightens leg at knee; raises thigh

Tibialis anterior:
turns foot upward, as when walking on heels

Masseter:
a chewing muscle; clinches teeth

Deltoid:
brings arm away from the side of body; moves arm up and down in front

Biceps brachii:
bends forearm at elbow

Rectus abdominis:
bends vertebral column; compresses abdomen

Flexor carpi group:
bends wrist and hand

Adductor longus:
moves thigh toward midline; raises thigh

Sartorius:
moves the thigh away from the midline; raises and rotates leg close to body; these combined actions occur when "crossing legs" or soccer kick

Extensor digitorum longus:
raises toes; raises foot

Trapezius:
raises scapula, as when shrugging shoulders; pulls head backward

Latissimus dorsi:
brings arm down and backward behind the body

Triceps brachii:
straightens forearm at elbow

Extensor carpi group:
straightens wrist and hand

Extensor digitorum:
straightens fingers and wrist

Gluteus maximus:
extends thigh back

Biceps femoris:
bends leg at knee; extends thigh back

Gastrocnemius:
turns foot downward, as when standing on toes; bends leg at knee

Achilles tendon

a.

b.

Limbs	
arm: above the elbow	thigh: above the knee
forearm: below the elbow	leg: below the knee

Antagonistic Pairs

Skeletal muscles are attached to the skeleton, and their contraction causes the movement of bones at a joint. Muscles shorten when they contract, so they can only pull; they cannot push. Therefore, muscles work in **antagonistic pairs.** Usually, contraction of one member of the pair causes a bone to move in one direction, and contraction of the other member of the pair causes the same bone to move in an opposite direction.

Figure 12.6 Joint movements.
a. Flexion and extension. **b.** Adduction and abduction. **c.** Rotation and circumduction. **d.** Inversion and eversion. Circles indicate pivot points.

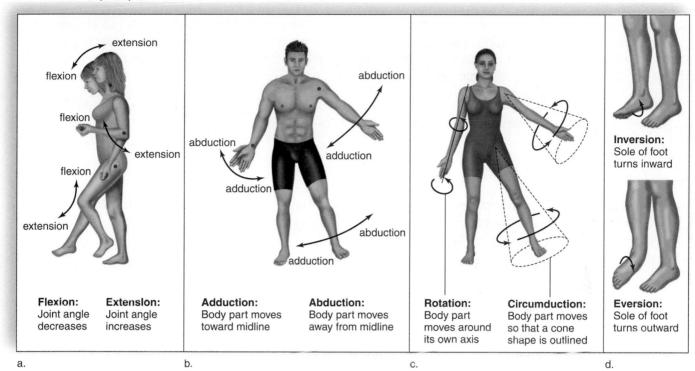

a.   b.   c.   d.

Figure 12.6 demonstrates the following types of joint movements:

Flexion   Moving jointed body parts toward each other

Extension Moving jointed body parts away from each other

Adduction Moving a part toward a vertical plane running through the longitudinal midline of the body

Abduction Moving a part away from a vertical plane running through the longitudinal midline of the body

Rotation   Moving a body part around its own axis; **circumduction** is moving a body part in a wide circle

Inversion A movement of the foot in which the sole is turned inward

Eversion   A movement of the foot in which the sole is turned outward

Observation: Antagonistic Pairs

Locate the following antagonistic pairs in Figure 12.5. In each case, state their opposing actions by inserting one of these functions: *flexes, extends, adducts,* or *abducts.*

1. The biceps brachii _____ the forearm.

   The triceps brachii _____ the forearm.

2. The sartorius _____ the thigh.

   The adductor longus _____ the thigh.

3. The quadriceps femoris _____ the leg.

   The biceps femoris _____ the leg.

Isometric and Isotonic Contractions

A muscle contains many muscle fibers. When a muscle contracts, usually some fibers undergo isotonic contraction, and others undergo isometric contraction. When the tension of muscle fibers is sufficient to lift a load, many fibers change length as they lift the load. The muscle contraction is said to be **isotonic** (same tension). In contrast, when the tension of muscle fibers is used only to support rather than lift a load, the muscle contraction is said to be **isometric** (same length). The length of many fibers remains the same, but their tension still changes.

Experimental Procedure: Isometric and Isotonic Contractions

Note: The upper limb is composed of the arm plus the forearm.

Isotonic Contraction

1. Start with your left forearm resting on a table. Watch the anterior surface of your left arm while you slowly bend your elbow and bring your left forearm toward the arm. An isotonic contraction of the biceps brachii produces this movement.

2. If muscle contraction produces movement, is this an isometric or isotonic contraction? _____

_____

Isometric Contraction

1. Place the palm of your left hand underneath a tabletop. Push up against the table while you have your right hand cupped over the anterior surface of your left arm so that you can feel the muscle there undergo an isometric contraction.

2. Is the biceps brachii or the triceps brachii located on the anterior surface of the arm?

_____

3. What change did you notice in the firmness of this muscle as it contracted? _____

_____

4. Did your hand or forearm move as you pushed up against the table? _____

5. Given your answer to question 4, did this muscle's fibers shorten as you pushed up against the tabletop? _____

12.4 Mechanism of Skeletal Muscle Fiber Contraction

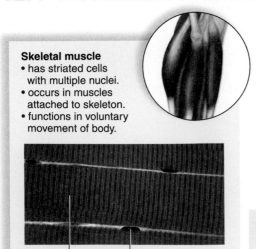

Skeletal muscle
- has striated cells with multiple nuclei.
- occurs in muscles attached to skeleton.
- functions in voluntary movement of body.

striation   nucleus

A whole skeletal muscle is made up of many cells, usually called muscle fibers.

Light Microscopy

Muscle fibers are striated—that is, they have alternating light and dark bands. These striations can be observed in a light micrograph of muscle fibers in longitudinal section.

Observation: Skeletal Muscle

Examine a prepared slide of skeletal muscle, and identify the long, multinucleated fibers arranged in a parallel fashion. How do you know the muscle fibers are striated?

_____

Muscle Contraction

Electron microscopy helped investigators determine what causes the striated appearance of a muscle fiber and its contraction (Fig. 12.7). A muscle fiber contains hundreds, even thousands, of contractile portions called **myofibrils** divided into units called **sarcomeres**. Each sarcomere contains **myosin filaments** and **actin filaments**. The sarcomeres contract when myosin cross-bridges attach to and pull the actin filaments to the center of the sarcomeres.

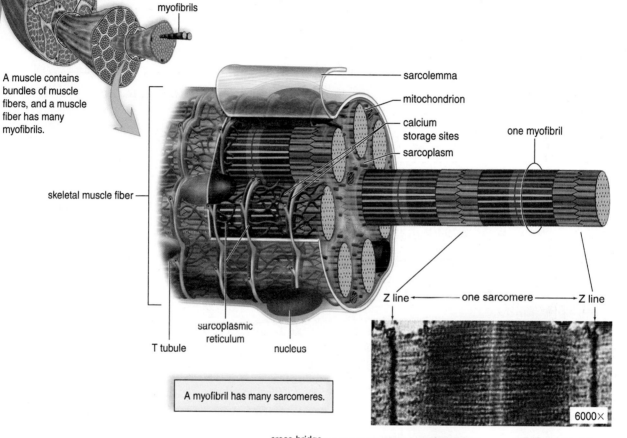

bundle of muscle fibers

myofibrils

A muscle contains bundles of muscle fibers, and a muscle fiber has many myofibrils.

sarcolemma

mitochondrion

calcium storage sites

sarcoplasm

one myofibril

skeletal muscle fiber

Z line ← one sarcomere → Z line

sarcoplasmic reticulum

T tubule

nucleus

A myofibril has many sarcomeres.

6000×

Figure 12.7   Microscopic structure of a skeletal muscle fiber.

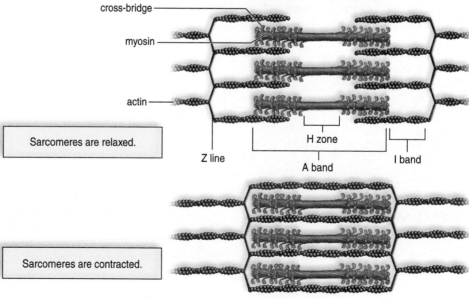

cross-bridge

myosin

actin

Sarcomeres are relaxed.

H zone

Z line

A band

I band

Sarcomeres are contracted.

We are going to study muscle contraction with this data in mind:

1. Myosin is an enzyme that can break down ATP as an energy source for muscle contraction.
2. Enzymes often require cofactors, which can be coenzymes or certain ions, such as the K^+ and Mg^{2+} required by myosin.
3. When ATP, K^+ and Mg^{2+} are present, myosin cross-bridges will attach to actin filaments and pull them to the center of sarcomeres within myofibrils. In this way, the actin filaments slide past myosin filaments and the sarcomeres and a muscle fiber contracts.

In the following Experimental Procedure, we are going to expose muscle fibers to different solutions:

1. No salt solution and no ATP;
2. Salt solution (contains K^+ and Mg^{2+}) only;
3. ATP solution only;
4. ATP solution and salt solution.
   Hypothesize which of these will produce contraction and explain. _____

_____

Experimental Procedure: Muscle Fiber Contraction

1. Label two slides, slide 1 and slide 2. Mount a strand of muscle fibers in a drop of *glycerol* on each slide. Place each slide on a millimeter ruler, and measure the length of the strand. Record these lengths in the first row in Table 12.1. If there is more than a small drop of glycerol on the slides, soak up the excess on a piece of lens paper held at the edge of the glycerol farthest from the fiber strand.
2. To slide 1, add a few drops of a *salt solution* containing potassium (K^+) and magnesium (Mg^{2+}) ions, and note any change in strand length. Record your results in Table 12.1.
3. To slide 2, add a few drops of *ATP solution*, and note any change in strand length. Record your results in Table 12.1.
4. Now add *ATP solution* to slide 1. Note any change in strand length, and record your results in Table 12.1. To slide 2, add a few drops of the K^+/Mg^{2+} *salt solution*, and note any change in strand length. Record your results in Table 12.1.

Table 12.1 Glycerinated Muscle Contraction

Solution	Length of Muscle Fiber	
	Slide 1	Slide 2
1. Glycerol alone	mm	mm
2. K^+/Mg^{2+} salt solution alone	mm	—
3. ATP alone	—	mm
4. Both ATP and salt solution	mm	mm

Conclusion: Muscle Fiber Contraction

- To demonstrate that you understand the requirements for contraction, state the function of each of the substances listed in Table 12.2.

Table 12.2 Summary of Muscle Fiber Contraction	
Substance	**Function**
Myosin	
Actin	
K^+/Mg^{2+} salt solution	
ATP	

- Was your hypothesis stated on page 162 supported? _____ Why or why not? _____

_____

Application for Daily Living

Bone Marrow Transplants

We are accustomed to thinking of a transplant as a procedure that replaces a nonfunctioning organ with one that works properly. A red bone marrow transplant doesn't quite work like that. Instead, red bone marrow is injected into the bloodstream and the recipient is receiving the cells that occur in the red bone marrow. The red bone marrow contains the precious stem cells capable of producing all the various cells in the blood. And they aren't ordinarily in the blood! However, these cells usually find their way home—the bones that ordinarily contain red bone marrow in adults, such as the sternum, breast bone, skull, hips, ribs, and spine.

The health reasons for needing a red bone marrow transplant are numerous, but chief among them are cancer patients whose own bone marrow was destroyed by treatment of cancer. As with any transplant, a careful match between donor and recipient is required.

_____ 1. Is compact bone located in the diaphysis or in the epiphyses?

_____ 2. Does compact bone or spongy bone contain red bone marrow?

_____ 3. What are bone cells called?

_____ 4. What are the vertebrae in the neck region called?

_____ 5. Name the strongest bone in the lower limb.

_____ 6. What bones are part of a pectoral girdle?

_____ 7. What type of joint movement occurs when a muscle moves a limb toward the midline of the body?

_____ 8. What type of joint movement occurs when a muscle moves a body part around its own axis?

_____ 9. Skeletal muscle is voluntary, and its appearance is _____ because of the placement of actin and myosin filaments.

_____ 10. Glycerinated muscle requires the addition of what molecule to supply the energy for muscle contraction?

_____ 11. Actin and myosin are what type of biological molecule?

_____ 12. Does the quadriceps femoris flex or extend the leg?

_____ 13. Does the biceps brachii flex or extend the forearm?

_____ 14. What muscle forms the buttocks?

_____ 15. Name the muscle group antagonistic to the quadriceps femoris group.

Thought Questions

16. What bones protect the thoracic cavity?

17. When you see glycerinated muscle shorten, what is happening microscopically?

Human Biology Website

The companion website for _Human Biology_ provides a wealth of information organized and integrated by chapter. You will find practice tests, animations, and much more that will complement your learning and understanding of general biology.

www.mhhe.com/maderhuman11

McGraw-Hill Access Science Website

An online encyclopedia of science and technology that provides information, including videos, that can enhance the laboratory experience.

www.accessscience.com

13

Nervous System and Senses

Learning Outcomes

13.1 The Mammalian Brain
- Identify the parts of the brain studied, and state the functions of each part.
- Give examples to show that the parts of the brain work together.

Question: Distinguish between the cerebral cortex and the cerebrum.

13.2 Spinal Nerves and Spinal Cord
- Describe the anatomy of the spinal cord and tell how the cord functions as a relay station.
- Describe the anatomy and physiology of a spinal reflex arc.

Question: How does the brain become aware that you have removed your hand from a hot stove?

13.3 The Human Eye
- Identify the parts of the eye and state a function for each part.

Question: What part of the eye contains the sensory receptors for sight?

13.4 The Human Ear
- Using photographs, other images, or models, identify the parts of the ear and state a function for each part.

Question: What part of the ear contains the sensory receptors for hearing?

13.5 Sensory Receptors in Human Skin
- Describe the anatomy of the human skin and explain the distribution and function of sensory receptors.
- Relate the abundance of touch receptors to the ability to distinguish between two different touch points.

Question: What part of the skin contains sensory receptors?

13.6 Human Chemoreceptors
- Relate the ability to distinguish tastes to the distribution of taste receptors on the human tongue.
- Relate the ability to distinguish foods to the senses of smell and taste.

Question: Taste is dependent on what types of chemical stimuli?

Application for Daily Living: LASIK Surgery

Introduction

The human nervous system consists of the brain, spinal cord, and nerves. Sensory receptors detect changes in environmental stimuli, and nerve impulses move along sensory nerve fibers to the brain and the spinal cord. The brain and spinal cord sum up the data before sending impulses via motor neurons to effectors (muscles and glands) so a response to stimuli is possible. Nervous tissue consists of neurons; whereas the brain and spinal cord contain all parts of neurons, nerves contain only axons (Fig. 13.1).

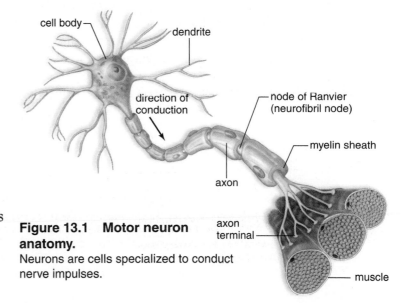

Figure 13.1 Motor neuron anatomy.
Neurons are cells specialized to conduct nerve impulses.

13.1 The Mammalian Brain

The brain is the enlarged anterior end of the spinal cord containing parts and centers that receive input from, and can command other regions of, the nervous system.

> ⚠ **Latex gloves** Wear protective latex gloves when handling preserved animal organs. Use protective eyewear and exercise caution when using sharp instruments during this laboratory. Wash hands thoroughly upon completion of this laboratory.

Preserved Sheep Brain

The sheep brain (Fig. 13.2) is often used to study the mammalian brain. It is easily available and large enough that individual parts can be identified.

Observation: Preserved Sheep Brain

Examine the exterior and a midsaggital (longitudinal) section of a preserved sheep brain or a model of the human brain, and with the help of Figure 13.2, identify the following.

1. **Ventricles:** Interconnecting spaces that produce and serve as a reservoir for cerebrospinal fluid, which cushions the brain. Toward the anterior, note the large lateral ventricle (on one longitudinal section) and the lateral ventricle (on the other longitudinal section). Trace the second ventricle to the third and then the fourth ventricles.
2. **Medulla oblongata** (or simply **medulla**): The most posterior portion of the brain stem. It controls internal organs; for example, cardiac and breathing control centers are present in the medulla. Nerve impulses pass from the spinal cord through the medulla to higher brain regions.
3. **Pons:** The ventral, bulblike enlargement on the brain stem. It serves as a passageway for nerve impulses running between the medulla and the higher brain regions.
4. **Midbrain:** Anterior to the pons, the midbrain serves as a relay station for sensory input and motor output. It also contains a reflex center for eye muscles.
5. **Diencephalon:** The portion of the brain where the third ventricle is located. The hypothalamus and thalamus are also located here.
6. **Hypothalamus:** Forms the floor of the third ventricle and contains control centers for appetite, body temperature, and water balance. Its primary function is homeostasis. The hypothalamus also has centers for pleasure, reproductive behavior, hostility, and pain.
7. **Thalamus:** Two connected lobes located in the roof of the third ventricle. The thalamus is the highest portion of the brain to receive sensory impulses before the cerebrum. It is believed to control which of the received impulses is passed on to the cerebrum. For this reason, the thalamus sometimes is called the "gatekeeper to the cerebrum."
8. **Cerebellum:** Located just posterior to the cerebrum as you observe the brain dorsally, the cerebellum's two lobes make it appear rather like a butterfly. In cross section, the cerebellum has an internal pattern that looks like a tree. The cerebellum coordinates equilibrium and motor activity to produce smooth movements.

Figure 13.2 The sheep brain.

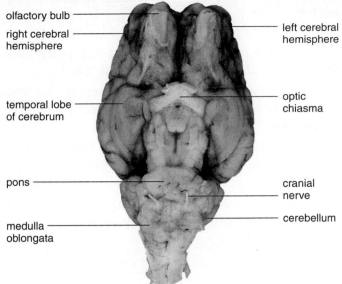

olfactory bulb

right cerebral hemisphere

temporal lobe of cerebrum

pons

medulla oblongata

left cerebral hemisphere

optic chiasma

cranial nerve

cerebellum

a. Ventral view

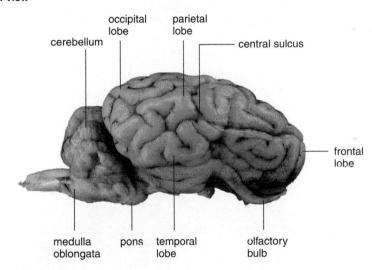

occipital lobe

parietal lobe

cerebellum

central sulcus

frontal lobe

medulla oblongata

pons

temporal lobe

olfactory bulb

b. Lateral view

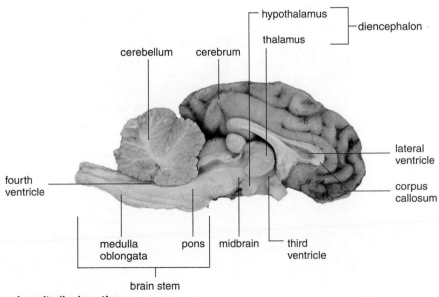

hypothalamus

diencephalon

thalamus

cerebellum

cerebrum

lateral ventricle

corpus callosum

fourth ventricle

medulla oblongata

pons

midbrain

third ventricle

brain stem

c. Longitudinal section

9. **Cerebrum:** The most developed area of the brain and responsible for higher mental capabilities. The cerebrum is divided into the right and left **cerebral hemispheres,** joined by the **corpus callosum,** a broad sheet of white matter. The outer portion of the cerebrum is highly convoluted and divided into the following surface lobes:

a. **Frontal lobe:** Controls motor functions and permits voluntary muscle control. It also is responsible for abilities to think, problem solve, and speak.

b. **Parietal lobe:** Receives information from sensory receptors located in the skin. It also helps in the understanding of speech. A groove called the **central sulcus** separates the frontal lobe from the parietal lobe.

c. **Occipital lobe:** Interprets visual input and combines visual images with other sensory experiences. The optic nerves split and enter opposite sides of the brain at the optic chiasma, located in the diencephalon.

d. **Temporal lobe:** Has sensory areas for hearing and smelling. The olfactory bulb contains nerve fibers that communicate with the olfactory cells in the nasal passages and take nerve impulses to the temporal lobe.

The Human Brain

Based on your knowledge of the sheep brain, label Figure 13.3 and complete Table 13.1 by stating the major functions of each part of the brain listed.

Figure 13.3   The human brain (longitudinal section).
The cerebrum is larger in humans than in sheep. *Label where indicated.*

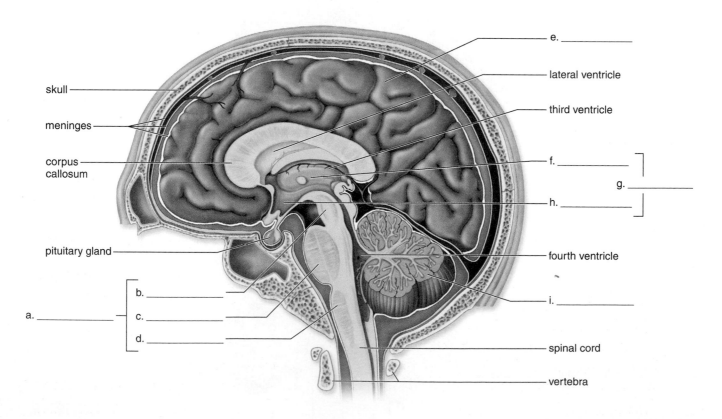

Table 13.1 Summary of Brain Functions

Part	Major Functions
Cerebrum	
Cerebellum	
Diencephalon Thalamus	
Hypothalamus	
Brain Stem Midbrain	
Pons	
Medulla Oblongata	

Which parts of the brain would work together to achieve:

1. Good eye-hand coordination _____

2. Concentrating on homework when TV is playing _____

3. Avoiding dark alleys while walking home at night _____

4. Keeping the blood pressure constant _____

13.2 Spinal Nerves and Spinal Cord

The spinal nerves and spinal cord function below the level of consciousness, the reflex actions allowing quick responses to environmental stimuli without communicating with the brain.

Spinal Nerves

Pairs of spinal nerves are connected to the spinal cord, which lies in the middorsal region of the body and is protected by the vertebral column. Each spinal nerve contains long fibers of sensory neurons and long fibers of motor neurons. In Figure 13.4, identify the following:

1. **Sensory neuron** takes nerve impulses from a sensory receptor to the spinal cord. The cell body of the sensory neuron is in the dorsal-root ganglion.
2. **Interneuron,** which lies completely within the spinal cord. Some interneurons have long fibers and take nerve impulses to and from the brain. The neuron in Figure 13.4 transmits nerve impulses from the sensory neurons to the motor neuron.
3. **Motor neuron** takes nerve impulses from the spinal cord to an effector—in this case, a muscle. Muscle contraction is one type of response to stimuli.

Suppose you were walking barefoot and stepped on a prickly sand burr. Describe the pathway of information, starting with the pain receptor in your foot, that would allow you to both feel and respond

to this unwelcome stimulus. _____

_____

_____

_____

Figure 13.4 Spinal nerves and spinal cord.
The arrows mark the path of nerve impulses from a sensory receptor to an effector.

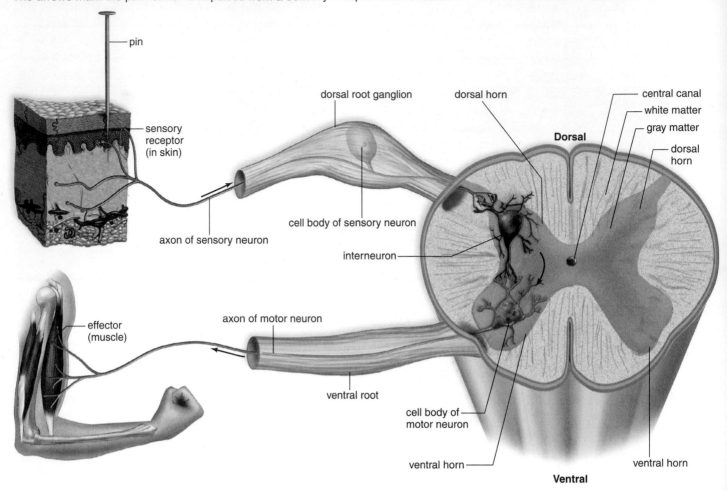

The Spinal Cord

The spinal cord is a part of the central nervous system. It lies in the middorsal region of the body and is protected by the vertebral column.

Observation: The Spinal Cord

1. Examine a prepared slide of a cross section of the spinal cord under the lowest magnification possible. For example, some microscopes are equipped with a short scanning objective that enlarges about 3.5×, with a total magnification of 35×. If a scanning objective is not available, observe the slide against a white background with the naked eye.

2. Identify the following with the help of Figure 13.5:

   a. **Gray matter:** A central, butterfly-shaped area composed of masses of short nerve fibers, interneurons, and motor neuron cell bodies.

   b. **White matter:** Masses of long fibers that lie outside the gray matter and carry impulses up and down the spinal cord. In living animals, white matter appears white because an insulating myelin sheath surrounds long fibers.

Figure 13.5 The spinal cord.
Photomicrograph of spinal cord cross section.

Spinal Reflexes

A **reflex** is an involuntary and predictable response to a given stimulus. When you touch a sharp tack, you immediately withdraw your hand (see Fig. 13.4). When a spinal reflex occurs, a sensory receptor is stimulated and generates nerve impulses that pass along the three neurons mentioned earlier—the sensory neuron, interneuron, and motor neuron—until the effector responds. In the spinal reflexes below, stretch receptors detect the tap, and sensory neurons conduct nerve impulses to interneurons in the spinal cord. The interneurons send a message via motor neurons to the effectors, muscles in the leg or foot. These reflexes are involuntary because the brain is not involved in formulating the response. *Consciousness* of the stimulus lags behind the response because information must be sent up the spinal cord to the brain before you can become aware of the tap.

Experimental Procedure: Spinal Reflex

Although many reflexes occur in the body, only a tendon reflex is investigated in this Experimental Procedure. One easily tested tendon reflex involves the **patellar tendon.** When this tendon is tapped with a reflex hammer (Fig. 13.6) or, in this experiment, with a meterstick, the attached muscle is stretched. The stretch receptor generates nerve impulses transmitted along sensory neurons to the spinal cord. Nerve impulses from the cord then pass along motor neurons and stimulate the muscle, causing it to contract. As the muscle contracts, it tugs on the tendon, causing movement of a bone opposite the joint. Receptors in other tendons, such as the Achilles tendon, respond similarly.

Knee-Jerk (Patellar) Reflex

1. Have the subject sit on a table so that his or her legs hang freely.
2. Sharply tap one of the patellar tendons just below the patella (kneecap) with a meterstick.
3. In this relaxed state, does the leg flex (move toward the buttocks) or extend (move away from the buttocks)? _____

Figure 13.6   Knee-jerk reflex.
The quick response when the patellar tendon is stimulated by tapping with a reflex hammer indicates that a reflex has occurred.

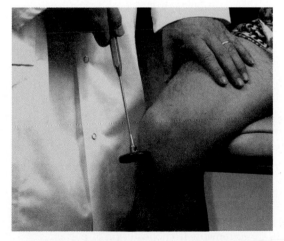

Knee-jerk (patellar) reflex

13.3 The Human Eye

The human eye is responsible for sight. Light rays enter the eye and strike the **rod cells** and **cone cells,** the photoreceptors for sight. The rods and cones generate nerve impulses that go to the brain via the optic nerve.

Observation: The Human Eye

1. Examine a human eye model, and identify the structures listed in Table 13.2 and depicted in Figure 13.7.
2. Trace the path of light from outside the eye to the retina.

_____

_____

3. During **accommodation,** the lens rounds up to aid in viewing near objects or flattens to aid in viewing distant objects. Which structure holds the lens and is involved in accommodation?

_____

4. **Refraction** is the bending of light rays so that they can be brought to a single focus. Which of the structures listed in Table 13.2 aid in refracting and focusing light rays?

_____

5. Specifically, what are the sensory receptors for sight, and where are they located in the eye?

_____

6. What structure takes nerve impulses to the brain from the rod cells and cone cells?

_____

Table 13.2 Parts of the Human Eye

Part	Location	Function
Sclera	Outer layer of eye	Protects and supports eyeball
Cornea	Transparent portion of sclera	Refracts light rays
Choroid	Middle layer of eye	Absorbs stray light rays
Retina	Inner layer of eye	Contains receptors for sight
Rod cells	In retina	Make black-and-white vision possible
Cone cells	Concentrated in fovea centralis	Make color vision possible
Fovea centralis	Special region of retina	Makes acute vision possible
Lens	Interior of eye between cavities	Refracts and focuses light rays
Ciliary body	Extension from choroid	Holds lens in place; functions in accommodation
Iris	More anterior extension of choroid	Regulates light entrance
Pupil	Opening in middle of iris	Admits light
Humors (aqueous and vitreous)	Fluid media in anterior and posterior compartments, respectively, of eye	Transmit and refract light rays; support eyeball
Optic nerve	Extension from posterior of eye	Transmits impulses to brain

Figure 13.7 Anatomy of the human eye.
The sensory receptors for vision are the rod cells and cone cells present in the retina of the eye.

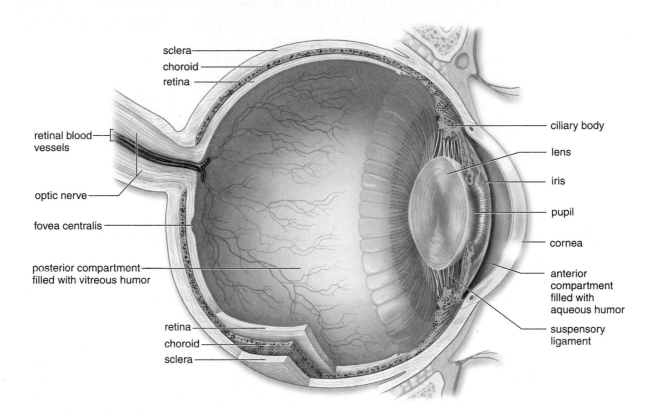

The Blind Spot of the Eye

The **blind spot** occurs where the optic nerve fibers exit the retina. No vision is possible at this location because of the absence of rod cells and cone cells.

Experimental Procedure: Blind Spot of the Eye

This Experimental Procedure requires a laboratory partner. Figure 13.8 shows a small circle and a cross several centimeters apart.

Left Eye

1. Hold Figure 13.8 approximately 30 cm from your eyes. The cross should be directly in front of your left eye. If you wear glasses, keep them on.
2. Close your right eye.

Figure 13.8 Blind spot.
This dark circle (or cross) will disappear at one location because there are no rod cells or cone cells at each eye's blind spot, where vision does not occur.

3. Stare only at the cross with your left eye. You should also be able to see the circle in the same field of vision. Slowly move the paper toward you until the circle disappears.
4. Repeat the procedure as many times as needed to find the blind spot.
5. Then slowly move the paper closer to your eyes until the circle reappears. Because only your left eye is open, you have found the blind spot of your left eye.
6. With your partner's help, measure the distance from your eye to the paper when the circle first

    disappeared. Left eye: _____ cm

Right Eye

1. Hold Figure 13.8 approximately 30 cm from your eyes. The circle should be directly in front of your right eye. If you wear glasses, keep them on.
2. Close your left eye.
3. Stare only at the circle with your right eye. You should also be able to see the cross in the same field of vision. Slowly move the paper toward you until the cross disappears.
4. Repeat the procedure as many times as needed to find the blind spot.
5. Then slowly move the paper closer to your eyes until the cross reappears. Because only your right eye is open, you have found the blind spot of your right eye.
6. With your partner's help, measure the distance from your eye to the paper when the cross first

    disappeared. Right eye: _____ cm

Accommodation of the Eye

When the eye accommodates to see objects at different distances, the shape of the lens changes. The lens shape is controlled by the ciliary muscles attached to it. When you are looking at a distant object, the lens is in a flattened state. When you are looking at a closer object, the lens becomes more rounded. The elasticity of the lens determines how well the eye can accommodate. Lens elasticity decreases with increasing age, a condition called **presbyopia.** Presbyopia is the reason many older people need bifocals to see near objects.

Experimental Procedure: Accommodation of the Eye

This Experimental Procedure requires a laboratory partner. It tests accommodation of either your left or right eye.

1. Hold a pencil upright by the eraser and at arm's length in front of whichever of your eyes you are testing (Fig. 13.9).
2. Close the opposite eye.
3. Move the pencil from arm's length toward your eye.
4. Focus on the end of the pencil.
5. Move the pencil toward you until the end is out of focus. Measure the distance (in centimeters)

    between the pencil and your eye: _____ cm
6. At what distance can your eye no longer

    accommodate for distance? _____ cm
7. If you wear glasses, repeat this experiment without your glasses, and note the accommodation distance of your eye without glasses:

    _____cm. (Contact lens wearers need not make these determinations, and they should write the words *contact lens* in this blank.)

Figure 13.9   Accommodation.
When testing the ability of your eyes to accommodate to see a near object, always keep the pencil in this position.

8. The "younger" lens can easily accommodate for closer distances. The nearest point at which the end of the pencil can be clearly seen is called the **near point.** The more elastic the lens, the "younger" the eye (Table 13.3). How "old" is the eye you tested? _____

Table 13.3 Near Point and Age Correlation						
Age (Years)	10	20	30	40	50	60
Near Point (cm)	9	10	13	18	50	83

Why are you unaware of a blind spot under normal conditions? While the eye detects patterns of light and color, it is the brain that determines what we visually perceive. The brain interprets the visual input based in part on past experiences. In this exercise, you created an artificial situation in which you became aware of how your perception of the world is constrained by the eye's anatomy. Your brain filled in the area of missing information and you saw the blank page.

13.4 The Human Ear

The human ear, whose parts are listed and depicted in Figure 13.10 and Table 13.4, serves two functions: hearing and balance. When you hear, sound waves are picked up by the **tympanic**

Figure 13.10 Anatomy of the human ear.
The outer ear extends from the pinna to the tympanic membrane. The middle ear extends from the tympanic membrane to the oval window. The inner ear encompasses the semicircular canals, the vestibule, and the cochlea.

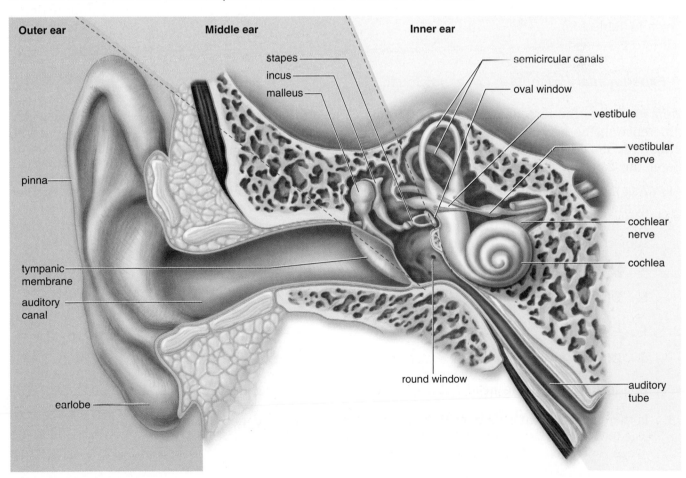

Table 13.4 Parts of the Human Ear

Part	Medium	Function	Mechanoreceptor
Outer ear	Air		
Pinna		Collects sound waves	—
Auditory canal		Filters air	—
Middle ear	Air		
Tympanic membrane and ossicles		Amplify sound waves	—
Auditory tube		Equalizes air pressure	—
Inner ear	Fluid		
Semicircular canals		Rotational equilibrium	Stereocilia embedded in cupula
Vestibule (contains utricle and saccule)		Gravitational equilibrium	Stereocilia embedded in otolithic membrane
Cochlea (spiral organ)		Hearing	Stereocilia embedded in tectorial membrane

membrane and amplified by the **malleus, incus,** and **stapes.** This creates pressure waves in the canals of the **cochlea** that lead to stimulation of **hair cells,** the receptors for hearing. Nerve impulses travel by way of the **cochlear nerve** to the brain. Hair cells in the utricle and saccule of the vestibule and in semicircular canals are receptors for balance.

Observation: The Human Ear

Examine a human ear model, and find the structures depicted in Figure 13.10 based on the information given in Table 13.4.

Experimental Procedure: Locating Sound

Humans locate the direction of sound according to how fast it is detected by either or both ears. A difference in the hearing ability of the two ears can lead to a mistaken judgment about the direction of sound. You and a laboratory partner should perform this Experimental Procedure on each other. Enter the data for *your* ears, not your partner's ears, in the spaces provided.

1. Ask the subject to be seated, with eyes closed. Then strike a tuning fork or rap two spoons together at the five locations listed in number 2. Use a random order.
2. Ask the subject to give the exact location of the sound in relation to his or her head. Record the subject's perceptions when the sound is:

   a. Directly below and behind the head _____

   b. Directly behind the head _____

   c. Directly above the head _____

   d. Directly in front of the face _____

   e. To the side of the head _____

3. Is there an apparent difference in hearing between your two ears? _____

13.5 Sensory Receptors in Human Skin

The sensory receptors in human skin respond to touch, pain, temperature, and pressure. There are individual sensory receptors for each of these stimuli, as well as free nerve endings able to respond to pressure, pain, and temperature.

Sense of Touch

The dermis of the skin contains touch receptors, whose concentration differs in various parts of the body.

Experimental Procedure: Sense of Touch

You will need a laboratory partner to perform this Experimental Procedure. Enter *your* data, not the data of your partner, in the spaces provided.

1. Ask the subject to be seated, with eyes closed.
2. Then test the subject's ability to discriminate between the two points of a hairpin or a pair of scissors at the four locations listed in number 5.
3. Hold the points of the hairpin or scissors on the given skin area, with both of the points simultaneously and gently touching the subject.
4. Ask the subject whether the experience involves one or two touch sensations.
5. Record the shortest distance between the hairpin or scissor points for a two-point discrimination.

    a. Forearm: _____ mm

    b. Back of the neck: _____ mm

    c. Index finger: _____ mm

    d. Back of the hand: _____ mm

6. Which of these areas apparently contains the greatest density of touch receptors? _____
   Why is this useful? _____
7. Do you have a sense of touch at every point in your skin? _____ Explain. _____
   _____

Sense of Heat and Cold

Temperature receptors respond to a change in temperature.

Experimental Procedure: Sense of Heat and Cold

1. Obtain three 1,000 ml beakers, and fill one with *ice water,* one with *tap water* at room temperature, and one with *warm water* (45°–50°C).
2. Immerse your left hand in the ice-water beaker and your right hand in the warm-water beaker for 30 seconds.
3. Then place both hands in the beaker with room-temperature tap water.
4. Record the sensation in the right and left hands.

    a. Right hand: _____

    b. Left hand: _____

5. Explain your results: _____
   _____

13.6 Human Chemoreceptors

The taste receptors, located in the mouth, and the smell receptors, located in the nasal cavities, are the chemoreceptors that respond to molecules in the air and water.

Experimental Procedure: Sense of Taste

You will need a laboratory partner to perform the following procedures. It will not be necessary for all tests to be performed on both partners. You should take turns being either the subject or the experimenter. Dispose of used cotton swabs in a hazardous waste container or as directed by your instructor.

Taste

1. The experimenter should be sure to use a clean cotton swab *each* time. The subject should be sure to rinse the mouth between applications.
2. For the sensation of sweet, apply *5% sucrose* to the tip, sides, and back of the tongue, and record on the first drawing in Figure 13.11 where the subject tastes the solution.
3. For the sensation of sour, apply *5% acetic acid* to the tip, sides, and back of the tongue, and record on the second drawing in Figure 13.11 where the subject tastes the solution.
4. For the sensation of salty, apply *10% NaCl* to the tip, sides, and back of the tongue, and record on the third drawing in Figure 13.11 where the subject tastes the solution.
5. For the sensation of bitter, apply *0.1% quinine sulfate* to the tip, sides, and back of the tongue, and record on the fourth drawing in Figure 13.11 where the subject tastes the solution.

Figure 13.11   Human tongue.
Recordings of where a subject tastes the solutions indicated.

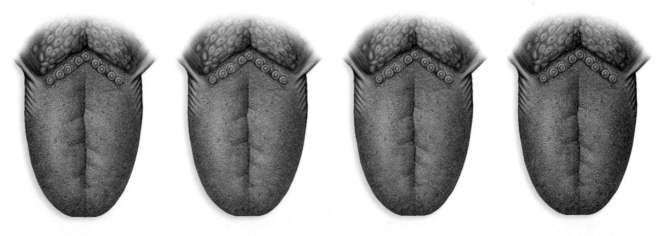

Conclusions: Sense of Taste

- Do your results agree with those of other students in your laboratory? _____
  Explain: _____
- Give two general reasons the results might not agree, and explain your reasons based upon the technique used and the subject of the test.
  a. Technique: _____
  b. Subject: _____

Taste and Smell

1. Students work in groups. Each group has one experimenter and several subjects.
2. The experimenter should obtain a LifeSavers candy from the various flavors available, without letting the subject know what flavor it is.
3. The subject closes both eyes and holds his or her nose.
4. The experimenter gives the LifeSavers candy to the subject, who places it on his or her tongue.
5. The subject, while still holding his or her nose, guesses the flavor of the candy. The experimenter records the guess in Table 13.5.
6. The subject releases his or her nose and guesses the flavor again. The experimenter records the guess and the actual flavor in Table 13.5.

Table 13.5 Taste and Smell Experiment

Subject	Actual Flavor	Flavor While Holding Nose	Flavor After Releasing Nose
1			
2			
3			
4			
5			

Conclusions: Sense of Taste and Smell

- From your results, how would you say that smell affects the taste of LifeSavers candy?

- What do you conclude about the effect of smell on your sense of taste?

Application for Daily Living

LASIK Surgery

The focusing ability of the lens to place an image on the retina so we can see is assisted by the cornea. The cornea refracts or bends the light rays, and then the lens takes on the chore from then on. This accounts for why LASIK eye surgery, which reshapes the cornea, works. The traditional LASIK vision correction involves two steps: (1) First, the surgeon has to make a flap in the outer surface of the eye to expose the underlying cornea. (2) Then, the cornea is reshaped.

Anyone considering undergoing LASIK eye surgery should be aware that various side effects have been seen from dry eyes to severe glare when driving at night. Therefore, the procedure should be discussed with a physician or optician first. They can recommend a reliable clinic and surgeon and will also be able to advise whether there is any reason why LASIK eye surgery might not work for you.

_____ 1. What portion of the brain is largest in humans?

_____ 2. What portion of the brain controls muscular coordination?

_____ 3. What is the most inferior portion of the brain stem?

_____ 4. What structures protect the spinal cord?

_____ 5. Are motor neuron cell bodies located in the gray or white matter of the spinal cord?

_____ 6. What type of neuron is found completely within the central nervous system?

_____ 7. Which neuron's cell body is in the dorsal root ganglion?

_____ 8. What part of the eye contains the sensory receptors for sight?

_____ 9. Where on the retina is the blind spot located?

_____ 10. What do you call the outer layer of the eye?

_____ 11. What part of the ear contains the sensory receptors for hearing?

_____ 12. Where in relation to the head is it most difficult to detect the location of a sound?

_____ 13. In which portion of the ear are the malleus, incus, and stapes located?

_____ 14. What layer of the skin contains sensory receptors?

_____ 15. Are touch receptors distributed evenly or unevenly in the skin?

_____ 16. What senses are dependent on chemoreceptors?

_____ 17. The four taste sensations are sour, salty, bitter, and _____.

_____ 18. What advantages are associated with the spinal cord and spinal nerves functioning below the level of consciousness?

_____ 19. Identify the type of neuron responsible for transmitting nerve impulses from the spinal cord to an effector.

Thought Questions

20. Trace the path of light in the human eye through each structure or compartment—from the exterior to the retina. How do nerve impulses from the retina reach the brain?

21. Trace the path of sound waves in the human ear—from the tympanic membrane to the sensory receptors for hearing.

Human Biology Website

The companion website for _Human Biology_ provides a wealth of information organized and integrated by chapter. You will find practice tests, animations, and much more that will complement your learning and understanding of general biology.

www.mhhe.com/maderhuman11

McGraw-Hill Access Science Website

An Online encyclopedia of science and technology that provides information, including videos, that can enhance the laboratory experience.

www.accessscience.com

14

Development

Learning Outcomes

14.1 Embryonic Development
- Identify the cellular stages of development with reference to slides of early sea star development.
- Identify the tissue stages of development with reference to slides of frog development.
- Associate the germ layers with the development of various organs.
- Identify which organs develop first in a vertebrate embryo (e.g., frog, chick, and human).
- When presented with a sequence of human embryos, point out and discuss aspects of their increasing complexity.

Question: Which human organs develop first during development?

14.2 Extraembryonic Membranes, the Placenta, and the Umbilical Cord
- Distinguish between and give a function for the extraembryonic membranes, the placenta, and the umbilical cord.
- Trace the development of the extraembryonic membranes during embryonic development, and state a function for each membrane.

Question: Which extraembryonic membrane becomes the placenta?

14.3 Fetal Development
- Trace the main events of human fetal development.

Question: Account for why the respiratory system is not functional until the sixth month or later.

Application for Daily Living: Cord Around Baby's Neck

Introduction

Human development is divided into **embryonic development** (first two months) and **fetal development** (third through ninth month). Development begins when the sperm fertilizes the egg and a **zygote** is formed. This event takes place in an oviduct of the female. As the zygote makes its way to the uterus, it divides and becomes multicellular. At about the seventh day following fertilization, the embryo implants in the uterine lining. In some cases, this early developmental period is given its own designation, the preembryonic period of development. After an embryo becomes a multicellular ball, its cells begin to arrange themselves into three layers, called the **germ layers.** It is possible to associate the development of particular organs with a specific germ layer. Embryonic development comes to a close when all the basic organs have formed.

The human embryo is dependent upon **extraembryonic membranes,** specialized tissues that protect the embryo and serve various useful functions. One of the extraembryonic membranes, the chorion, along with the lining of the uterus, contributes to the formation of the placenta. The **placenta** is the region of exchange between the mother and the embryo, and later the fetus. Waste molecules and carbon dioxide are exchanged for nutrients and oxygen at the placenta.

In humans, the final events of development include a maturation process where the organs that have been formed during embryonic development are able to mature into their final functional state. During this final fetal development period, the fetus takes on a human appearance and gains weight as the organs grow and mature prior to birth.

14.1 Embryonic Development

We will divide embryonic development into three stages: cellular, tissue layer, and organ development. In human beings, it takes two months to complete embryonic development. It is impossible for us to view the stages of embryonic development in a human being, so we will use the sea star, frog, and chick as our observational material.

Cellular Stages of Development

The cellular stages of development include:

- Zygote formation: A single sperm fertilizes an egg and the result is a zygote, the first cell of the new individual.
- Morula formation: Zygote divides into a number of smaller cells until there is a cluster of 16–32 cells called a morula.
- Blastula formation: The morula becomes a blastula, a hollow ball of cells.

Observation: Cellular Stages of Development in the Sea Star

The cellular stages of development are remarkably similar in all animals. Therefore, we can view slides of sea star development to study the cellular stages of human development (Fig. 14.1). A sea star is an invertebrate that develops in the ocean, and therefore will develop easily in the laboratory where it can be observed.

Obtain slides or view a model of sea star development and note:

1. **Zygote.** Both plants and animals begin life as a single cell, a zygote. A zygote contains genes of a different combination than either parent. Explain. _____

    _____

2. **Cleavage.** View slides showing various numbers of cells due to the process of cleavage, cell division without growth until the morula stage. Is the morula about the same size as the zygote?_____ Explain. _____

    _____

3. **Blastula.** The cavity of a blastula is called the blastocoel. *Label blastocoel in Figure 14.1.* The formation of a hollow cavity is important to the next stage of development.

Figure 14.1 Starfish development.
All animals, including starfish and humans, go through the same cellular stages from cleavage to blastula. (Magnification × 75.)

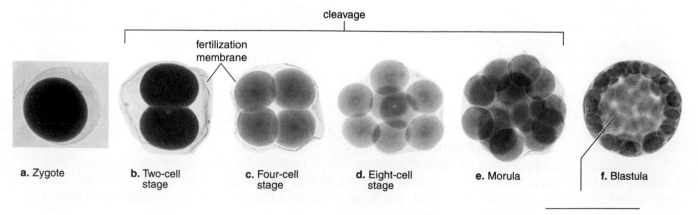

a. Zygote   b. Two-cell stage   c. Four-cell stage   d. Eight-cell stage   e. Morula   f. Blastula

Observation: Cellular Stages of Development in Humans

In Figure 14.2, or in a model of human development, observe the same stages of development already observed in sea star slides. Also, observe that fertilization in humans occurs in an oviduct following ovulation. As the embryo undergoes cleavage, it travels in the oviduct to the uterus.

If the embryo splits at the 2-cell stage, the result is identical twins. (Fraternal twins arise when two separate eggs are fertilized.) How might you account for the development of identical

triplets? _____

_____

The blastula in humans is called a blastocyst. The blastocyst contains an **inner cell mass** that becomes the embryo, while the outer group of cells will become membranes that nourish and protect it. At about day 6, the blastocyst has reached the uterus and implants into the uterine wall, where it will receive nourishment from the mother's bloodstream.

What's the main difference between the cellular stages in a sea star and in a human? _____

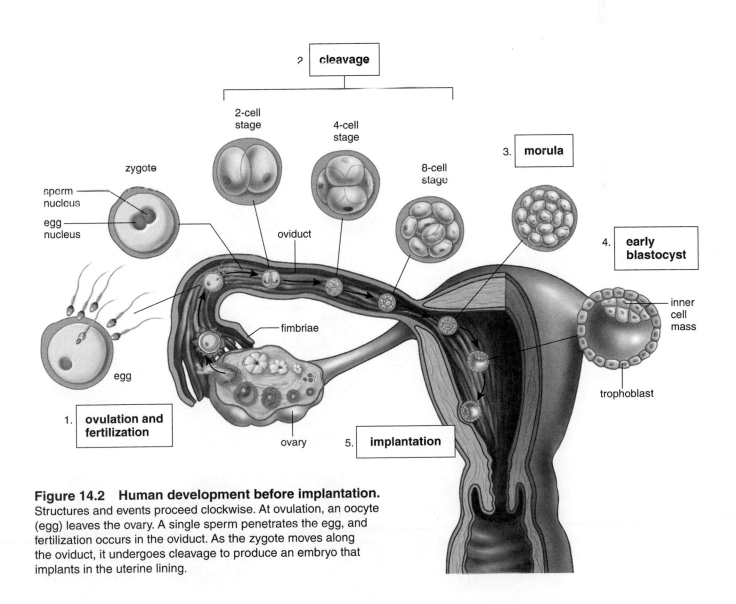

Figure 14.2 Human development before implantation.
Structures and events proceed clockwise. At ovulation, an oocyte (egg) leaves the ovary. A single sperm penetrates the egg, and fertilization occurs in the oviduct. As the zygote moves along the oviduct, it undergoes cleavage to produce an embryo that implants in the uterine lining.

Tissue Stages of Development

The tissue stages of development include:

- **Early gastrula stage.** This stage begins when certain cells begin to push or invaginate into the blastocoel, creating a double layer of cells. The outer layer is called the ectoderm and the inner layer is called the endoderm.
- **Late gastrula stage.** Gastrulation is not complete until there are three layers of cells. The third layer called mesoderm occurs between the other two layers already mentioned.

Observation: Tissue Stages of Development in a Frog

It is traditional to view frog gastrulation. A frog is a vertebrate, and so its development is expected to be closer to that of a human than is a sea star. In Figure 14.3, note that the yellow (vegetal pole) cells are heavily laden with yolk, while the blue (animal pole) cells are the ones that invaginate into the blastocoel forming the early gastrula.

1. Early gastrula stage. Obtain a cross section of a frog gastrula. Most likely, your slide is the equivalent of Figure 14.3*b* number 3, in which case you will see two cavities, the old blastocoel and newly forming *archenteron*, which forms once the animal pole cells have invaginated. The archenteron will become the digestive tract.
2. Late gastrula stage. In Figure 14.3, note that a third layer of cells, the mesoderm, is colored red and that it develops between the ectoderm and endoderm.

Figure 14.3   Drawings of frog developmental stages.
a. During cleavage, the number of cells increases but overall size remains the same. **b.** During gastrulation, three tissue layers form. **c.** During neurulation, the notochord and neural tube form.

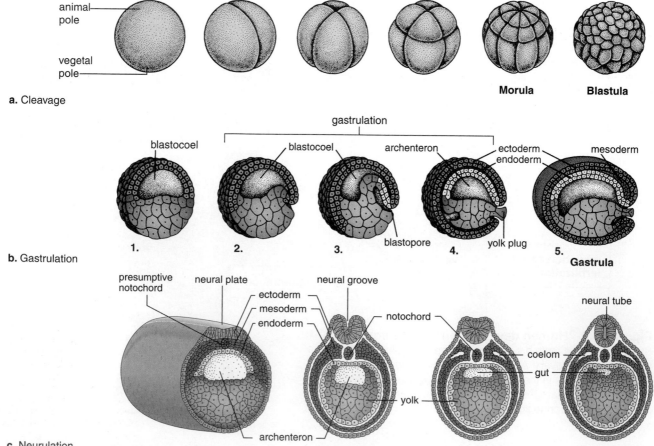

a. Cleavage

b. Gastrulation

c. Neurulation

In a model of human development, observe the same stages of development already observed in frog slides. After implantation, gastrulation in humans turns the inner cell mass into the **embryonic disk.** Figure 14.4 shows the embryonic disk, which has the three layers of cells we have been discussing: the ectoderm, mesoderm, and endoderm. Figure 14.4 also shows the significance of these layers, often called the **germ layers.** The future organs of an individual can be traced back to one of the germ layers.

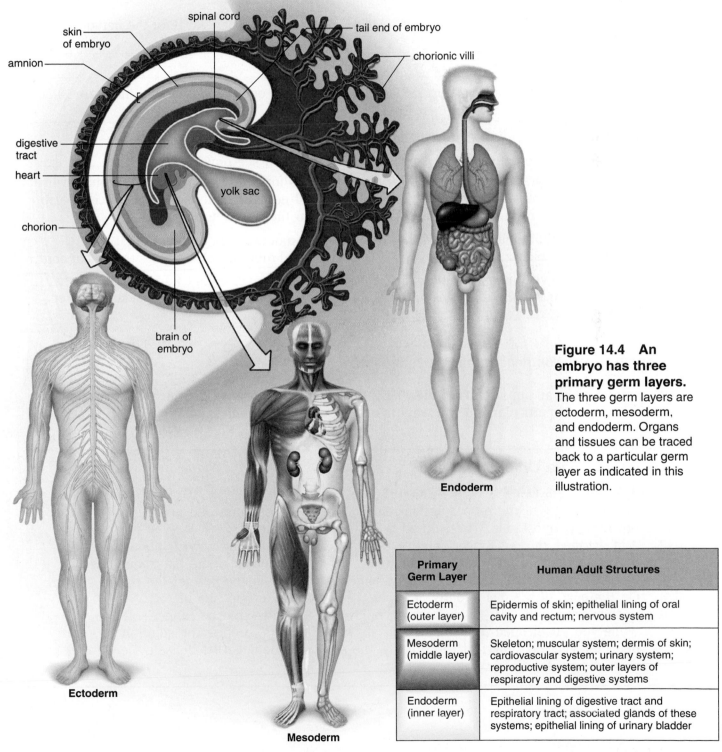

Figure 14.4   An embryo has three primary germ layers. The three germ layers are ectoderm, mesoderm, and endoderm. Organs and tissues can be traced back to a particular germ layer as indicated in this illustration.

Primary Germ Layer	Human Adult Structures
Ectoderm (outer layer)	Epidermis of skin; epithelial lining of oral cavity and rectum; nervous system
Mesoderm (middle layer)	Skeleton; muscular system; dermis of skin; cardiovascular system; urinary system; reproductive system; outer layers of respiratory and digestive systems
Endoderm (inner layer)	Epithelial lining of digestive tract and respiratory tract; associated glands of these systems; epithelial lining of urinary bladder

Organ Stages of Development

As soon as all three embryonic tissue layers (ectoderm, endoderm and mesoderm) are established, the organ level of development begins. It continues until development is complete. The first organs to develop are the

- Digestive tract. You have already observed the start of the archenteron during gastrulation.
- Spinal cord and brain
- Heart

Observation: Development of the Spinal Cord and Brain

One of the first systems to form is the nervous system. Why might it be beneficial for the nervous system to begin development first? _____

_____

1. Obtain a cross section of a frog neurula stage, and match it to one of the drawings in Figure 14.3c.

   Which drawing seems to best match your slide? _____
   Your instructor will confirm your match for you.

2. A neural tube develops from ectoderm (Fig. 14.3c). Can you see how? _____
   When neural folds rise up and fuse, the neural tube has formed. The neural tube, which runs the length of the embryo, is the first sign of the central nervous system. The nerve cord, also called the spinal cord, and the brain both develop from the neural tube.

   Notice how the neural tube develops above the notochord, a dorsal supporting rod that later becomes the vertebral column. Why would you expect the neural tube, which becomes the spinal cord, to develop in the same vicinity as the notochord, which becomes the vertebral column? _____
   If you are uncertain, review the functions of the skull and vertebral column in the axial skeleton (see page 154).

Observation: Development of the Heart

A chick embryo offers an opportunity to view a beating heart in an embryo. Your instructor may show you various stages. In particular you will want to observe the 48-hour chick embryo.

Observing Live Chick Embryos
Use the following procedure for selecting and opening the eggs of live chick embryos:

1. Choose an egg of the proper age to remove from the incubator, and put a penciled × on the uppermost side. The embryo is just below the shell.
2. Add warmed chicken Ringer solution to a finger bowl until the bowl is about half full. (Chicken Ringer solution is an isotonic salt solution for chick tissue that maintains the living state.) The chicken Ringer solution should not cover the yolk of the egg.
3. On the edge of the dish, gently crack the egg on the side opposite the ×.
4. With your thumbs placed over the ×, hold the egg in the chicken Ringer solution while you pry it open from below and allow its contents to enter the solution. If you open the egg too slowly or too quickly, the shell may damage the delicate membranes surrounding the embryo.

Observation: Forty-Eight-Hour Chick Embryo

1. Follow the standard procedure (see page 186) for selecting and opening an egg containing a 48-hour chick embryo.
2. The embryo has turned so that the head region is lying on its side. Refer to Figure 14.5, and identify the following:

   a. **Shape of the embryo,** which has started to bend. The head is now almost touching the heart.

   b. **Heart,** contracting and circulating blood. Can you make out a ventricle, an atrium, and the aortic arches in the region below the head? Later, only one aortic arch will remain.

   c. **Vitelline arteries** and **veins,** which extend over the yolk. The vitelline veins carry nutrients from the yolk sac to the embryo.

   d. **Brain** with several distinct regions.

   e. **Eye,** which has a developing lens.

   f. **Margin (edge) of the amnion,** which can be seen above the vitelline arteries (see next section for amnion).

   g. **Somites,** blocks of developing muscle tissue that differentiate from mesoderm, which now number 24 pairs.

   h. **Caudal fold** of the amnion. The embryo will be completely enveloped when the head fold and caudal fold meet the margin of the amnion.

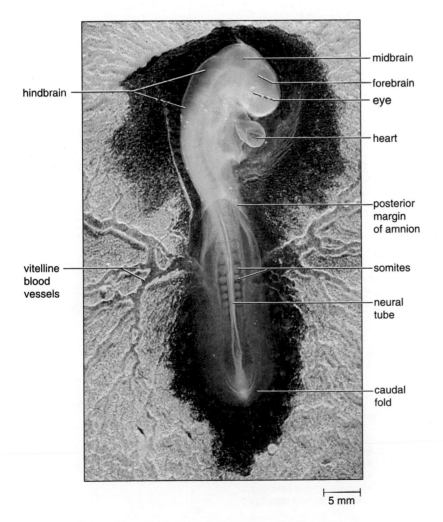

hindbrain

vitelline blood vessels

midbrain
forebrain
eye

heart

posterior margin of amnion

somites

neural tube

caudal fold

5 mm

Figure 14.5   Forty-eight-hour chick embryo.
The most prominent organs are labeled.

Study models or other study aids available that show the development of the nervous system and the heart in human beings and/or show models of human embryos of different ages. Also view Figure 14.6, which depicts the external appearance of the embryo from the fourth to the seventh week of development.

During the embryonic period of development, the growing baby is susceptible to environmental influences, including the following:

- Drugs, such as alcohol; certain prescriptions; and recreational drugs. These can cause birth defects.
- Infections such as rubella, also called German measles, and other viral infections.
- Nutritional deficiencies.
- X-rays or radiation therapy.

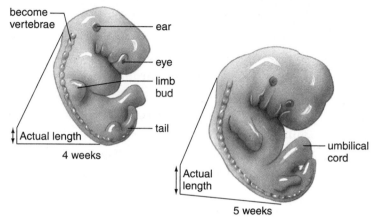

Figure 14.6   External appearance of the embryo.
a. Weeks 4 to 5 and (**b**) Weeks 6 to 7.

a. Weeks 4 and 5
- Head dominant, but body getting longer.
- Limb buds are visible.
- Eyes and ears begin to form.
- Tissue for vertebrae extend into tail.

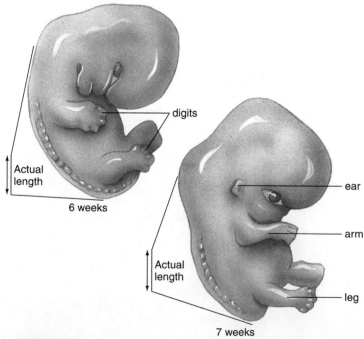

b. Weeks 6 and 7
- Head still dominant, but tail has disappeared.
- Facial features continue to develop.
- Hands and feet have digits.
- All organs more developed.

14.2 Extraembryonic Membranes, the Placenta, and the Umbilical Cord

- The **extraembryonic membranes** take their name from the observation that they are not part of the embryo proper. They are outside the embryo, and therefore they are "extra."
- The **placenta** is the structure that provides the embryo with nutrient molecules and oxygen and takes away its waste molecules, such as carbon dioxide. The fetal half of the placenta is the chorionic villi, which contain fetal capillaries. The maternal half of the placenta is capillaries in the uterine wall.
- The **umbilical cord** is a tubular structure that contains two of the extraembryonic membranes (the allantois and the yolk sac) and also the umbilical blood vessels. The umbilical blood vessels bring fetal blood to and from the placenta. When a baby is born and begins to breathe on its own, the umbilical cord is cut and the remnants become the navel.

In this drawing, label the umbilical cord, which contains the umbilical blood vessels. Also label the placenta, which contains the maternal blood vessels.

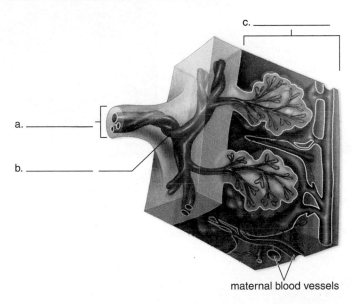

maternal blood vessels

Observation: The Extraembryonic Membranes

In a model, and in Figure 14.7, trace the development of the extraembryonic membranes. Also, note the development of the placenta and the umbilical cord. The extraembryonic membranes are the:

- **Chorion.** The chorion begins to form at the blastocyst stage of development. The outer layer of cells surrounding the inner cell mass of the blastocyst becomes the chorion. Notice in Figures 14.4 and 14.6, the tree-like **chorionic villi** are a part of the chorion that will become the placenta.
- **Amnion.** Forms the amniotic cavity, which envelops the fetus and contains the amniotic fluid that cushions and protects the fetus (Fig. 14.8). All animals, whether the sea star, the frog, the chick, or a human, develop in an aqueous environment. Birth of a human is imminent when "the water breaks," the loss of the amniotic fluid.
- **Allantois.** The allantois extends into the umbilical cord. It accumulates the small amount of urine produced by the fetal kidneys and later gives rise to the urinary bladder. Its blood vessels become the umbilical blood vessels.
- **Yolk sac.** The yolk sac is the first embryonic membrane to appear. In the chick, the yolk sac does contain yolk, food for the developing embryo. In humans, the yolk sac contains plentiful blood vessels and is the first site of blood cell formation.

Figure 14.7 Development of extraembryonic membranes.

a. At first, no organs are present in the embryo, only tissues. The amniotic cavity is above the embryonic disk, and the yolk sac is below. The chorionic villi are present. **b, c.** The allantois and yolk sac, two more extraembryonic membranes, are positioned inside the body stalk as it becomes the umbilical cord. **d.** At 35+ days, all membranes are present, and the umbilical cord takes blood vessels between the embryo and the chorion (placenta).

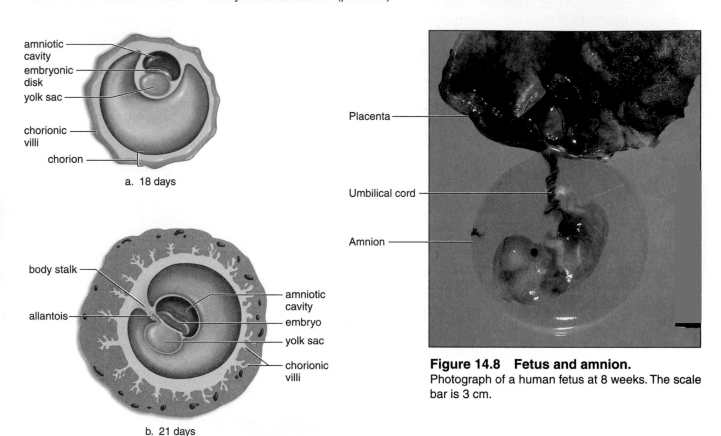

a. 18 days

b. 21 days

Figure 14.8 Fetus and amnion.

Photograph of a human fetus at 8 weeks. The scale bar is 3 cm.

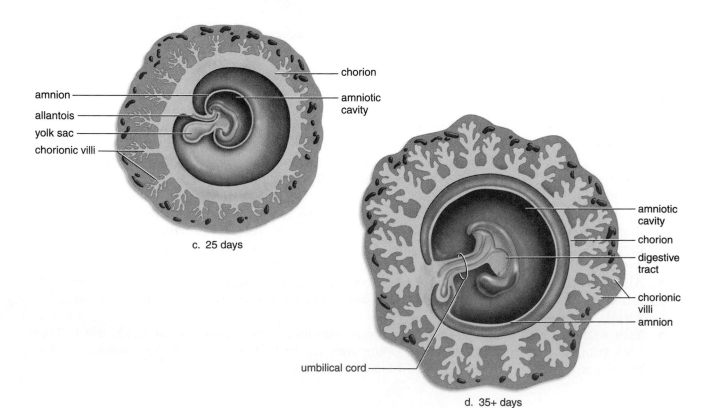

c. 25 days

d. 35+ days

14.3 Fetal Development

During fetal development (last seven months), the skeleton becomes ossified (bony), reproductive organs form, arms and legs develop fully, and the fetus enlarges in size and gains weight.

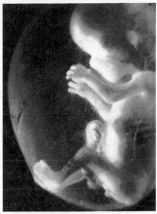

Three- to four-month-old fetus

Observation: Fetal Development

1. Using Table 14.1 as a guide, examine models of fetal development.
2. In Table 14.1, note the following.
   a. **External genitals:** About the third month, it is possible to tell male from female if an ultrasound is done.
   b. **Quickening:** Fetal movement is felt during the fourth or fifth months.
   c. **Vernix caseosa:** Beginning with the fifth month, the skin is covered with a cheesy coating called vernix caseosa.
   d. **Lanugo:** During the sixth and seventh months, the body is covered with fine, downy hair termed lanugo.

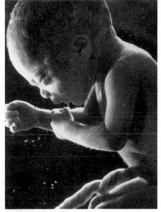

Seven- to eight-month-old fetus

Table 14.1 Fetal Development

Month	Events for Mother	Events for Baby
Third month	Uterus is the size of a grapefruit.	Possible to distinguish sex. Fingernails appear.
Fourth month	Fetal movement is felt by those who have been previously pregnant. Heartbeat is heard by stethoscope.	Bony skeleton visible. Hair begins to appear. 150 mm (6 in), 170 g (6 oz).
Fifth month	Fetal movement is felt by those who have not been previously pregnant. Uterus reaches up to level of umbilicus and pregnancy is obvious.	Protective cheesy coating, called vernix caseosa, begins to be deposited. Heartbeat can be heard.
Sixth month	Doctor can tell where baby's head, back, and limbs are. Breasts have enlarged, nipples and areolae are darkly pigmented, and colostrum is produced.	Body is covered with fine hair called lanugo. Skin is wrinkled and reddish.
Seventh month	Uterus reaches halfway between umbilicus and rib cage.	Testes descend into scrotum. Eyes are open. 300 mm (12 in), 1,350 g (3 lb).
Eighth month	Weight gain is averaging about a pound a week. Difficulty in standing and walking because center of gravity is thrown forward.	Body hair begins to disappear. Subcutaneous fat begins to be deposited.
Ninth month	Uterus is up to rib cage, causing shortness of breath and heartburn. Sleeping becomes difficult.	Ready for birth. 530 mm (20½ in), 3,400 g (7½ lb).

Fetal Circulation

Figure 14.9 depicts the special features of fetal circulation.

1. The pulmonary circuit is not used in the fetus because of the
   - **Oval opening:** a shunt that takes most fetal blood from the right to the left side of the heart. This shunt closes at birth when the baby takes its first breath.
   - **Arterial duct:** a shunt that takes any blood that enters the pulmonary trunk to the artery. This shunt becomes connective tissue soon after birth.

   Why aren't the pulmonary circuit and the lungs operative in the fetus?

   _____

2. The **umbilical arteries** take O_2-poor blood to the placenta, and the **umbilical vein** brings O_2-rich blood back to the inferior vena cava.

   In what way is this similar to the pulmonary circuit? _____ In what way is it different? _____

Figure 14.9 Human fetal circulation.

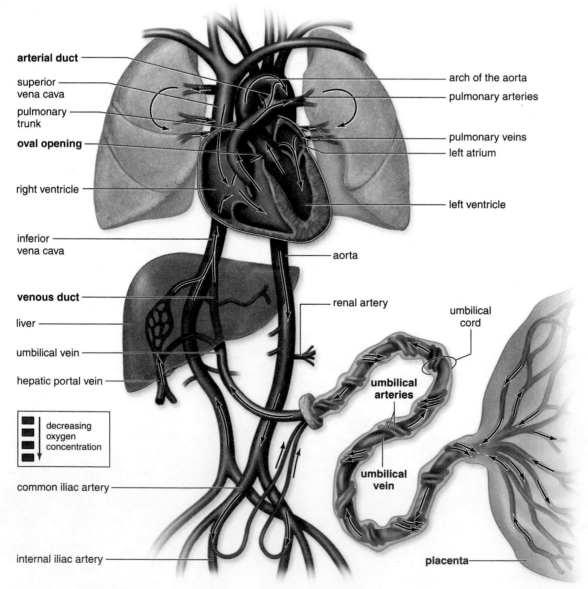

Cord Around Baby's Neck

Babies are sometimes born with the umbilical cord wrapped around the neck. There isn't much room in the uterus, and this is a common place for the cord to be located. The umbilical cord around the neck is not as dangerous as it sounds because the baby gets its oxygen by way of the placenta and the umbilical blood vessels and not the lungs. If the umbilical chord becomes overly stretched, oxygen may not be delivered as it should. This will cause the fetal heart to slow down. First, the mother can change her position and/or be given oxygen but if the baby's heart slows to below 100 beats for any length of time, then a cesarean delivery may be in order.

Laboratory Review 14

_____ 1. Name the stage when the embryo is a ball of cells.

_____ 2. Name the stage when the embryo has just formed a neural tube.

_____ 3. The nervous system develops from which germ layer?

_____ 4. The digestive system develops from which germ layer?

_____ 5. Which extraembryonic membrane participates in the formation of the placenta?

_____ 6. Which extraembryonic membrane is the first site for red blood cell formation?

_____ 7. What process directly follows the zygote stage?

_____ 8. Which fetal blood vessels take blood to and from the placenta and to and from the fetus?

_____ 9. What is the earliest month for quickening to occur?

_____ 10. Is the skeleton cartilaginous or bony during fetal development?

_____ 11. Do the lungs function during fetal development?

_____ 12. In what month is it possible to distinguish the sex of the developing child?

_____ 13. What is the function of the placenta?

Thought Questions

14. List the three stages of embryonic development (p. 182), and explain.

15. Does the overall size of the organism increase as a result of cleavage? If not, what is the significance of the cleavage process?

16. Why isn't the pulmonary circuit used in fetal circulation?

Human Biology Website

The companion website for *Human Biology* provides a wealth of information organized and integrated by chapter. You will find practice tests, animations, and much more that will complement your learning and understanding of general biology.

www.mhhe.com/maderhuman11

McGraw-Hill Access Science Website

An online encyclopedia of science and technology that provides information, including videos, that can enhance the laboratory experience.

www.accessscience.com

15
Mitosis and Meiosis

Learning Outcomes

15.1 The Cell Cycle
- Name and describe the stages of the cell cycle.
- Identify the phases of mitosis in models and microscope slides. Explain how the chromosome number stays constant.
- Describe cytokinesis.

Question: During what stage of the cell cycle does chromosome duplication occur, and why is this critical to mitosis?

15.2 Meiosis
- Name and describe the phases of meiosis I and meiosis II with attention to the movement of chromosomes.
- Explain how the chromosome number is reduced.

Question: What is synapsis, and why is it critical to meiosis?

15.3 Mitosis Versus Meiosis
- Compare the effects of mitosis to meiosis.
- Contrast the behavior of chromosomes during mitosis with the behavior of chromosomes during meiosis I and II.

Question: How are mitosis I and meiosis II similar? How are they different?

15.4 Karyotype Abnormalities
- Recognize that abnormalities in chromosome number and structure can occur when cells divide.

Question: What happenings could account for a male that has an XXY karyotype?

15.5 Gametogenesis
- Contrast spermatogenesis with oogenesis using diagrams and models.

Question: What differences between spermatogenesis and oogenesis help explain why males produce so many more sperm than females produce eggs?

Application for Daily Living: Mitosis and Cancer

Introduction

Dividing cells experience nuclear division, cytoplasmic division, and a period between divisions called interphase. During **interphase,** the nucleus appears normal, and the cell is performing its usual cellular functions. Also, the cell is increasing all of its components, including such organelles as the mitochondria, ribosomes, and centrioles, if present. DNA replication (making an exact copy of the DNA) occurs toward the end of interphase. Thereafter, the chromosomes, which contain DNA, are duplicated and contain two chromatids held together at a **centromere.** These chromatids are called **sister chromatids.**

When the nucleus divides during **mitosis,** the daughter nuclei receive the same number of chromosomes and genetic material as the parent cell. When the cytoplasm divides, a process called cytokinesis, two daughter cells are produced. Mitosis in humans permits growth and repair of tissues. During sexual reproduction, another form of division called **meiosis** occurs. Meiosis is a part of **gametogenesis,** the production of gametes (sex cells). The gametes are sperm in males and eggs in females. As a result of meiosis, the daughter cells have half the number of chromosomes as the parent cell. Also, the chromosomes can exchange genetic material during crossing-over; therefore, the daughter cells do not have the same number of chromosomes and are not genetically identical to the parent cell, following meiosis.

15.1 The Cell Cycle

As stated in the Introduction, the period between cell divisions is known as interphase. Early investigators noted little visible activity between cell divisions, so they dismissed this period as a resting state. But when they discovered that DNA replication and chromosome duplication occur during interphase, the **cell cycle** concept was proposed. Investigators have also discovered that cytoplasmic organelle duplication occurs during interphase, as does synthesis of the proteins involved in regulating cell division. Thus, the cell cycle can be broken down into four stages (Fig. 15.1). State the event of each stage on the line provided:

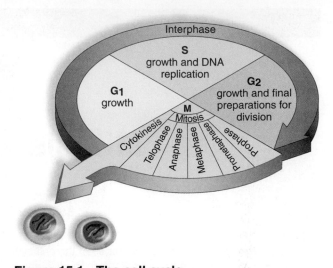

Figure 15.1 The cell cycle.
Immature cells go through a cycle that consists of four stages: G1, S (for synthesis), G2, and M (for mitosis). Eventually, some daughter cells "break out" of the cell cycle and become specialized cells.

G_1 _____

S _____

G_2 _____

M _____

Explain why the entire process is called the "cell cycle."

The length of time required for the entire cell cycle varies according to the organism, but 18–24 hours is typical for animal cells. Mitosis (including cytokinesis, if it occurs) lasts less than an hour to slightly more than 2 hours; for the rest of the time, the cell is in interphase.

Mitosis

Mitosis is nuclear division that results in two new nuclei, each having the same number of chromosomes as the original nucleus. The **parental cell** is the cell that divides, and the resulting cells are called **daughter cells.** If a parental cell has 46 chromosomes how many chromosomes does each daughter cell have following mitosis? _____

When cell division is about to begin, chromatin starts to condense and compact to form visible, rodlike **sister chromatids** held together at the centromere (Fig. 15.2a). Label the sister chromatids and the centromere in the drawing of a duplicated chromosome in Figure 15.2b. This illustration represents a chromosome as it would appear just before nuclear division occurs.

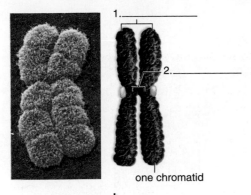

1._____

2._____

one chromatid

a.   b.

Spindle

Table 15.1 lists the structures that play a role during mitosis. The spindle is a structure that appears and brings about an orderly distribution of chromosomes to the daughter cell nuclei. A spindle has fibers that stretch between two poles (ends). Spindle fibers are bundles of microtubules, protein cylinders found in the cytoplasm that can assemble and disassemble. The **centrosome,** which is the main microtubule-organizing center of the cell, divides before mitosis so that each pole of the spindle has a pair of centrosomes. Animal cells contain two barrel-shaped organelles called centrioles in each centrosome and asters, arrays of short microtubules radiating from the poles (see Fig. 15.3). Plant cells lack centrioles suggesting that centrioles are not required for spindle formation.

Table 15.1	Structures Associated with Mitosis
Structure	**Description**
Nucleus	A large organelle containing the chromosomes and acting as a control center for the cells
Chromosome	Rod-shaped body in the nucleus seen during mitosis and meiosis that contains DNA and therefore the hereditary units, or genes
Nucleolus	An organelle found inside the nucleus; composed largely of RNA for ribosome formation
Spindle	Microtubule structure that brings about chromosome movement during cell division
Chromatids	The two identical parts of a chromosome following DNA replication
Centromere	A constriction where duplicates (sister chromatids) of a chromosome are held together
Centrosome	The central microtubule-organizing center of cells; consists of granular material; in animal cells, contains two centrioles
Centriole*	A short, cylindrical organelle in animal cells that contains microtubules and is associated with the formation of the spindle during cell division
Aster*	Short, radiating fibers produced by the centrioles; important during mitosis and meiosis

*Animal cells only

Observation: Mitosis

Mitosis Models

1. Using the descriptions given in Figure 15.3 as a guide, identify the phases of animal cell mitosis in models of animal cell mitosis.
2. Each species has its own chromosome number. Counting the number of centromeres tells you the number of chromosomes in the models. What is the number of chromosomes observed in each nucleus of the cells? _____

Figure 15.3   Phases of mitosis in animal cells.

The colors signify that the chromosomes were inherited from different parents.

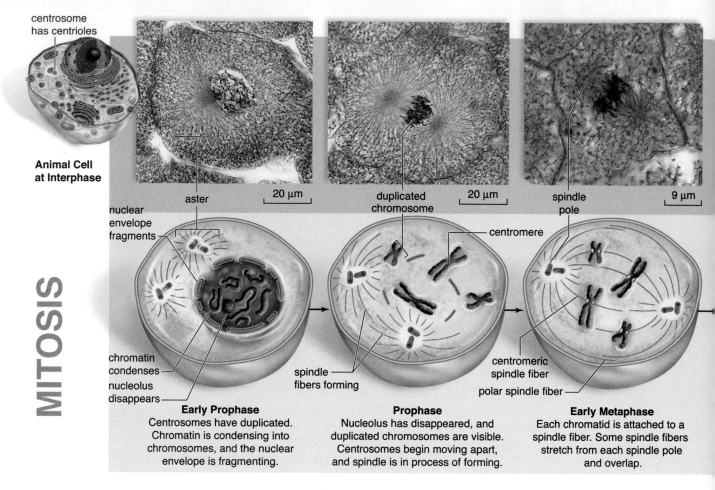

MITOSIS

centrosome has centrioles

Animal Cell at Interphase

aster   20 μm   duplicated chromosome   20 μm   spindle pole   9 μm

nuclear envelope fragments

centromere

chromatin condenses
nucleolus disappears

spindle fibers forming

centromeric spindle fiber
polar spindle fiber

Early Prophase
Centrosomes have duplicated. Chromatin is condensing into chromosomes, and the nuclear envelope is fragmenting.

Prophase
Nucleolus has disappeared, and duplicated chromosomes are visible. Centrosomes begin moving apart, and spindle is in process of forming.

Early Metaphase
Each chromatid is attached to a spindle fiber. Some spindle fibers stretch from each spindle pole and overlap.

Whitefish Blastula Slide

The blastula is an early embryonic stage in the development of animals. The **blastomeres** (blastula cells) that make up the top row in Figure 15.3 are in different phases of mitosis.

1. Examine a prepared slide of whitefish blastula cells undergoing mitotic cell division.
2. Try to find a cell in each phase of mitosis. Have a partner or your instructor check your identification.

Mitosis Phases

The phases of mitosis are **prophase, metaphase, anaphase,** and **telophase**—in that order (Fig. 15.3). Early and transitional stages of prophase are also shown in this figure.

Prophase

During early prophase, the chromosomes continue to condense, the nucleolus disappears, and the nuclear envelope fragments. The spindle begins to assemble as the centrosomes, each containing two centrioles, migrate to the poles.

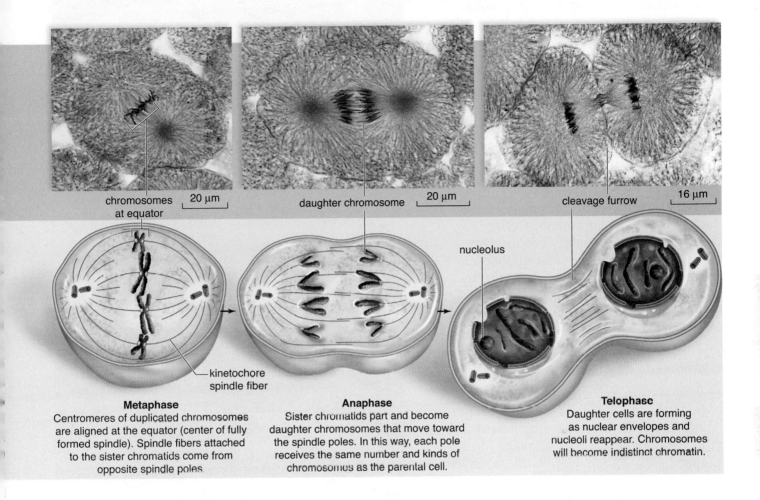

chromosomes at equator | 20 μm

daughter chromosome | 20 μm

cleavage furrow | 16 μm

nucleolus

kinetochore
spindle fiber

Metaphase
Centromeres of duplicated chromosomes are aligned at the equator (center of fully formed spindle). Spindle fibers attached to the sister chromatids come from opposite spindle poles

Anaphase
Sister chromatids part and become daughter chromosomes that move toward the spindle poles. In this way, each pole receives the same number and kinds of chromosomes as the parental cell.

Telophase
Daughter cells are forming as nuclear envelopes and nucleoli reappear. Chromosomes will become indistinct chromatin.

During prophase, the chromosomes have no apparent orientation within the cell. The already duplicated chromosomes are composed of two sister chromatids held together at a centromere. Counting the number of *centromeres* in diagrammatic drawings gives the number of chromosomes for the cell.

What is the chromosome number for the cells in Figure 15.3? _____

During late prophase, the mitotic spindle occupies the region formerly occupied by the nucleus. Short microtubules radiate out in a starlike aster from the pair of centrioles located in each centrosome. The spindle consists of poles, asters, and fibers, bundles of parallel microtubules. The chromosomes become attached to spindle fibers coming from opposite poles.

Metaphase

The sister chromatids are now attached to the spindle and the chromosomes are aligned at the equator of the spindle.

Anaphase

At the start of anaphase, the centromeres split, and the sister chromatids of each chromosome separate, giving rise to two daughter chromosomes. The daughter chromosomes begin to move toward opposite poles of the spindle. Each pole receives the diploid number of daughter chromosomes.

Telophase

New nuclear envelopes form around the daughter chromosomes at the poles. Each daughter nucleus contains the same number and types of chromosomes as the parental cell. The chromosomes become more diffuse chromatin once again, and a nucleolus appears in each daughter nucleus. Division of the cytoplasm by formation of a **cleavage furrow** is nearly complete.

Cytokinesis

Cytokinesis, division of the cytoplasm, usually accompanies mitosis. During cytokinesis, each daughter cell receives a share of the organelles that duplicated during interphase. Cytokinesis begins in anaphase, continues in telophase, and reaches completion by the start of the next interphase.

Cytokinesis in Animal Cells

In animal cells, a cleavage furrow, an indentation of the membrane between the daughter nuclei, begins as anaphase draws to a close (Fig. 15.4). The cleavage furrow deepens as a band of actin filaments called the contractile ring slowly constricts the cell, forming two daughter cells.

Were any of the cells of the whitefish blastula slide undergoing cytokinesis?

_____

How do you know? _____

_____

_____

Summary of Mitotic Cell Division

1. The nuclei in the daughter cells have the _____ number of chromosomes as the parental cell had.
2. Mitosis is cell division in which the chromosome number _____.

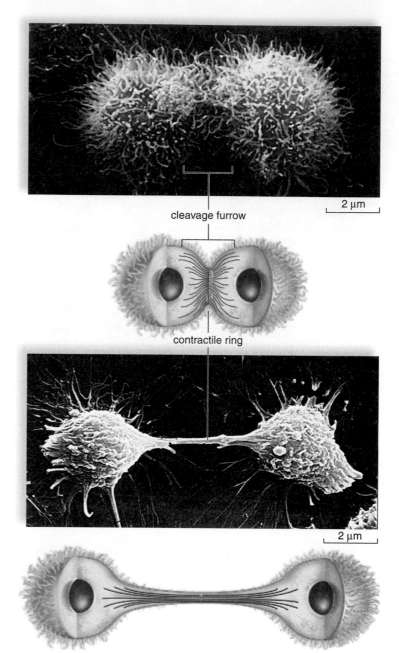

cleavage furrow

contractile ring

Figure 15.4 Cytokinesis in animal cells.
A single cell becomes two cells by a furrowing process. A contractile ring composed of actin filaments gradually gets smaller, and the cleavage furrow pinches the cell into two cells.
Copyright by R. G. Kessel and C. Y. Shih, *Scanning Electron Microscopy in Biology: A Students' Atlas on Biological Organization*, Springer-Verlag, 1974.

15.2 Meiosis

Meiosis is a form of nuclear division in which the chromosome number is reduced by half (see Fig. 15.6). While the nucleus of the parental cell has the diploid (2n) number of chromosomes, the daughter nuclei, after meiosis is complete, have the haploid number (n) of chromosomes. In sexually reproducing species, meiosis must occur or the chromosome number would double with each generation.

A diploid cell nucleus contains **homologues,** also called homologous chromosomes. Homologues look alike and carry the genes for the same traits. Before meiosis begins, the chromosomes are already double stranded—they contain sister chromatids. Meiosis requires two divisions, called **meiosis I** and **meiosis II.**

Experimental Procedure: Meiosis

In this exercise, you will use pop beads to construct chromosomes and move the chromosomes to simulate meiosis.

Building Chromosomes to Simulate Meiosis

1. Obtain the following materials: 48 pop beads of one color (e.g., red) and 48 pop beads of another color (e.g., blue) for a total of 96 beads; eight magnetic centromeres; and four centriole groups.
2. Build a homologous pair of duplicated chromosomes using Figure 15.5a as a guide. Each chromatid will have 16 beads. Be sure to bring the centromeres of two units of the same color together so that they attract and link to form one duplicated chromosome. (One member of the pair will be red, and the other will be blue.)
3. Build another homologous pair of duplicated chromosomes using Figure 15.5b as a guide. Each chromatid will have eight beads. Be sure to bring the centromeres of two units of the same color together so that they attract. (One member of the pair will be red, and the other will be blue.)
4. Your chromosomes are the same as those in Figure 15.6. The red chromosomes were inherited from one parent, and the blue chromosomes were inherited from the other parent.

Figure 15.5 Two pairs of homologues.
The chromosomes of these homologous pairs are duplicated.

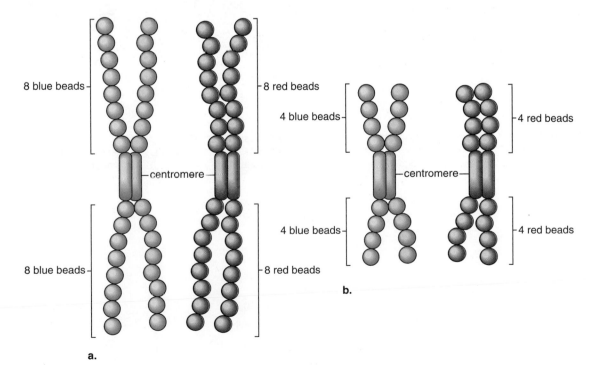

8 blue beads · 8 red beads · 4 blue beads · 4 red beads · centromere · 8 blue beads · 8 red beads · 4 blue beads · 4 red beads · centromere

a.

b.

Figure 15.6   Meiosis I and II in animal cell drawings.

Note the effects of crossing-over during meiosis I.

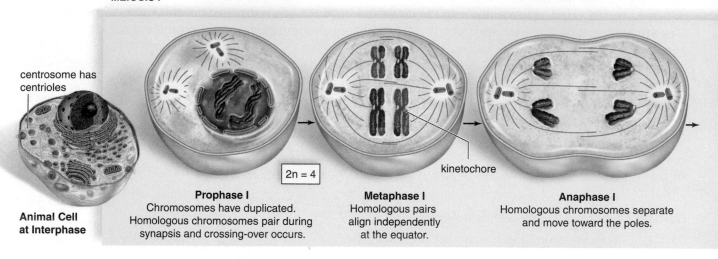

MEIOSIS I

$2n = 4$

kinetochore

centrosome has centrioles

Animal Cell at Interphase

Prophase I
Chromosomes have duplicated.
Homologous chromosomes pair during synapsis and crossing-over occurs.

Metaphase I
Homologous pairs align independently at the equator.

Anaphase I
Homologous chromosomes separate and move toward the poles.

MEIOSIS II

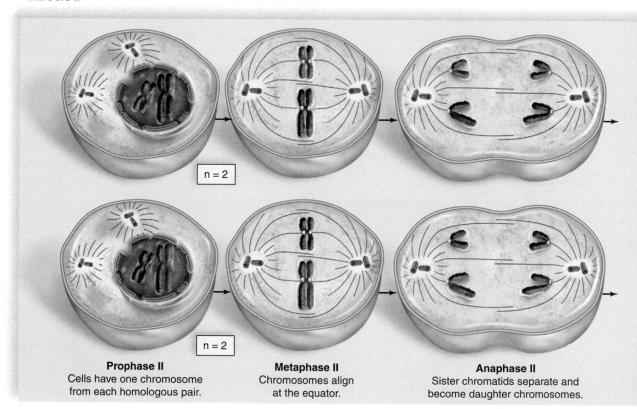

$n = 2$

$n = 2$

Prophase II
Cells have one chromosome from each homologous pair.

Metaphase II
Chromosomes align at the equator.

Anaphase II
Sister chromatids separate and become daughter chromosomes.

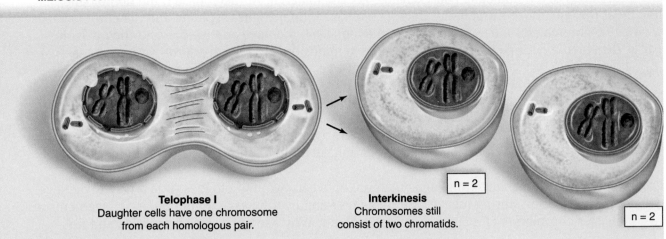

Telophase I
Daughter cells have one chromosome
from each homologous pair.

Interkinesis
Chromosomes still
consist of two chromatids.

n = 2

n = 2

MEIOSIS II cont'd

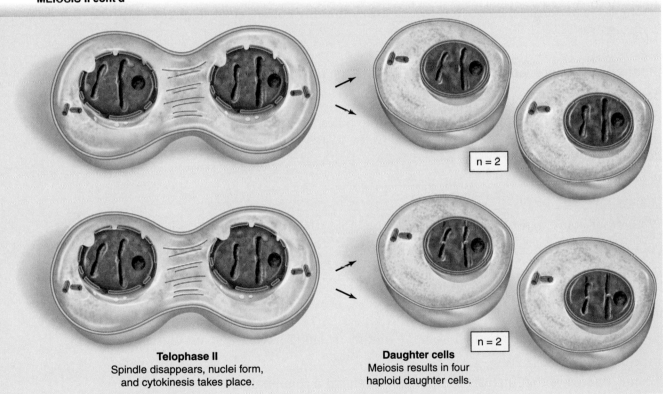

n = 2

Telophase II
Spindle disappears, nuclei form,
and cytokinesis takes place.

Daughter cells
Meiosis results in four
haploid daughter cells.

n = 2

Meiosis I

During prophase of meiosis I, the spindle appears while the nuclear envelope and nucleolus disappear. Homologues line up next to one another during a process called synapsis. During **crossing-over,** the nonsister chromatids of a homologue pair exchange genetic material. At metaphase I, the homologue pairs line up at the equator of the spindle. During anaphase I, homologues separate and the chromosomes (still having two chromatids) move to each pole. In telophase I, the nuclear envelope and the nucleolus reappear as the spindle disappears. Each new nucleus contains one from each pair of chromosomes.

Prophase I

5. Using Figure 15.6 as a guide, put all four of the chromosomes you built in the center of your work area, which represents the nucleus. Place your two pairs of centrioles outside the nucleus.
6. Separate the pairs of centrioles, and move one pair to opposite poles of the nucleus.
7. Synapsis is the pairing of homologues during prophase I. Simulate synapsis by bringing the homologues together.
8. **Crossing-over** is an exchange of genetic material between two homologues. It is a way to achieve genetic recombination during meiosis. Simulate crossing-over by exchanging the exact segments of two nonsister chromatids of a single homologous pair. Why use nonsister chromatids and not

    sister chromatids? _____

Metaphase I

Position the homologues at the equator in such a way that the homologues are prepared to move apart toward the centrioles.

Anaphase I

Separate the homologues, and move each one toward the opposite pole.

Telophase I

9. During telophase I, the chromosomes are at the poles. What combinations of chromosomes are at the poles? Fill in the following blanks with the words *red-long, red-short, blue-long,* and *blue-short:*

    Pole A: _____ and _____

    Pole B: _____ and _____

10. What other combinations would have been possible? (*Hint:* Alternate the colors at metaphase I.)

    Pole A: _____ and _____

    Pole B: _____ and _____

Conclusions: Meiosis I

- Do the chromosomes inherited from the mother or father have to remain together following

    meiosis I? _____

- Name two ways that meiosis contributes to genetic recombination:

    a. _____

    b. _____

Interkinesis

Interkinesis is the period between meiosis I and meiosis II. In some species, daughter cells do not form, and meiosis II follows right after meiosis I. Does DNA replication occur during interkinesis? _____

Explain. _____

Meiosis II

During prophase of meiosis II, a spindle appears. Each chromosome attaches to the spindle independently. During metaphase II, the chromosomes are lined up at the equator. During anaphase II, the centromeres divide and the chromatids separate, becoming daughter chromosomes that move toward the poles. In telophase II, the spindle disappears as the nuclear envelope reappears. Meiosis II is exactly like mitosis except that the nuclei of the parental cell and the daughter cells are haploid.

Prophase II

1. Using Figure 15.6 as a guide, choose the chromosomes from one pole to represent those in the new parental cell undergoing meiosis II.
2. Place two pairs of centrioles at opposite sides of these chromosomes to form the new spindle.

Metaphase II

Move the duplicated chromosomes to the metaphase II equator. How many chromosomes are at the

metaphase II equator? _____

Anaphase II

Pull the two magnets of each duplicated chromosome apart. What does this action represent? _____

_____

Telophase II

Put the chromosomes—each having one chromatid—at the poles (the new centrioles).

Conclusions: Meiosis II

- You worked with only one daughter cell from meiosis I as the new parental cell. Suppose you had worked with both daughter cells. How many cells would have been present when

  meiosis II was complete? _____ _____

- How many chromosomes are in the parental cell undergoing meiosis II? _____
- How many chromosomes are in the daughter cell? _____ Explain. _____

  _____

Summary of Meiotic Cell Division

1. The parental cell has the diploid (2n) number of chromosomes, and the daughter cells have the

   _____ _____(n) number of chromosomes.

2. Meiosis is cell division in which the chromosome number _____.
3. If a parent cell has 16 chromosomes, the daughter cells will have how many chromosomes

   following meiosis? _____

4. Whereas meiosis reduces the chromosome number, **fertilization** restores the chromosome number. A zygote contains the same number of chromosomes as the parent, but are these exactly the

   same chromosomes? _____

5. What is another way that sexual reproduction results in genetic recombination?

   _____

15.3 Mitosis Versus Meiosis

Examine Figure 15.7, and note the differences between mitosis and meiosis.

General Differences

Given that a parental cell is diploid (2n), fill in Table 15.2 to indicate general differences between mitosis and meiosis.

Table 15.2 Differences Between Mitosis and Meiosis	Mitosis	Meiosis
1. Number of divisions		
2. Chromosome number in daughter cells		
3. Number of daughter cells		

Figure 15.7   Meiosis I compared to mitosis.

Compare metaphase I of meiosis I to metaphase of mitosis. Only in metaphase I are the homologous chromosomes paired at the equator. Members of homologous chromosome pairs separate during anaphase I, and therefore the daughter cells are haploid. The blue chromosomes were inherited from one parent, and the red chromosomes were inherited from the other parent. The exchange of color between nonsister chromatids represents the crossing-over that occurred during meiosis I.

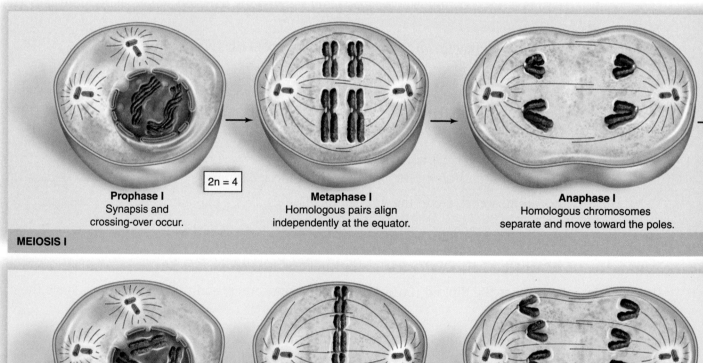

MEIOSIS I

Prophase I
Synapsis and
crossing-over occur.

2n = 4

Metaphase I
Homologous pairs align
independently at the equator.

Anaphase I
Homologous chromosomes
separate and move toward the poles.

MITOSIS

Prophase

2n = 4

Metaphase
Chromosomes align
at the equator.

Anaphase
Sister chromatids separate and
become daughter chromosomes.

Specific Differences

1. Complete Table 15.3 to indicate specific differences between mitosis and meiosis I.

Table 15.3 Mitosis Compared with Meiosis I	
Mitosis	**Meiosis I**
Prophase: no pairing of chromosomes	Prophase I: _____
Metaphase: duplicated chromosomes at equator	Metaphase I: _____
Anaphase: sister chromatids separate	Anaphase I: _____
Telophase: chromosomes have one chromatid	Telophase I: _____

2. Complete Table 15.4 to indicate specific differences between mitosis and meiosis II.

Table 15.4 Mitosis Compared with Meiosis II	
Mitosis	**Meiosis II**
Prophase: no pairing of chromosomes	Prophase II: _____
Metaphase: duplicated chromosomes at equator	Metaphase II: _____
Anaphase: sister chromatids separate	Anaphase II: _____
Telophase: two diploid daughter cells	Telophase II: _____

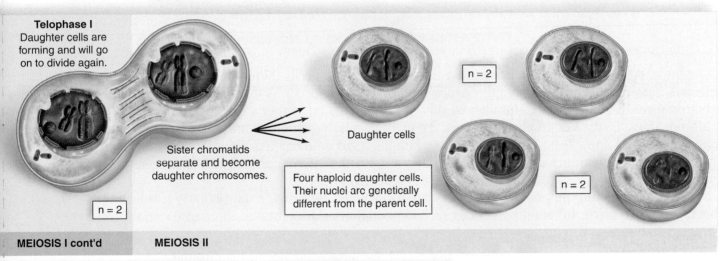

Telophase I
Daughter cells are forming and will go on to divide again.

n = 2

Sister chromatids separate and become daughter chromosomes.

Daughter cells

n = 2

n = 2

Four haploid daughter cells. Their nuclei are genetically different from the parent cell.

MEIOSIS I cont'd   **MEIOSIS II**

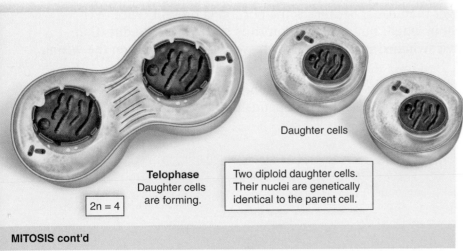

Telophase
Daughter cells are forming.

2n = 4

Daughter cells

Two diploid daughter cells. Their nuclei are genetically identical to the parent cell.

MITOSIS cont'd

15.4 Karyotype Abnormalities

In a karyotype, the chromosomes of an organism are arranged so that the pairs of chromosomes can be seen (Fig. 15.8). At that time, it is possible to observe any possible abnormalities in chromosome number and structure.

Figure 15.8 Human karyotypes.
The chromosomes are arranged according to size and banding patterns.

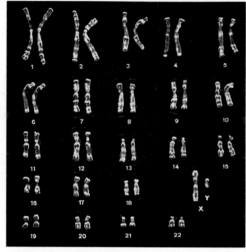

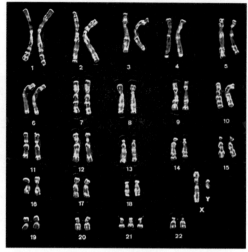

a. Normal male karyotype with 46 chromosomes. **b.** Down syndrome karyotype with an extra chromosome 21.

Abnormalities of chromosome number usually occur when cells divide during mitosis or during meiosis, signifying that these complex processes don't always occur as expected. The most common abnormal result is a change in number so that the individual has either 45 chromosomes or 47 chromosomes, instead of 46 chromosomes. An extra or missing chromosome can cause a fetus and/or a child to develop apparent abnormalities. For example, a girl who has a missing X chromosome may fail to develop the appearance of a female and may not have the internal organs of a female. Either sex that has an extra chromosome 21 has the symptoms of Down syndrome.

Abnormalities of chromosome structure can occur when cells divide, particularly if cells have been subject to environmental influences such as radiation or drug intake. Some of the more common structural abnormalities are:

Deletion: The chromosome is shorter than usual because some portion is missing.
Duplication: The chromosome is longer than usual because some portion is present twice over.
Inversion: The chromosome is normal in length but some portion runs in the opposite direction.
Translocation: Two chromosomes have switched portions and each switched portion is on the wrong chromosome.

Abnormalities of chromosome structure can result in recognized syndromes, a collection of symptoms that always occur together. Which syndrome appears depends on the abnormality.

Sex Chromosome Abnormalities

Nondisjunction (failure to separate) of the X chromosome can occur in humans during oogenesis. Three viable abnormal chromosomal types can occur: Turner syndrome (XO), poly-X syndrome (XXX), and Klinefelter syndrome (XXY). In addition to the three abnormal chromosomal types already mentioned, Jacobs syndrome (XYY) is possible.

A female with **Turner syndrome** (XO) has only one sex chromosome, an X chromosome; the O signifies the absence of the second sex chromosome. The ovaries never become functional, so these females do not undergo puberty or menstruation, and their breasts do not develop. Generally, females with Turner syndrome have a short build, folds of skin on the back of the neck, difficulty recognizing various spatial patterns, and normal intelligence. With hormone supplements, they can lead fairly normal lives.

When an egg having two X chromosomes is fertilized by an X-bearing sperm, an individual with **poly-X syndrome** results. The body cells have three X chromosomes, and therefore 47 chromosomes. It might be supposed that poly-X females are especially feminine, but this is not the case. Although they tend to have learning disabilities, poly-X females have no apparent physical abnormalities, and many are fertile and have children with a normal chromosome count.

When an egg having two X chromosomes is fertilized by a Y-bearing sperm, a male with **Klinefelter syndrome** results. This individual is male in general appearance, but the testes are underdeveloped, and the breasts may be enlarged. The limbs of XXY males tend to be longer than average, muscular development is poor, body hair is sparse, and many XXY males have learning disabilities.

Jacobs syndrome can be due to nondisjunction during meiosis II of spermatogenesis. These males are usually taller than average, suffer from persistent acne, and tend to have speech and reading problems. At one time, it was suggested that XYY males were likely to be criminally aggressive, but the incidence of such behavior has been shown to be no greater than that among normal XY males.

Complete Table 15.5 to show how a physician would recognize each of these syndromes from a karyotype.

Table 15.5 Numerical Sex Chromosome Abnormalities

Syndrome	Karyotype
Turner	
Poly-X	
Klinefelter	
Jacobs	

15.5 Gametogenesis

Gametogenesis is the formation of **gamete**s (sex cells), the sperm and egg. **Fertilization** occurs when the nucleus of a sperm fuses with the nucleus of an egg.

Gametogenesis

Gametogenesis occurs in the testes of males, where **spermatogenesis** produces sperm. Gametogenesis occurs in the ovaries of females, where **oogenesis** produces oocytes (eggs).

A **diploid** (2n) nucleus contains the full number of chromosomes, and a **haploid** (n) nucleus contains half as many. Gametogenesis involves **meiosis,** the process that reduces the chromosome number from 2n to n. In sexually reproducing species, if meiosis did not occur, the chromosome number would double with each generation. Meiosis consists of two divisions: the first meiotic division (meiosis I) and the second meiotic division (meiosis II). Therefore, you would expect four haploid cells at the end of the process. Indeed, there are four sperm as a result of spermatogenesis (Fig. 15.9). However, in females, meiosis I results in a secondary oocyte and one polar body. **A polar body** is a nonfunctioning cell that will disintegrate. A secondary oocyte does not undergo meiosis II unless fertilization (fusion of egg and sperm) occurs. At the completion of oogenesis, there is a single egg and at least two polar bodies (Fig. 15.9).

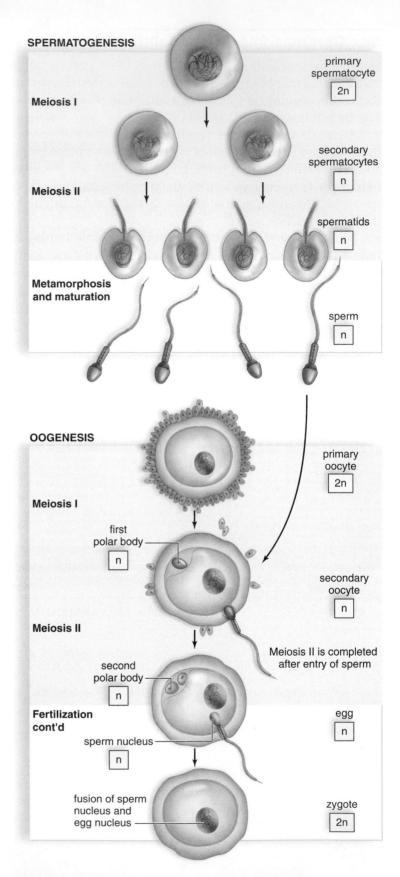

Figure 15.9   Spermatogenesis and oogenesis.
Spermatogenesis produces four viable sperm, whereas oogenesis produces one egg and two polar bodies. In humans, both sperm and egg have 23 chromosomes each; therefore, following fertilization, the zygote has 46 chromosomes.

Gametogenesis Models

Examine any available gametogenesis models, and determine the diploid number of the parental cell and the haploid number of a gamete. Remember that counting the number of centromeres tells you the number of chromosomes.

Slide of Ovary

1. With the help of Figure 15.10, examine a prepared slide of an ovary. Under low power, you will see a large number of small, primary follicles near the outer edge. A primary follicle contains a primary oocyte.
2. Find a secondary follicle, and switch to high power. Note the secondary oocyte, surrounded by numerous cells, to one side of the liquid-filled follicle.
3. Also look for a large, fluid-filled vesicular (Graafian) follicle, which contains a mature secondary oocyte to one side. The vesicular follicle will be next to the outer surface of the ovary because this type of follicle releases the secondary oocyte during ovulation.
4. How many secondary follicles can you find on your slide? _____

   How many vesicular follicles can you find? _____
   How does this number compare with the number of sperm cells seen in the testis cross section?

   _____

Figure 15.10 Microscopic ovary anatomy.

The stages of follicle and oocyte (egg) development are shown in sequence. Each follicle goes through all the stages. Following ovulation, a follicle becomes the corpus luteum.

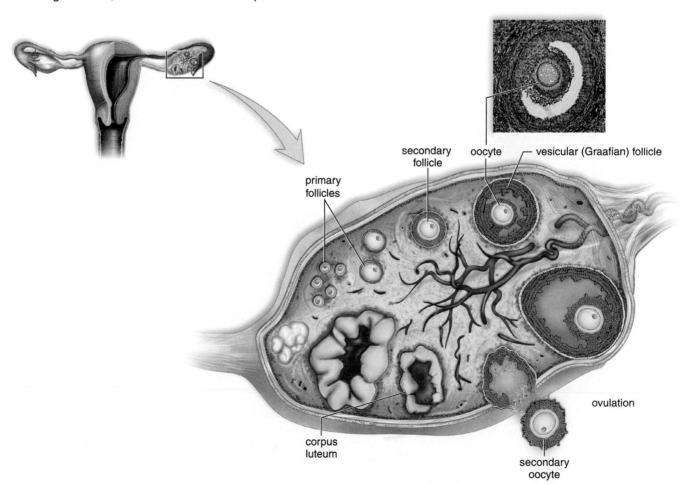

1. With the help of Figure 15.11, examine a prepared slide of a testis. Under low power, note the many circular structures. These are the **seminiferous tubules,** where sperm formation takes place.

2. Switch to high power, and observe one tubule in particular. Find mature sperm (which look like thin, fine, dark lines) in the middle of the tubule. **Interstitial cells,** which produce the male sex hormone testosterone, are between the tubules.

Summary of Gametogenesis

1. What is gametogenesis? _____

    In general, how many chromosomes are in a gamete?_____

2. What is spermatogenesis? _____

    How many chromosomes does a human sperm have? _____

3. What is oogenesis? _____

    How many chromosomes does an egg have? _____

4. Following fertilization, how many chromosomes does the zygote, the first cell of the

    new individual, have? _____

Figure 15.11   Microscopic testis anatomy.

a. A testis contains many seminiferous tubules. **b.** Scanning electron micrograph of a cross section of the seminiferous tubules, where spermatogenesis occurs. Note the location of interstitial cells in clumps among the seminiferous tubules in this light micrograph.

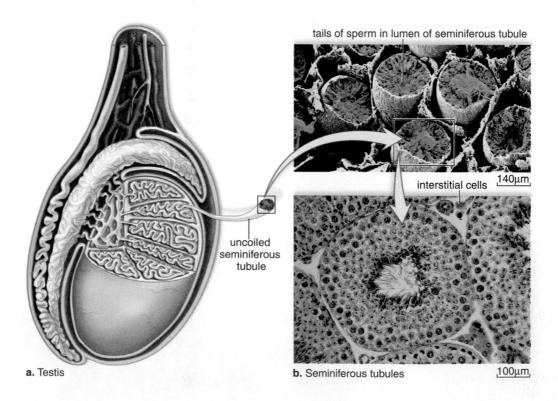

tails of sperm in lumen of seminiferous tubule

interstitial cells   140µm

uncoiled seminiferous tubule

a. Testis

b. Seminiferous tubules   100µm

Mitosis and Cancer

Mutations can upset the cell cycle and cause body cells to divide uncontrollably. Such mutations often lead to cancer. Two of the frequent causes of mutations are exposure to radiation or organic chemicals. Radiation is in sunlight, and we are all well aware, that sitting in the sun for long hours can lead to skin cancer. Frequent X-rays can also be a matter of concern, and we should avoid any that are not medically necessary. Mutagenic organic chemicals can be found in certain food additives, industrial chemicals, and pesticides. That's why lawns sprayed with pesticides often carry a warning label. People sometimes show extreme concern about industrial chemicals and pesticides in our water supply, and yet they still smoke. Tobacco smoke contains a number of organic chemicals that are known carcinogens, and it is estimated that one-third of cancer deaths can be attributed to smoking. Lung cancer is the most frequently lethal cancer in the United States, and smoking is also implicated in the development of cancers of the mouth, larynx, bladder, kidney, and pancreas. When smoking is combined with drinking alcohol, the risk of cancer increases.

Laboratory Review 15

_____ 1. During what stage of the cell cycle does DNA replication occur?

_____ 2. Name the phase of cell division during which separation of sister chromatids occurs.

_____ 3. By what process does the cytoplasm of a human cell separate?

_____ 4. Name the phase of cell division when duplicated chromosomes first appear.

_____ 5. Where in humans would you expect to find meiosis taking place?

_____ 6. If there are 13 pairs of homologues in a primary spermatocyte, how many chromosomes are there in a sperm?

_____ 7. What term refers to the production of an egg?

_____ 8. During which type of gametogenesis would you see polar bodies?

_____ 9. What do you call chromosomes that look alike and carry genes for the same traits?

_____ 10. If homologues are separating, what phase is this?

_____ 11. If the parental cell has 24 chromosomes, how many does each daughter cell have at the completion of meiosis II?

_____ 12. Name the type of cell division during which homologues pair.

_____ 13. Name the type of cell division described by 2n → 2n.

_____ 14. Does metaphase of mitosis, meiosis I, or meiosis II have the haploid number of chromosomes at the equator of the spindle?

Thought Questions

15. Meiosis functions to reduce chromosome number. When, during the human life cycle, is the diploid number of chromosomes restored?

16. How does the alignment of chromosomes differ between metaphase of mitosis and metaphase of meiosis I?

17. A student is simulating meiosis I with homologues that are red-long and yellow-long. Describe the appearance of two nonsister chromatids following crossing-over.

Human Biology Website

The companion website for *Human Biology* provides a wealth of information organized and integrated by chapter. You will find practice tests, animations and much more that will complement your learning and understanding of general biology.

www.mhhe.com/maderhuman11

McGraw-Hill Access Science Website

An online encyclopedia of science and technology that provides information, including videos, that can enhance the laboratory experience.

www.accessscience.com

16

Patterns of Genetic Inheritance

Learning Outcomes

16.1 Determining the Genotype
- Determine students' genotypes by observing themselves and their relatives.

Question: Both Nancy and Jim are homozygous for freckles, a dominant trait. Using letters, what is their genotype?

16.2 Determining Inheritance
- Do genetics problems involving autosomal dominant, autosomal recessive, and X-linked recessive alleles.

Question: What are the chances that Nancy and Jim will have children with freckles?

16.3 Determining the Pedigree
- Determine whether a pedigree represents a pattern of autosomal dominant, autosomal recessive, or X-linked recessive inheritance.

Question: In the pedigree of Nancy's family and Jim's family, would you expect to find few or many people with freckles? Explain.

Application for Daily Living: Choosing the Gender of Your Child

Introduction

Particulate genetics, which views the genes as particles located on the chromosomes, is no longer supported by molecular genetics. Still, its principles can be used to understand patterns of inheritance. First, a gene has two alternate forms called alleles for any trait such as hair line, finger length, and so on. One possible allele designated by a capital letter is dominant over the other allele designated by a lowercase letter. An individual can be homozygous dominant (two dominant alleles, *EE*), homozygous recessive (two recessive alleles, *ee*) or heterozygous (one dominant and one recessive allele, *Ee*). Genotype refers to an individual's alleles, while phenotype refers to an individual's appearance (Fig. 16.1). Homozygous dominant and heterozygous individuals show the dominant phenotype; homozygous recessive individuals show the recessive phenotype.

Figure 16.1 Genotype versus phenotype.
Unattached earlobes (*E*) are dominant over attached earlobes (*e*). **a.** Homozygous dominant individuals have unattached earlobes. **b.** Homozygous recessive individuals have attached earlobes. **c.** Heterozygous individuals have unattached earlobes.

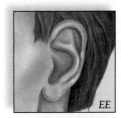
a. unattached earlobe

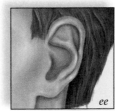
b. attached earlobe

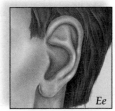
c. unattached earlobe

16.1 Determining the Genotype

Autosomal traits are determined by alleles on the autosomal chromosomes, all chromosomes except the sex chromosomes. Humans have 46 chromosomes. How many pairs of autosomal chromosomes are there? _____ Are most traits autosomal? _____ Explain. _____

_____

Autosomal Dominant and Recessive Traits

Figure 16.2 shows a few human traits. If individuals are homozygous dominant (*AA*) or heterozygous (*Aa*), their phenotype is the dominant trait. If individuals are homozygous recessive (*aa*), their phenotype is the recessive trait.

Figure 16.2   Commonly inherited traits in human beings.
The alleles indicate which traits are dominant and which are recessive.

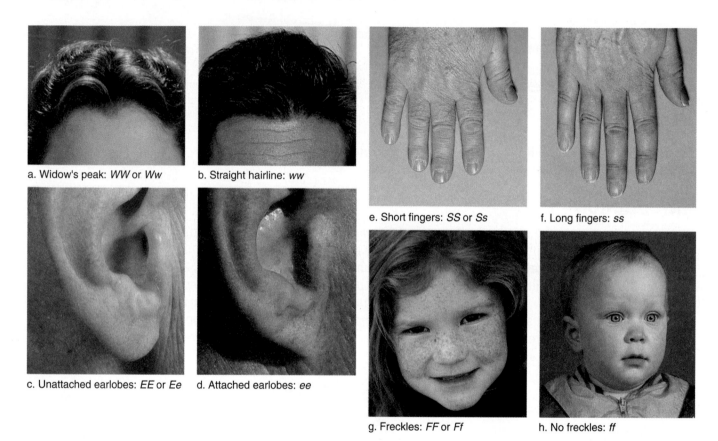

a. Widow's peak: *WW* or *Ww*   b. Straight hairline: *ww*

e. Short fingers: *SS* or *Ss*   f. Long fingers: *ss*

c. Unattached earlobes: *EE* or *Ee*   d. Attached earlobes: *ee*

g. Freckles: *FF* or *Ff*   h. No freckles: *ff*

Cystic fibrosis, characterized by respiratory and digestive difficulties, is the most common autosomal recessive genetic disorder in Caucasians. The most usual key used for cystic fibrosis is: *C* = normal, *c* = cystic fibrosis.

1. How is this key contrary to the described methodology for selecting a key when the trait is not a genetic disease? _____

2. Use letters for the genotype of an individual who is heterozygous? _____ Does this person have cystic fibrosis? _____

3. Use letters for the geotype of a person who has cystic fibrosis? _____ Use words for this geotype: _____

Experimental Procedure: Human Traits

1. For this Experimental Procedure, you will need a lab partner to help you determine your phenotype for the traits listed in the first column of Table 16.1.
2. Determine your probable genotype. If you have the recessive phenotype, you know your genotype. If you have the dominant phenotype, you may be able to decide whether you are homozygous dominant or heterozygous by recalling the phenotype of your parents, siblings, or children. Circle your probable genotype in the second column of Table 16.1.
3. Your instructor will tally the class's phenotypes for each trait so that you can complete the third column of Table 16.1.
4. Complete Table 16.1 by calculating the percentage of the class with each trait. Are dominant phenotypes always the most common in a population? _____ Explain. _____
_____

Table 16.1 Autosomal Human Traits

Trait: d = Dominant r = Recessive	Possible Genotypes	Number in Class	Percentage of Class with Trait
Hairline: Widow's peak (d) Straight hairline (r)	*WW* or *Ww* *ww*	_____	
Earlobes: Unattached (d) Attached (r)	*UU* or *Uu* *uu*	_____	
Skin pigmentation: Freckles (d) No freckles (r)	*FF* or *Ff* *ff*	_____	
Hair on back of hand: Present (d) Absent (r)	*HH* or *Hh* *hh*	_____	
Thumb hyperextension—"hitchhiker's thumb": Last segment cannot be bent backward (d) Last segment can be bent back to 60° (r)	*TT* or *Tt* *tt*	_____	
Bent little finger: Little finger bends toward ring finger (d) Straight little finger (r)	*LL* or *Ll* *ll*	_____	
Interlacing of fingers: Left thumb over right (d) Right thumb over left (r)	*II* or *Ii* *ii*	_____	

16.2 Determining Inheritance

A Punnett square is a means to determine inheritance if the genotype of both parents are known. Figure 16.3 *a* and *b* show two common Punnett squares when autosomal alleles are involved. In a **Punnett square**, all possible types of sperm are lined up vertically, and all possible types of eggs are lined up horizontally, or vice versa, so that every possible combination of gametes occurs within the square. As you will discover, sometimes it is not necessary to do a Punnett square when solving a genetics problem. Therefore, first see if you can determine the answer without doing a Punnett square. And then, if necessary, do a Punnett square to determine inheritance.

One Trait Autosomal Inheritance

These genetic problems are based on Figure 16.2 and Table 16.1.

1. Nancy and the members of her immediate family have attached earlobes. Her maternal grandfather has unattached earlobes. What is the genotype of her maternal grandfather? _____ Nancy's maternal grandmother is no longer living. What could have been the genotype of her maternal grandmother? _____

2. *Joe does not have a bent little finger, but his parents do. What is the expected phenotypic ratio among the parents' children? _____

3. *Henry is adopted. He has hair on the back of his hand. Could both of his parents have had hair on the back of the hand? _____ Could both of his parents have had no hair on the back of the hand? _____ Explain. _____
_____

Inheritance of Genetic Disorders

Examine the cross in Figure 16.3*a* and notice the Punnett square has four divisions and only one of these is a homozygous recessive. Therefore, the chances of a homozygous recessive offspring is 25%.

1. **a.** With reference to Figure 16.3*a*, if a genetic disorder is recessive and the parents are heterozygous, what are the chances that an offspring will have the disorder? _____

   b. With reference to Figure 16.3*a*, if a genetic disorder is dominant and the parents are heterozygous, what are the chances that an offspring will have the disorder? _____

2. **a.** With reference to Figure 16.3*b*, if the parents are heterozygous by homozygous recessive, and the genetic disorder is recessive, what are the chances that the offspring will have the disorder? _____

   b. With reference to Figure 16.3*b*, if the parents are heterozygous by homozygous recessive, and the genetic disorder is dominant, what are the chances that an offspring will have the disorder? _____

Autosomal Disorders

Neurofibromatosis (NF), sometimes called von Recklinghausen disease, is one of the most common genetic disorders. It affects roughly 1 in 3,000 people. It is seen equally in every racial and ethnic group throughout the world.

At birth or later, the affected individual may have six or more large tan spots on the skin. Such spots may increase in size and number and become darker. Small benign tumors (lumps) called neurofibromas may occur under the skin or in the muscles. Neurofibromas are made up of nerve cells and other cell types.

*If necessary see Figure 16.3*a*.

Figure 16.3 Two common patterns of autosomal inheritance in humans.

a. Both parents are heterozygous. **b.** One parent is heterozygous and the other is homozygous recessive. The letter *A* stands for any trait that is dominant and the letter *a* stands for any trait that is recessive. Substitute in the correct key for the problem you are working on.

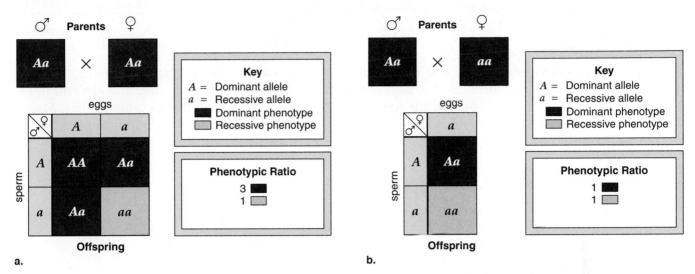

1. Neurofibromatosis is a dominant disorder. If a heterozygous woman reproduces with a homozygous normal man, what are the chances a child will have neurofibromatosis? _____

Cystic fibrosis, is due to abnormal mucus-secreting tissues. At first the infant may have difficulty regaining the birth weight despite good appetite and vigor. A cough associated with a rapid respiratory rate but no fever indicates lung involvement. Large, frequent, and foul-smelling stools are due to abnormal pancreatic secretions. Whereas children previously died in infancy due to infections, they now often survive because of antibiotic therapy.

2. Cystic fibrosis is a recessive disorder. A **carrier** is an individual that appears to be normal but carries a recessive allele for a genetic disorder. A man and a woman are both carriers for cystic fibrosis. What are the chances a child will have cystic fibrosis? _____

Huntington disease does not appear until the thirties or early forties. There is a progressive deterioration of the individual's nervous system that eventually leads to constant thrashing and writhing movements until insanity precedes death. Studies suggest that Huntington disease is due to a single faulty gene that has multiple effects, in which case there is now hope for a cure.

People with Huntington disease seem to be more fertile than others. It is amazing that more than a thousand of the cases in the United States in the past century can be traced to one man born in 1831.

3. Huntington disease is a dominant disorder. Mary is 25 years old and as yet has no signs of Huntington disease. However, her mother does have Huntington disease, but her father is free of the disorder. What are the chances that Mary will develop Huntington disease? _____

Phenylketonuria (PKU) is characterized by severe mental retardation due to an abnormal accumulation of the common amino acid phenylalanine within cells, including neurons. The disorder takes its name from the presence of a breakdown product, phenylketone, in the urine and blood. Newborn babies are routinely tested at the hospital and, if necessary, are placed on a diet low in phenylalanine.

4. Phenylketonuria (PKU) is a recessive disorder. Mr. and Mrs. Smith appear to be normal, but they have a child with PKU. What are the genotypes of Mr. and Mrs. Smith? _____

Tay-Sachs disease is caused by the inability to break down a certain type of fat molecule that accumulates around nerve cells until they are destroyed. Afflicted newborns appear normal and healthy at birth, but they do not develop normally. At first, they may learn to sit up and stand, but later they regress and become mentally retarded, blind, and paralyzed. Death usually occurs between ages three and four.

5. Tay-Sachs is an autosomal recessive disorder. Is it possible for two individuals who do not have Tay-Sachs to have a child with the disorder? Explain. _____

X-Linked Disorders

The sex chromosomes designated X and Y carry genes just like the autosomal chromosomes. Some genes, particularly on the X chromosome, have nothing to do with gender inheritance and are said to be X-linked. **X-linked recessive disorders** are due to recessive genes carried on the X chromosomes. Males are more likely to have an X-linked recessive disorder than females because the Y chromosome is blank for this trait. Does a color-blind male give his son a recessive-bearing X or a Y that is blank for the recessive allele? _____

The possible genotypes and phenotypes for an x-linked recessive disorder are as follows:

Females
$X^B X^B$ = normal vision
$X^B X^b$ = normal vision (carrier)
$X^b X^b$ = color blindness

Males
$X^B Y$ = normal vision
$X^b Y$ = color blindness

An X-linked recessive disorder in males is always inherited from his mother. Most likely, his mother is heterozygous and therefore does not show the disorder. She is designated a carrier for the disorder. Figure 16.4 shows how females can become carriers.

1. **a.** What is the genotype for a color-blind female?_____ How many recessive alleles does a female inherit to be color-blind? _____

   b. What is the genotype for a color-blind male? _____ How many recessive alleles does a male inherit to be color-blind? _____

2. **a.** With reference to Figure 16.4a, if the mother is a carrier and the father has normal vision, what are the chances that a daughter will be color blind? _____

   b. A daughter will be a carrier? _____ **c.** A son will be color blind? _____

3. **a.** With reference to Figure 16.4b, if the mother has normal vision and the father is color blind, what are the chances that a daughter will be color blind? _____

   b. A daughter will be a carrier? _____ **c.** A son will be color blind? _____

Figure 16.4 Two common patterns of X-linked inheritance in humans.

a. The sons of a carrier mother have a 50% chance of being color blind. **b.** A color-blind father has carrier daughters.

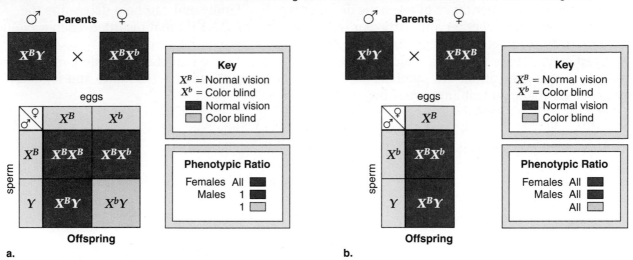

X-Linked Genetics Problems

For **color blindness,** there are two possible x-linked alleles involved. One affects the green-sensitive cones, whereas the other affects the red-sensitive cones. About 6% of men in the United States are color blind due to a mutation involving green perception, and about 2% are color blind due to a mutation involving red perception.

1. A woman with normal color vision, whose father was color blind, marries a man with normal color vision. What do you expect to see among their offspring? _____

   _____

   What would you expect to see if it was the normal-visioned man's father who was color blind?

   _____

2. John's father is color blind but his mother is not color blind. Is John necessarily color blind? _____ Why? _____ Could he be color blind? _____ Why? _____

   Hemophilia is called the bleeder's disease because the affected person's blood is unable to clot. Although hemophiliacs do bleed externally after an injury, they also suffer from internal bleeding, particularly around joints. Hemorrhages can be checked with transfusions of fresh blood (or plasma) or concentrates of the clotting protein. The most common type of hemophilia is hemophilia A, due to absence or minimal presence of a particular clotting factor called factor VIII.

3. Make up a cross involving hemophilia that could be answered by a Punnett square, as in Figure 16.4a or b. _____

   _____

   What is the answer to your genetics problem? _____

16.3 Determining the Pedigree

A **pedigree** shows the inheritance of a genetic disorder within a family and can help determine the inheritance pattern and whether any particular individual has an allele for that disorder. Then a Punnett square can be done to determine the chances of a couple producing an affected child.

In a pedigree, Roman numerals indicate the generation, and Arabic numerals indicate particular individuals in that generation. The symbols used to indicate normal and affected males and females, reproductive partners, and siblings are shown in Figure 16.5.

Figure 16.5   Pedigree symbols.

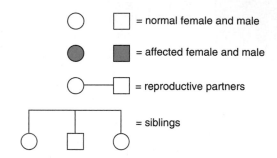

Pedigree Analyses

For each of the following pedigrees, determine how a genetic disorder is inherited. Is the inheritance pattern autosomal dominant, autosomal recessive, or X-linked recessive? Also, decide the genotype of particular individuals in the pedigree. Remember that the *genotype* indicates the dominant and recessive alleles present and the *phenotype* is the actual physical appearance of the trait in the individual. A pedigree indicates the phenotype, and you can reason out the genotype.

1. Study the following pedigree:

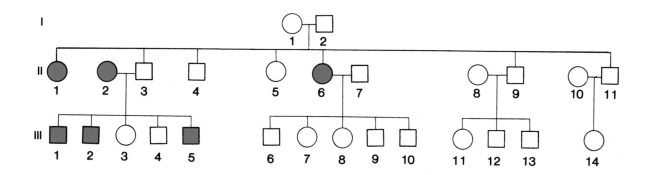

a. What is the inheritance pattern for this genetic disorder? _____

b. What is the genotype of the following individuals? Use *A* for the dominant allele and *a* for the recessive allele.

Generation I, individual 1: _____

Generation II, individual 1: _____

Generation III, individual 8: _____

2. Study the following pedigree:

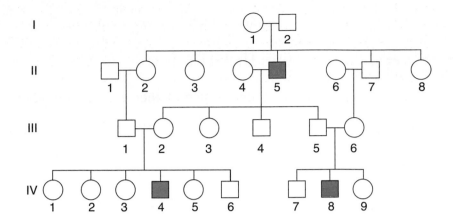

a. What is the inheritance pattern for this genetic disorder?_____
b. What is the genotype of the following individuals?

   Generation I, individual 1: _____

   Generation II, individual 8: _____

   Generation III, individual 1: _____

3. Study the following pedigree:

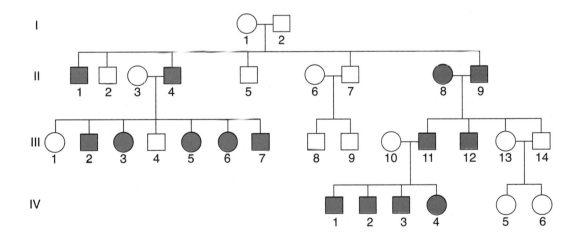

a. What is the inheritance pattern for this genetic disorder? _____
b. What is the genotype of the following individuals?

   Generation I, individual 1: _____

   Generation II, individual 7: _____

   Generation III, individual 4: _____

   Generation III, individual 11: _____

Construction of a Pedigree

You are a genetic counselor who has been given the following information from which you will construct a pedigree.

Your data: Henry has a double row of eyelashes, which is a dominant trait. Both his maternal grandfather and his mother have double eyelashes. Their spouses do not. Henry is married to Isabella, and their first child Polly has normal eyelashes. The couple wants to know the chances of any child having a double row of eyelashes.

1. Construct the pedigree. Begin with the maternal grandfather and grandmother, and end with Polly.

2. Try out a pattern of autosomal dominant inheritance by assigning appropriate genotypes for this pattern of inheritance to each person in your pedigree. Then try out a pattern of X-linked dominant inheritance by assigning appropriate genotypes for this pattern of inheritance to each person in your pedigree. Which pattern is correct?

   _____

3. What is your key for this trait?

Key:

   _____ normal eyelashes

   _____ double row of eyelashes

4. Use correct genotypes to show the cross between Henry and Isabella and perform a Punnett square for this cross.

   Henry   Isabella

   _____ X _____

5. What are the chances of a child of Henry and Isabella having double eyelashes? _____

Choosing the Gender of Your Child

The gender of a child depends upon whether an X-bearing sperm or a Y-bearing sperm enters the egg. A new technology that can separate X-bearing and Y-bearing sperm offers prospective parents the opportunity to choose the sex of their child. The results are not perfect. Following artificial insemination, there's about an 85% success rate for a girl and about a 65% success rate for a boy.

Proponents of sex-selection technology argue that there are many instances in which the ability to choose the sex of a child may benefit society. For example, if a mother is a carrier of an X-linked genetic disorder, such as hemophilia or Duchenne muscular distrophy, this would be the simplest way to ensure a healthy child. Previously, a pregnant woman with these concerns had to wait for the results of an amniocentesis test and then decide whether to abort the pregnancy if it were a boy. In such cases, is it better to ensure that the child will not have a specific genetic disorder than to take the risk?

Also, it's possible for parents to use this technology simply because they choose to have a child of one particular gender. Do you think it is acceptable to select the sex of your child? Some are concerned that allowing parents to select the sex of their children could lead to selecting specific traits for their children. Should this be a concern?

Laboratory Review 16

_____ 1. Mary's father does not have freckles but Mary does. What genotypes could Mary's mother have?

_____ 2. What is the genotype of a man who has unattached earlobes but whose mother has attached earlobes?

_____ 3. A cross gives a 3:1 phenotypic ratio. What are the genotypes of the parents?

_____ 4. What does a geneticist construct to show the inheritance pattern of a genetic disorder within a family?

_____ 5. The alleles of which parent, regardless of the phenotype, determine color blindness in a son?

_____ 6. If only males are affected in a pedigree chart, what is the likely inheritance pattern for the trait?

_____ 7. Which cross gives the better chance of an offspring with the recessive phenotype? Aa × Aa or Aa × aa?

_____ 8. Mary has a widow's peak but her sister has a smooth hairline. Is either one of Mary's parents homozygous dominant or recessive?

_____ 9. Both parents have attached earlobes (recessive). What percentage of children will have unattached earlobes?

_____ 10. If only your mother had Huntington disease (dominant) what are your chances of escaping the disorder which develops later in life?

_____ 11. A woman is a carrier for hemophilia. What are the chances for sons with hemophilia if the father has hemophilia?

_____ 12. A woman is a carrier for hemophilia. What are the chances for sons with hemophilia if the father does not have hemophilia?

_____ 13. If the parents are not affected and a child is affected, what is the inheritance pattern?

_____ 14. The parents are homozygous recessive for freckles. What are the chances the children will have freckles?

_____ 15. A man has Huntington disease (autosomal dominant). He cannot assume his mother passed him the gene. Why not?

_____ 16. A boy is a hemophiliac but his mother is not. What is her genotype?

_____ 17. The trait is autosomal recessive and the results of a cross are 1:1. Using A = dominant and a = recessive, give the genotypes of the parents.

_____ 18. Give the genotype of a girl that is a hemophiliac.

Thought Questions

19. What would be the genotype of a man who is homozygous dominant for widow's peak and is color blind. (Hint: First do the genotype for widow's peak, and then do the genotype of color blindness.)

20. If the pedigree shows that the daughters of affected males are affected but there is no male to male transmission, what could be the pattern of inheritance, assuming the offending allele is on the X chormosome? Construct a pedigree showing three generations and putting in the genotypes to show that you are correct.

17
DNA and Biotechnology

Learning Outcomes

17.1 DNA Structure and Replication
- Explain how the structure of DNA facilitates replication.
- Explain how DNA replication is semiconservative.
Question: What does semiconservative replication mean?

17.2 RNA Structure
- Compare DNA and RNA, discussing their similarities as well as what distinguishes one from the other.
Question: The "R" in RNA stands for what?

17.3 DNA and Protein Synthesis
- Compare the events of transcription with those of translation during protein synthesis.
- Describe how DNA is able to store so much varied information.
Question: Which one, transcription or translation, produces a protein?

17.4 Isolation of DNA
- Explain the importance of DNA technology in modern science.
- Describe how DNA can be isolated, and explain the procedure testing the DNA.
Question: Give an example to show that DNA can be manipulated in the laboratory like any other chemical.

17.5 Detecting Genetic Disorders
- Understand the relationship between an abnormal DNA base sequence and a genetic disorder.
- Understand the process of gel electrophoresis.
Question: If the DNA base sequence changes, the protein changes. How?

Application for Daily Living: Personal DNA Sequencing

Introduction

This laboratory pertains to molecular genetics and biotechnology. Molecular genetics is the study of the structure and function of **DNA (deoxyribonucleic acid),** the genetic material. Biotechnology is the manipulation of DNA for the benefit of human beings and other organisms. Significant advances in medicine, agriculture, and science in general can be attributed to the fields of molecular genetics and biotechnology.

First we will study the structure of DNA and see how that structure facilitates DNA replication in the nucleus of cells. DNA replicates prior to cell division; following cell division, each daughter cell has a complete copy of the genetic material. DNA replication is also needed to pass genetic material from one generation to the next. You may have an opportunity to use models to see how replication occurs.

Then we will study the structure of **RNA (ribonucleic acid)** and how it differs from that of DNA, before examining how DNA and RNA specify protein synthesis. The linear construction of DNA, in which nucleotide is linked to nucleotide, is paralleled by the linear construction of the primary structure of protein, in which amino acid is linked to amino acid. Essentially, we will see that the sequence of nucleotides in DNA codes for the sequence of amino acids in a protein. We will also review the role of three types of RNA in protein synthesis. DNA's code is passed to messenger RNA (mRNA), which moves to the ribosomes containing ribosomal RNA (rRNA). Transfer RNA (tRNA) brings the amino acids to the ribosomes.

We now understand that a mutated gene has an altered DNA base sequence, which can lead to a genetic disorder. You will have an opportunity to carry out a laboratory procedure that detects whether an individual is normal, has sickle-cell disease, or is a carrier.

17.1 DNA Structure and Replication

The structure of DNA lends itself to **replication**, the process that makes a copy of a DNA molecule. Accurate DNA replication is a necessary part of chromosome duplication, which precedes cell division. It also makes possible the passage of DNA from one generation to the next. It is this process that makes identical copies of DNA during the S stage of the cell cycle, allowing each new daughter cell to have exactly the same genetic information that was in the original cell.

DNA Structure

DNA is a polymer of nucleotide subunits (Fig. 17.1). Each nucleotide is composed of three molecules: deoxyribose (a 5-carbon sugar), a phosphate, and a nitrogen-containing base, and is attached to its complementary nucleotide by hydrogen bonds.

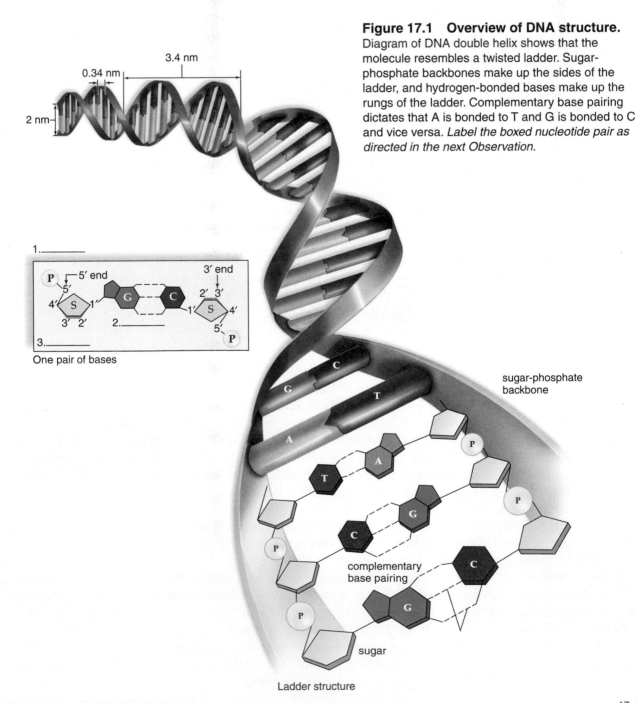

Figure 17.1 Overview of DNA structure. Diagram of DNA double helix shows that the molecule resembles a twisted ladder. Sugar-phosphate backbones make up the sides of the ladder, and hydrogen-bonded bases make up the rungs of the ladder. Complementary base pairing dictates that A is bonded to T and G is bonded to C and vice versa. *Label the boxed nucleotide pair as directed in the next Observation.*

One pair of bases

sugar-phosphate backbone

complementary base pairing

sugar

Ladder structure

1. A nucleotide pair is shown in Figure 17.1. If you are working with a kit, draw a representation of one of your nucleotides here. *Label phosphate, base, and deoxyribose in your drawing and in Figure 17.1.*

2. Notice the four types of bases: cytosine (C), thymine (T), adenine (A), and guanine (G). What is the color of the four types of bases in Figure 17.1? In your kit? Complete Table 17.1 by writing in the colors of the bases.

Table 17.1	Base Colors	
	In Figure 17.1	**In Your Kit**
Cytosine		
Thymine		
Adenine		
Guanine		

3. Using Figure 17.1 as a guide, join several nucleotides together. Observe the entire DNA molecule. What types of molecules make up the backbone (uprights of ladder) of DNA (Fig. 17.1)?

    _____ and _____
    In the backbone, the phosphate of one nucleotide is bonded to a sugar of the next nucleotide by a covalent bond.

4. Using Figure 17.1 as a guide, join the bases together with hydrogen bonds. Label a hydrogen bond in Figure 17.1. Dots are used to represent hydrogen bonds in Figure 17.1 because

    hydrogen bonds are (strong or weak)? _____

5. In Figure 17.1 and in your model, the base A is always paired with the base _____,

    and the base C is always paired with the base _____. This is called complementary base pairing.

6. In Figure 17.1, what molecules make up the rungs of the ladder? _____

7. Each half of the DNA molecule is a DNA strand. Why is DNA also called a double helix

    (Fig. 17.1)? _____

DNA Replication

During replication, the DNA molecule is duplicated so that there are two DNA molecules. We will see that complementary base pairing makes replication possible.

Observation: DNA Replication

1. Before replication begins, DNA is unzipped. Using Figure 17.2*a* as a guide, break apart your two DNA strands. What bonds are broken to unzip the DNA strands? _____

2. Using Figure 17.2*b* as a guide, attach new complementary nucleotides to each strand using complementary base pairing.

3. Show that you understand complementary base pairing by completing Table 17.2. You now have two DNA molecules (Fig. 17.2*c*). Are your molecules identical? _____

4. Because of complementary base pairing, each new double helix is composed of an _____ strand and a _____ strand. *Write old or new beside each strand in Figure 17.2a, b, and c, 1–10. Conservative means to save something from the past.* Why is DNA replication called semiconservative?

_____

_____

_____

_____

Figure 17.2   DNA replication.
Use of the ladder configuration better illustrates how replication takes place. **a.** The parental DNA molecule. **b.** The "old" strands of the parental DNA molecule have separated. New complementary nucleotides available in the cell are pairing with those of each old strand. **c.** Replication is complete.

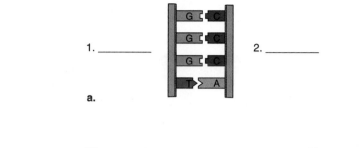

1. _____   2. _____

a.

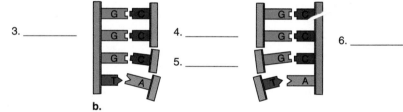

3. _____   4. _____   6. _____

5. _____

b.

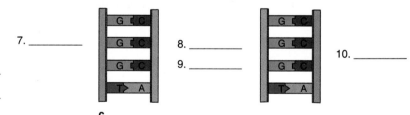

7. _____   8. _____   10. _____

9. _____

c.

Table 17.2   DNA Replication

Old strand	G G G T T C C A T T A A A T T C C A G A A A T C A T A
New strand	

5. Genetic material has to be inherited from cell to cell and organism to organism. Consider that because of DNA replication, a chromosome is composed of two chromatids, and each chromatid is a complete DNA molecule. The chromatids separate during cell division so that each daughter cell receives a copy of each chromosome. Does replication provide a means for passing DNA

from cell to cell and organism to organism? _____

Explain. _____

_____

17.2 RNA Structure

Like DNA, RNA is a polymer of nucleotides (Fig. 17.3). In an RNA nucleotide, the sugar ribose is attached to a phosphate molecule and to a nitrogen-containing base, C, U, A, or G. In RNA, the base uracil replaces thymine as one of the pyrimidine bases. RNA is single stranded, whereas DNA is double stranded.

Figure 17.3   Overview of RNA structure.
RNA is a single strand of nucleotides. *Label the boxed nucleotide as directed in the next Observation.*

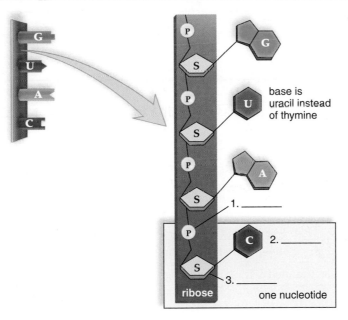

1. Describe the backbone of an RNA molecule. _____

2. Where are the bases located in an RNA molecule? _____

3. Complete Table 17.3 to show the complementary DNA bases for the RNA bases.

Table 17.3 DNA and RNA Bases			
RNA Bases	C	U	A	G
DNA Bases				

1. If you are using a kit, draw a nucleotide for the construction of mRNA. *Label the ribose (the sugar in RNA), the phosphate, and the base in your drawing and in Figure 17.3, p. 233.*

2. Complete Table 17.4 by writing in the colors of the bases in Figure 17.3 and in your kit.

Table 17.4 Base Colors

	In Figure 17.3	In Your Kit
Cytosine		
Uracil		
Adenine		
Guanine		

3. The base uracil substitutes for the base thymine in RNA. Complete Table 17.5 to show several other ways RNA differs from DNA.

Table 17.5 DNA Structure Compared with RNA Structure

	DNA	RNA
Sugar	Deoxyribose	
Bases	Adenine, guanine, thymine, cytosine	
Strands	Double stranded with base pairing	
Helix	Yes	

17.3 DNA and Protein Synthesis

Protein synthesis requires the processes of transcription and translation. During **transcription,** which takes place in the nucleus, an RNA molecule called **messenger RNA (mRNA)** is made complementary to one of the DNA strands. This mRNA leaves the nucleus and goes to the ribosomes in the cytoplasm. Ribosomes are composed of **ribosomal RNA (rRNA)** and proteins in two subunits.

During **translation,** RNA molecules called **transfer RNA (tRNA)** bring amino acids to the ribosome, and they join in the order prescribed by mRNA.

In the end, the final sequence of amino acids in a protein is specified by DNA. This is the information that DNA, the genetic material, stores.

Transcription

During transcription, complementary RNA is made from a DNA template (Fig. 17.4). A portion of DNA unwinds and unzips at the point of attachment of RNA polymerase. A strand of mRNA is produced when complementary nucleotides join in the order dictated by the sequence of bases in DNA. Transcription occurs in the nucleus, and the mRNA passes out of the nucleus to enter the cytoplasm. *Label Figure 17.4.*

Observation: Transcription

1. If you are using a kit, unzip your DNA model so that only one strand remains. This strand is the **template strand,** the strand transcribed or copied into complementary base pairs of RNA.
2. Using Figure 17.4 as a guide, construct a messenger RNA (mRNA) molecule by first lining up RNA nucleotides complementary to the template strand of your DNA molecule. Join the nucleotides together to form mRNA.
3. A portion of DNA has the sequence of bases shown in Table 17.6. *Complete Table 17.6 to show the sequence of bases in mRNA.*
4. If you are using a kit, unzip the mRNA transcript from the DNA. Locate the end of the strand that will move to the _____ in the cytoplasm.

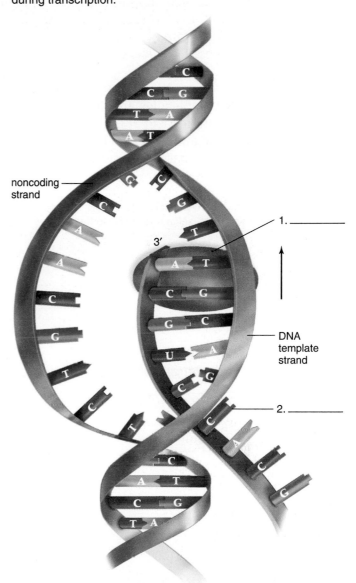

Figure 17.4   Messenger RNA (mRNA).
Messenger RNA complementary to a section of DNA forms during transcription.

noncoding strand

3′

1. _____

DNA template strand

2. _____

Table 17.6	Transcription
DNA	T A C A C G A G C A A C T A A C A T
mRNA	

Translation

DNA specifies the sequence of amino acids in a polypeptide because every three bases stands for an amino acid. Therefore, DNA is said to have a **triplet code.** The bases in mRNA are complementary to those in DNA, and therefore every three bases in mRNA (called a **codon**) stands for the same sequence of amino acids as does DNA. The correct sequence of amino acids in a polypeptide is the message that mRNA carries.

Messenger RNA leaves the nucleus and proceeds to the ribosomes, where protein synthesis occurs. Transfer RNA (tRNA) molecules are so named because they transfer amino acids to the ribosomes. Each tRNA has a specific amino acid at one end and a matching **anticodon** at the other end (Fig. 17.5). *Label Figure 17.5,* where the amino acid is represented as a colored ball, the tRNA is green, and the anticodon is the sequence of three bases.

Figure 17.5 Transfer RNA (tRNA).
Transfer RNA carries amino acids to the ribosomes.

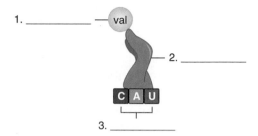

Observation: Translation

1. Figure 17.6 shows seven tRNA-amino acid complexes. Every amino acid has a name; in the figure, only the first three letters of the name are inside the ball. Using the mRNA sequence given in Table 17.7, number the tRNA-amino acid complexes in the order they will come to the ribosome.
2. If you are using a kit, arrange your tRNA-amino acid complexes in the proper order. Complete Table 17.7. Why are the codons and anticodons in groups of three? _____

_____

Figure 17.6 Transfer RNA diversity.
Each type of tRNA carries only one particular amino acid, designated here by the first three letters of its name.

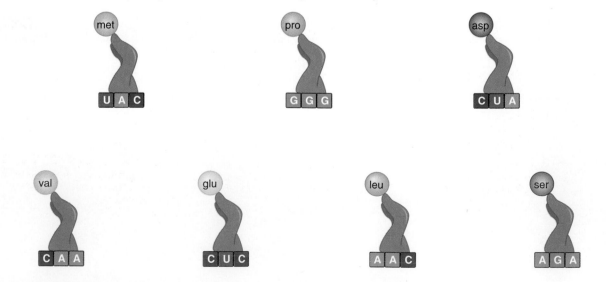

Table 17.7 Translation

mRNA codons	AUG	CCC	GAU	GUU	GAG	UUG	UCU
tRNA anticodons							
Amino acid*							

*Use three letters only. See Table 17.8 for the full names of these amino acids.

Table 17.8 Names of Amino Acids

Abbreviation	Name
met	methionine
pro	proline
asp	aspartate
val	valine
glu	glutamate
leu	leucine
ser	serine

3. Figure 17.7 shows the manner in which the polypeptide grows. A ribosome has room for two tRNA complexes at a time. As the first tRNA leaves, it passes its amino acid or peptide to the second tRNA-amino acid complex. Then the ribosome moves forward, making room for the next tRNA-amino acid complex. This sequence of events occurs over and over until the entire polypeptide is borne by the last tRNA to come to the ribosome. *In Figure 17.7, label the ribosome, the mRNA, and the peptide chain.*

Figure 17.7 Protein synthesis.

1. A ribosome has room for two tRNA-amino acid complexes. 2. Before tRNA leaves, an RNA passes its attached peptide to its neighboring tRNA-amino acid complex. 3. The ribosome moves forward, and the next tRNA-amino acid complex arrives.

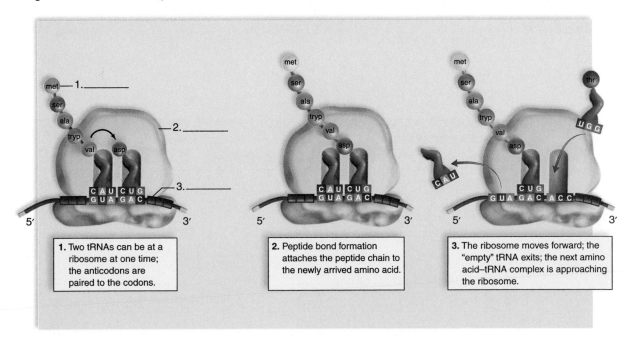

1. Two tRNAs can be at a ribosome at one time; the anticodons are paired to the codons.

2. Peptide bond formation attaches the peptide chain to the newly arrived amino acid.

3. The ribosome moves forward; the "empty" tRNA exits; the next amino acid–tRNA complex is approaching the ribosome.

Summary of Protein Synthesis

Examine Figure 17.8 and complete Table 17.9 to show that you understand the role of the particpants in protein synthesis.

Figure 17.8   Participants in synthesis.

The two steps required for proteins synthesis are transcription, which occurs in the nucleus, and translation, which occurs in the cytoplasm at the ribosomes.

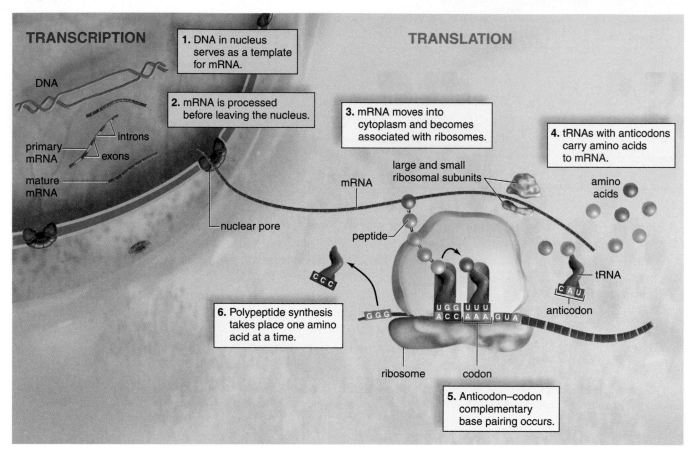

Table 17.9	Participants in Protein Synthesis	
	Special Role	**Description**
DNA		
mRNA		
tRNA		
rRNA		
Amino acid		
Protein		

17.4 Isolation of DNA

In the following Experimental Procedure, you will isolate DNA from the cells of an organism using a modified procedure like that used worldwide in biotechnology laboratories. You will extract DNA from an onion filtrate that contains DNA in solution. To prepare the filtrate, your instructor homogenized an onion with a detergent. The detergent emulsifies and forms complexes with the lipids and proteins of the plasma membrane, causing them to precipitate out of solution. Cell contents, including DNA, become suspended in solution. The cellular mixture is then filtered to produce the filtrate that contains DNA.

The DNA molecule is easily degraded (broken down), so it is important to follow all instructions closely. Handle glassware carefully to prevent nucleases in your skin from contaminating the glassware.

Experimental Procedure: Isolating DNA

1. Obtain a large, clean test tube, and place it in an ice bath. Let stand for a few minutes to make sure the test tube is cold. Everything must be kept very cold.
2. Obtain approximately 4 ml of the *onion filtrate*, and add it to your test tube while keeping the tube in the ice bath.
3. Obtain and add 2 ml of cold *meat tenderizer solution* to the solution in the test tube, and mix the contents slightly with a stirring rod or Pasteur pipette. Let stand for 10 minutes.
4. Use a graduated cylinder or pipette to slowly add an equal volume (approximately 6 ml) of ice-cold *95% ethanol* along the inside of the test tube. Keep the tube in the ice bath, and tilt it to a 45° angle. You should see a distinct layer of ethanol over the white filtrate. Let the tube sit for 2 to 3 minutes.
5. Insert a glass rod or a Pasteur pipette into the tube until it reaches the bottom of the tube. *Gently* swirl the glass rod or pipette, always in the same direction. (You are not trying to mix the two layers; you are trying to wind the DNA onto the glass rod like cotton candy.) This process is called "spooling" the DNA. The stringy, slightly gelatinous material that attaches to the pipette is DNA (Fig. 17.9). If the DNA has been damaged, it will still precipitate, but as white flakes that cannot be collected on the glass rod.
6. Answer the following questions:

   a. This procedure requires homogenization. When did homogenization occur? _____

   _____

   b. What was the purpose of homogenization? _____
   Next, deproteinization stripped proteins from the DNA. Which of the preceding steps represents deproteinization? _____

   c. Finally, DNA was precipitated out of solution. Which of the preceding steps represents the precipitation of DNA? _____

Figure 17.9 Isolation of DNA.
The addition of ethanol causes DNA to come out of solution so that it can be spooled onto a glass rod.

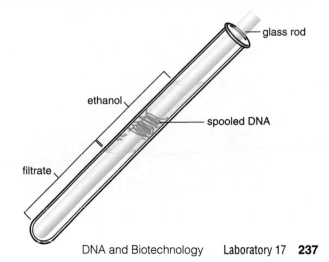

17.5 Detecting Genetic Disorders

The base sequence of DNA in all the chromosomes is an organism's genome. Now that the Human Genome Project is finished, we know the normal order of all the 3.6 billion nucleotide bases in the human genome. Someday it will be possible to sequence anyone's genome within a relatively short time, and thereby determine what particular base sequence alterations signify that he or she has a disorder or will have one in the future. In this laboratory, you will study the alteration in base sequence that causes a person to have sickle-cell disease.

In persons with sickle-cell disease, the red blood cells aren't biconcave disks like normal red blood cells—they are sickle shaped. Sickle-shaped cells can't pass along narrow capillary passageways. They clog the vessels and break down, causing the person to suffer from poor circulation, anemia, and poor resistance to infection. Internal hemorrhaging leads to further complications, such as jaundice, episodic pain in the abdomen and joints, and damage to internal organs.

Sickle-shaped red blood cells are caused by an abnormal hemoglobin (Hb^S). Individuals with the $Hb^A Hb^A$ genotype are normal; those with the $Hb^S Hb^S$ genotype have sickle-cell disease, and those with the $Hb^A Hb^S$ have sickle-cell trait. Persons with sickle-cell trait do not usually have sickle-shaped cells unless they experience dehydration or mild oxygen deprivation.

Sickle-Cell Disease

Examine Figure 17.10a and b, which show the DNA base sequence, the mRNA codons, and the amino acid sequence for a portion of the gene for Hb^A and the same portion for Hb^S.

Figure 17.10 Sickle-cell disease.
Sickle-cell disease occurs when **a.** the DNA base sequence in one location has changed from CTC **b.** to CAC in both alleles for Hb^A.

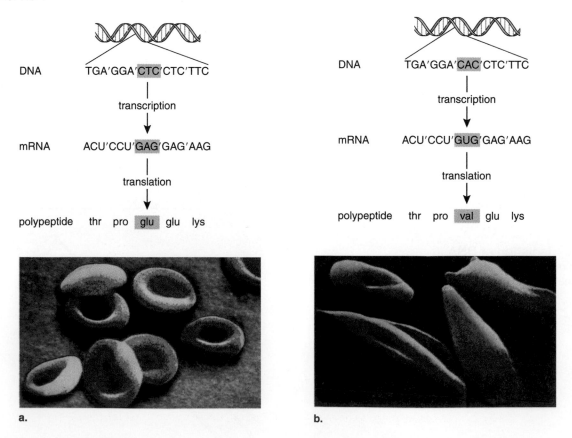

1. In what one base does Hb^A differ from Hb^S? Hb^A _____ Hb^S _____

2. What are the codons that contain this base? Hb^A _____ Hb^S _____

3. What is the amino acid difference? Hb^A _____ Hb^S _____

This amino acid difference causes the polypeptide chain in sickle-cell hemoglobin to pile up as firm rods that push against the plasma membrane and deform the red blood cell into a sickle shape:

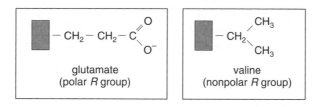

glutamate
(polar R group)

valine
(nonpolar R group)

Detection by Gel Electrophoresis

The two most widely used techniques for separating molecules in biotechnology are chromatography and gel electrophoresis. Chromatography separates molecules on the basis of their solubility and size. **Gel electrophoresis** separates molecules on the basis of their charge and size (Fig. 17.11).

During gel electrophoresis, charged molecules migrate across a span of gel (gelatinous slab) because they are placed in a powerful electrical field. In the present experiment, the fragment mixture for each DNA sample is placed in a small depression in the gel called a well. The gel is placed in a powerful electrical field. The electricity causes equal length DNA fragments, which are negatively charged, to move through the gel to the positive pole at a faster rate than those that have no charge.

Figure 17.11 Equipment and procedure for gel electrophoresis.

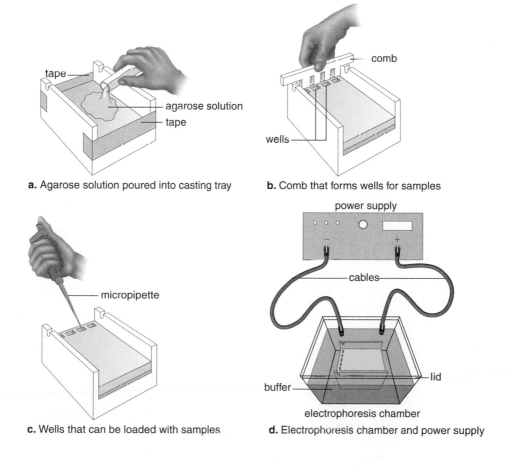

a. Agarose solution poured into casting tray

b. Comb that forms wells for samples

c. Wells that can be loaded with samples

d. Electrophoresis chamber and power supply

Almost all DNA gel electrophoresis is carried out using horizontal gel slabs. First, the gel is poured onto a glass plate, and the wells are formed. After the samples are added to the wells, the gel and the glass plate are put into an electrophoresis chamber, and buffer is added. The fragments begin to migrate after the electrical current is turned on. With staining, the fragments appear as a series of bands spread from one end of the gel to the other.

Experimental Procedure: Gel Electrophoresis

If so instructed, you will carry out gel electrophoresis as directed by a kit and described in Figure 17.11. Gel electrophoresis allows us to detect the molecule difference between hemoglobin in a person with sickle-cell disease, a normal person, and a person with sickle-cell trait (Fig. 17.12). If you are not doing the gel electrophoresis, continue with Analyzing the Electrophoresed Gel.

> ⚠ **Gel electrophoresis** Students should wear personal protective equipment. Safety goggles and smocks or aprons while loading gels and during electrophoresis and protective gloves while staining.

Obtain three samples of hemoglobin provided by your kit. They are labeled sample A, B, and C. Then, as directed by your kit, carry out electrophoresis of these samples.

Analyzing the Electrophoresed Gel

1. Sickle-cell hemoglobin (Hb^S) migrates slower toward the positive pole than normal hemoglobin (Hb^A) because the amino acid valine has no polar R groups, whereas the amino acid glutamate does have a polar R group.

2. In Figure 17.12, which lane contains only Hb^S, signifying that the individual is $Hb^S Hb^S$? _____

3. Which lane contains only Hb^A, signifying that the individual is $Hb^A Hb^A$? _____

4. Which lane contains both Hb^S and Hb^A, signifying that the individual is $Hb^A Hb^S$? _____

Figure 17.12   Gel electrophoresis of hemoglobins.

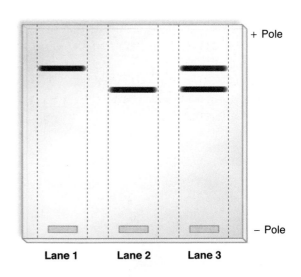

Detection by Genomic Sequencing

You are a genetic counselor. A young couple seeks your advice because sickle-cell disease occurs among the family members of each. You order DNA base sequencing to be done. The results come back that at one of the loci for normal hemoglobin, each has the abnormal sequence CAC instead of CTC. The other locus is normal. What are the chances that this couple will have a child with sickle-cell disease?

Conclusion: Detection of Genetic Disorders

* What two methods of detecting genetic disorders were described in this section?

* Which method is more direct and probably requires more expensive equipment to do?

* Which method probably preceded the other method as a means to detect sickle-cell disease?

Application for Daily Living

Personal DNA Sequencing

You may know that it took many years to get the human genome sequenced, but now personal DNA base sequencing can be done within days, and it is relatively affordable. The information can allow a trained geneticist to predict which genetic disorders you are susceptible to, and then you can choose either prevention and/or early detection to avoid a serious illness. DNA sequencing may also tell you which drugs might be especially useful to you in case of illness.

The move is on to require people to go through their personal physician to get their DNA sequenced. Why? It is always a good idea to have it done by a reputable company and to have someone help you sift through the data that might be made available. It's not always easy to learn that you may come down with a disorder, and you would want to know what your options are right away.

_____ 1. The DNA structure resembles a twisted ladder. What molecules make up the sides of the ladder?

_____ 2. What makes up the rungs of the ladder?

_____ 3. Do the two DNA double helices following DNA replication have the same, or a different, composition?

_____ 4. If DNA has 20% of adenine bases, what would be the percentage of thymine?

_____ 5. If the codons are AUG, CGC, and UAC, what are the anticodons?

_____ 6. Where does protein synthesis take place?

_____ 7. During transcription, what type of RNA is formed that carries the codons?

_____ 8. In what part of the cell does translation occur?

_____ 9. During translation, what type of RNA carries amino acids to the ribosomes?

_____ 10. A person with genotype Hb^SHb^S has what genetic disorder?

_____ 11. Sickle-cell disease illustrates that a mutation is a change in what?

_____ 12. Normal hemoglobin is separated from sickle-cell hemoglobin because of a _____ difference.

Thought Questions

13. What role does mRNA play in transcription and translation?

14. Explain the manner in which gel electrophoresis identifies a person with sickle-cell disease.

15. Below is a sequence of bases associated with the template DNA strand:

TAC CCC GAG CTT

a. Identify the sequence of bases in the mRNA resulting from the transcription of the above DNA sequence.

b. Identify the sequence of bases in the tRNA anticodon that will bind with the first codon on the mRNA identified above.

Human Biology Website

The companion website for _Human Biology_ provides a wealth of information organized and integrated by chapter. You will find practice tests, animations, and much more that will complement your learning and understanding of general biology.

www.mhhe.com/maderhuman11

McGraw-Hill Access Science Website

An online encyclopedia of science and technology that provides information, including videos, that can enhance the laboratory experience.

www.accessscience.com

18
Evolution

Learning Outcomes

18.1 Fossil Record
- Use the geologic timescale to trace the evolution of life in broad outline.
- Describe several types of fossils and explain how fossils help to establish the sequence in the evolution of living things.
- Explain how scientists use fossils to establish relationships between different forms of life.
Question: Explain in what way fossils allow biologists to trace the history of life.

18.2 Comparative Anatomy
- Explain how comparative anatomy provides evidence of common descent.
- Compare the human skeleton with the chimpanzee skeleton, and illustrate how the differences between the two reflect evolutionary adaptations.
Question: What anatomical features show that a chimpanzee skeleton and a human skeleton share a unity of plan?

18.3 Molecular Evidence
- Explain how biochemistry aids the study of the evolutionary relationships among organisms.
- Explain how biochemical evidence adds additional support to the concept of common descent.
Question: If a DNA sequence is the same between chimpanzees and humans, what other type sequence will be the same?

Introduction

Evolution is the process by which life has changed through time. A **species** is a group of similarly constructed organisms that share common genes, and a **population** is all the members of a species living in a particular area. When new variations arise that allow certain members of a population to capture more resources, these individuals tend to survive and have more offspring than the other, unchanged members. Therefore, each successive generation will include more members with the new variation. Eventually, most members of a population and then the species will have the same **adaptations,** structures, physiology, and behavior that make an organism suited to its environment.

Adaptations to various ways of life explain why life-forms are so diverse. However, evolution, which has been ongoing since the origin of life, is also an explanation for the unity of life and common descent. In this Laboratory, you will study three types of data that support the hypothesis of common descent from an original source: (1) the fossil record (Table 18.1), (2) comparative anatomy (embryological and adult), and (3) molecular comparison. **Fossils** are the remains or evidence of some organism that lived long ago. In the history of life as detected by fossils, prokaryotic cells preceded eukaryotic cells, and among animals, invertebrates preceded vertebrates. Humans began evolving about 5 million years ago, but modern humans do not appear in the fossil record until about 100,000 years ago. A comparative study of the anatomy of modern groups of organisms has shown that each group has homologous structures. For example, all vertebrate animals have essentially the same type of skeleton. Homologous structures signify relatedness through evolution. Almost all living organisms use the same basic molecules, including DNA, ATP, and many identical or nearly identical enzymes. Proteins and DNA are analyzed to determine how closely related the two groups are. In this Laboratory, you will use an antigen-antibody reaction to show the degree of evolutionary relatedness between different vertebrates.

Table 18.1 The Geologic Timescale: Major Divisions of Geologic Time and Some of the the Major Evolutionary Events of Each Time Period

Era	Period	Epoch	Million Years Ago (MYA)	Plant Life	Animal Life
Recent Time		Holocene	(0.01–0)	Human influence on plant life	Age of *Homo sapiens*
	Quaternary			**Significant Mammalian Extinction**	
		Pleistocene	(1.80–0.01)	Herbaceous plants spread and diversify.	Presence of Ice Age mammals. Modern humans appear.
Cenozoic		Pliocene	(5.33–1.80)	Herbaceous angiosperms flourish.	First hominids appear.
		Miocene	(23.03–5.33)	Grasslands spread as forests contract.	Apelike mammals and grazing mammals flourish; insects flourish.
	Tertiary	Oligocene	(33.9–23.03)	Many modern families of flowering plants evolve.	Browsing mammals and monkeylike primates appear.
		Eocene	(55.8–33.9)	Subtropical forests with heavy rainfall thrive.	All modern orders of mammals are represented.
		Paleocene	(65.5–55.8)	Flowering plants continue to diversify.	Primitive primates, mammalian herbivores, carnivores, and insectivores appear.
				Mass Extinction: Dinosaurs and Most Reptiles	
	Cretaceous		(145.5–65.5)	Flowering plants spread; conifers persist.	Placental mammals appear; modern insect groups appear.
Mesozoic	Jurassic		(199.6–145.5)	Flowering plants appear.	Dinosaurs flourish; birds appear.
				Mass Extinction	
	Triassic		(251–199.6)	Forests of conifers and cycads dominate.	First mammals appear; first dinosaurs appear; corals and molluscs dominate seas.

Era	Period	Million Years Ago (MYA)	Plant Life	Animal Life
Paleozoic			**Mass Extinction**	
	Permian	(299–251)	Gymnosperms diversify.	Reptiles diversify; amphibians decline.
	Carboniferous	(359.2–299)	Age of great coal-forming forests; ferns, club mosses, and horsetails flourish.	Amphibians diversify; first reptiles appear; first great radiation of insects.
			Mass Extinction	
	Devonian	(416–359.2)	First seed plants appear. Seedless vascular plants diversify.	First insects and first amphibians appear on land.
	Silurian	(443.7–416)	Seedless vascular plants appear.	Jawed fishes diversify and dominate the seas.
			Mass Extinction	
	Ordovician	(488.3–443.7)	Nonvascular plants appear on land.	First jawless and then jawed fishes appear.
	Cambrian	(542–488.3)	Marine algae flourish.	All invertebrate phyla present; first chordates appear.
Precambrian		630	Soft-bodied invertebrates	
		1,000	Protists evolve and diversify.	
		2,200	First eukaryotic cells	
		2,700	O_2 accumulates in atmosphere.	
		3,800	First prokaryotic cells	
Distant Time		4,570	Earth forms.	

18.1 Fossil Record

All life-forms evolved from the first cell or cells, so life has a history, and this history is revealed by the fossil record. The geologic timescale, developed by geologists and paleontologists, depicts the history of life based on the fossil record (see Table 18.1). In this section, we will study the geologic timescale and then examine some fossils.

Geologic Timescale

Divisions of the Timescale

The timescale divides the history of Earth into eras, then periods, and then epochs. The three eras span the greatest amounts of time, and the epochs are the shortest time frames. Only the periods of the Cenozoic era are divided into epochs, meaning that more attention is given to the evolution of primates and flowering plants than to the earlier evolving organisms. Modern civilization is given its own epoch, despite that humans have only been around about .04% of the history of life. List the four eras in the timescale starting with Precambrian time: _____

_____

How to Read the Timescale

Using the geologic timescale, you can trace the history of life by beginning with Precambrian time on page 245. The timescale indicates that the first cells (the prokaryotes) arose some 3,800 MYA. The prokaryotes evolved before any other group.

Why do you read the timescale starting with Precambrian time? _____

_____

The Precambrian time was very long, lasting from the time the Earth first formed until 542 MYA. The fossil record during the Precambrian time is meager, but the fossil record from the Cambrian period onward is rich (for reasons still being determined). This helps explain why the timescale usually does not show any periods until the Cambrian period of the Paleozoic era.

You can use the timescale to check when certain groups evolved and/or flourished. Examples:

1. During the Ordovician period, the nonvascular plants appear on land, and the first jawless and jawed fishes appear in the seas.

2. During the _____ era and the _____ period, the first flowering plants appear. How many million years ago was this? _____

3. On the timescale, note the Carboniferous period. During this period great swamp forests covered the land. These are also called coal-forming forests because with time they became the coal we burn today. How do you know that the plants in this forest were not flowering trees as most of our trees are today? _____

   What type animal was diversifying at this time? _____

4. You should associate the Cenozoic era with the evolution of humans. Among mammals, humans are primates. During what period and epoch did primitive primates appear?

   _____

5. Among primates, humans are hominids. During what period and epoch did hominids appear?

   _____

6. The scientific name for humans is *Homo sapiens*. What period and epoch is the age of *Homo sapiens*? _____

Dating Within the Timescale

The timescale provides both relative dates and absolute dates. When you say, for example, "Flowering plants evolved during the Jurassic period," you are using relative time, because flowering plants evolved earlier or later than groups in other periods. If you use the dates given in millions of years, you are using absolute time. Absolute dates are usually obtained by measuring the amount of a radioactive isotope in the rocks surrounding the fossils. Why wouldn't you expect to find human fossils and dinosaur fossils

together in rocks of the same date? _____

_____

Limitations of the Timescale

The timescale tells when various groups evolved and flourished, so it might seem that evolution has been a series of events leading only from the first cells to humans. This is not the case; for example, prokaryotes (bacteria and archaea) never declined and are still the most abundant and successful organisms on Earth. Even today, they constitute up to 90% of the total weight of living things.

Then, too, the timescale lists mass extinctions, but it doesn't tell when specific groups became extinct. **Extinction** is the total disappearance of a species or a higher group; **mass extinction** occurs when a large number of species disappear in a few million years or less. For lack of space, the geologic timescale can't give specific details.

1. Figure 18.1 does show how mass extinction affected a few groups of animals. Which of the animals shown in Figure 18.1 suffered the most during the P-T (Permian-Triassic) extinction?

    _____

2. The K-T extinction occurred between the Cretaceous and the Tertiary periods. Which animals shown in Figure 18.1 became extinct during the K-T extinction? _____

3. Figure 18.1 shows only periods and no eras. Fill in the eras on the lines provided in the figure.

Figure 18.1 Mass extinctions.
Five significant mass extinctions and their effects on the abundance of certain forms of marine and terrestrial life. The width of the horizontal bars indicates the varying abundance of each life-form considered.

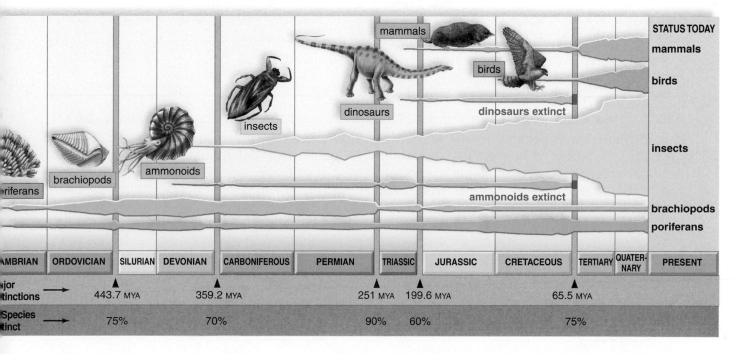

1. Obtain a box of selected fossils. If the fossils are embedded in rocks, examine the rock until you have found the fossil. Fossils are embedded in rocks because the sediment that originally surrounded them hardened over time. Most fossils consist of hard parts such as shells, bones, or teeth because these parts are not consumed or decomposed over time. One possible reason the Cambrian might be rich in fossils is because organisms before this time did not have

   _____ .

2. The kit you are using, or your instructor, will identify which of the fossils are invertebrate

   animals. These fossils date back to which era and period? _____
   Fill in the title of Table 18.2. List the names of these fossils in Table 18.2, and give a description of the hard part of the fossil that survived.

Table 18.2 Invertebrate Fossils	
Type of Fossil	**Description of Hard Part**

3. Which of the fossils available to you are vertebrates? _____
   Are any of the fossils mammals, as are humans? _____

Use the Geologic Timescale (Table 18.1) to associate each fossil with the particular era and period when this type of animal was most abundant. Fill in Table 18.3 according to sequence of the time frames from the latest *(top)* to earliest *(bottom)*.

Table 18.3 Vertebrate Fossils		
Type of Fossil	**Era, Period**	**Description of Hard Part**

4. Which of the fossils available to you are plants? _____ Plants that have no hard parts become fossils when their impressions are filled in by minerals. Use the Geologic Timescale (Table 18.1) to associate each plant with a particular era and period. Assume trees are flowering plants unless otherwise stated and associate them with the era and period when flowering plants were most abundant. Fill in Table 18.4 according to the sequence of the time frames from the latest *(top)* to earliest *(bottom)*.

Table 18.4 Plant Fossils		
Type of Fossil	**Era, Period**	**Description of Fossil**

18.2 Comparative Anatomy

In the study of evolutionary relationships, organisms or parts of organisms are said to be **homologous** if they exhibit similar basic structures and embryonic origins. If these organisms or parts of organisms are similar in function only (e.g., bird wings and butterfly wings), they are said to be **analogous.** Only homologous structures indicate an evolutionary relationship and are used to classify organisms.

Comparison of All Adult Vertebrate Forelimbs

The limbs of all vertebrates are homologous structures. Homologous structures share a basic pattern, although there may be specific differences. The similarity of homologous structures is explainable by descent from a common ancestor.

Observation: Vertebrate Forelimbs

1. The central diagram in Figure 18.2 represents the forelimb bones of the ancestral vertebrate. The basic components are the humerus (h), ulna (u), radius (r), carpals (c), metacarpals (m), and phalanges (p) in the five digits.
2. Carefully compare and label in Figure 18.2 the corresponding forelimb bones of the frog, the lizard, the bird, the bat, the cat, and the human. How do you know that of these vertebrates, the cat and bat are most closely related to humans? _____

_____

In particular, note the specific modifications that have occurred in some of the bones to meet the demands of a particular way of life.
3. Fill in Table 18.5 to indicate which bones in each specimen appear to most resemble the ancestral condition and which differ most from the ancestral condition.
4. Relate the change in bone structure to mode of locomotion in two examples.

Example 1: _____

Example 2: _____

Table 18.5 Comparison of Vertebrate Forelimbs		
Animal	**Bones That Resemble Common Ancestor**	**Bones That Differ from Common Ancestor**
Frog		
Lizard		
Bird		
Bat		
Cat		
Human		

Figure 18.2 Vertebrate forelimbs.

All vertebrates evolved from a common ancestor, so their forelimbs share homologous structures.

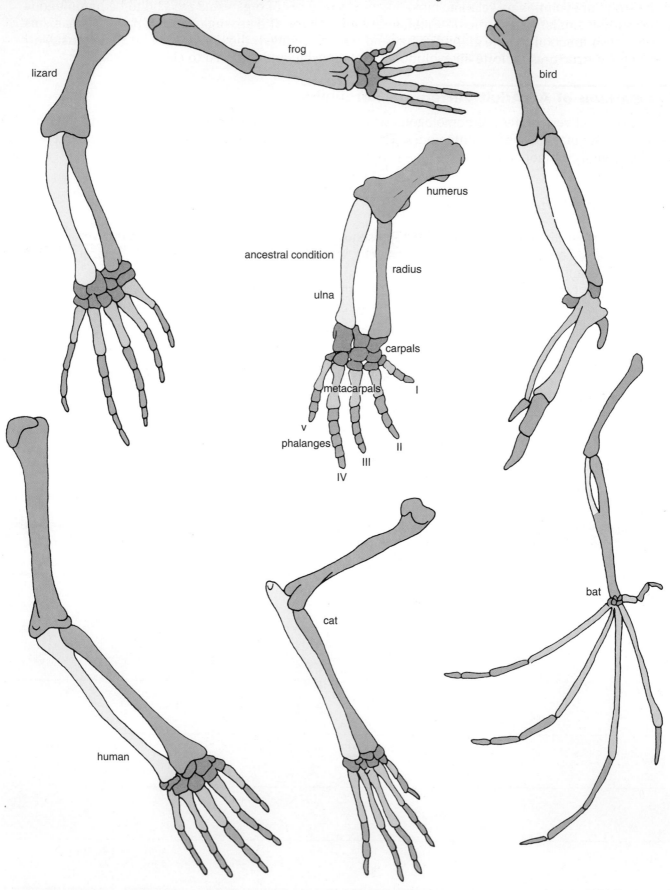

Comparison of Chimpanzee and Human Skeletons

Chimpanzees and humans are closely related, as is apparent from an examination of their skeletons. However, they are adapted to different ways of life. Chimpanzees are primates adapted to living in trees and are herbivores—they eat mainly plants. Humans are primates adapted to walking on the ground and are omnivores—they eat both plants and meat.

Observation: Chimpanzee and Human Skeletons

Chimpanzees are arboreal and climb in trees. While on the ground, they tend to knuckle-walk, with their hands bent. Humans are terrestrial and walk erect.

Compare the posture of a chimpanzee and human (Fig. 18.3) by answering the following questions:

Figure 18.3   Human and chimpanzee skeletons.
Differences in posture can be related to their adaptations to a different habitat. Humans now walk on land and chimpanzees primarily live in trees.

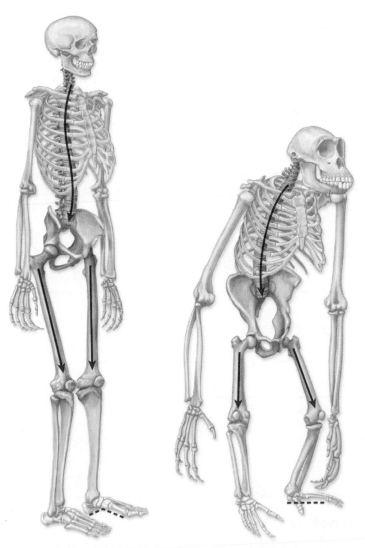

1. **Head and torso:** Where are the head and trunk with relation to the hips and legs—thrust forward over the hips and legs or balanced over the hips and legs? *Record your observation in Table 18.6.*
2. **Spine:** Which animal has a long and curved lumbar region, and which has a short and stiff lumbar region *Record your observation in Table 18.6.*
   How does this contribute to an erect posture in humans? _____
3. **Pelvis:** Chimpanzees sway when they walk because lifting one leg throws them off balance. Which animal has a narrow and long pelvis, and which has a broad and short pelvis? *Record your observation in Table 18.6.*
4. **Femur:** In humans, the femur better supports the trunk. In which animal is the femur angled to place the lower limbs under the trunk? *Record your observation in Table 18.6.*
5. **Knee joint:** In humans, the knee joint is modified to support the body's weight. In which animal is the femur larger at the bottom and the tibia larger at the top? *Record your observation in Table 18.6.*
6. **Foot:** In humans, the foot is adapted for walking long distances and running with less chance of injury. In which animal is the big toe opposable? How does an opposable toe assist chimpanzees? _____
   _____ Which foot has an
   arch? How does an arch assist humans? _____
   Record your observations in Table 18.6.
7. **Foramen magnum:** How does the difference in the position of the foramen magnum, a large opening in the base of the skull for the spinal cord, correlate with the posture and stance of
   the two organisms? _____
   Record your observation in Table 18.6.

Table 18.6 Comparison of Chimpanzee and Human Postures

Skeletal Part	Chimpanzee	Human
1. Head and torso		
2. Spine		
3. Pelvis		
4. Femur		
5. Knee joint		

6. Foot:
   Opposable toe
   Arch		

7. Foramen magnum		

Conclusion: Chimpanzee and Human Skeletons

- Do your observations show that the skeletal differences between chimpanzees and humans can be related to posture? _____ Explain. _____
  _____

Figure 18.4 Chimpanzee and human skulls.

Differences in facial features can be related to a difference in diet. Chimpanzees are herbivorous and humans are omnivores.

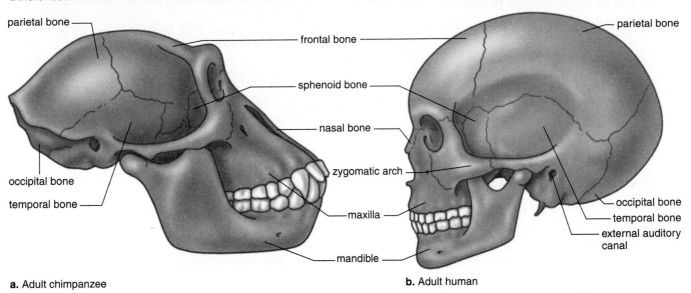

a. Adult chimpanzee

b. Adult human

Observation: Chimpanzee and Human Facial Features

Compare the skulls of the chimpanzee and the human in Figure 18.4, and answer the following questions:

1. **Supraorbital ridge:** For which skull is the supraorbital ridge (the region of frontal bone just above the eye socket) thicker? _____
   Record you observation in Table 18.7.
2. **Frontal bone:** Compare the slope of the frontal bones of the chimpanzee and human skulls. How are they different? _____
   Record your observation in Table 18.7.

Table 18.7 Facial Features of Chimpanzees and Humans

Feature	Chimpanzee	Human
1. Supraorbital ridge		
2. Frontal bone		
3. Teeth		
4. a. Mouth		
b. Chin		

3. **Teeth:** Examine the teeth in the adult chimpanzee and adult human skulls. Are the shapes and sizes of teeth similar in both? _____

Record your observations in Table 18.7. Humans are omnivorous. A diet rich in meat does not require strong grinding teeth or well-developed facial muscles. Chimpanzees are vegetarians, and a vegetarian diet requires strong teeth and strong facial muscles that attach to bony projections.

4. **Mouth and chin: a.** What is the position of the mouth and chin in relation to the profile for each skull? _____ *Record your observation in Table 18.7.*

b. What effect has the evolutionary change in the positions of these bones had on the shape of the face? _____ *Record your observation in Table 18.7.*

Conclusion: Chimpanzee and Human Facial Features

- Account for why a chimpanzee's face protrudes in the front and there are thick supraorbital ridges. _____
_____

Comparison of Vertebrate Embryos

The anatomy shared by vertebrates extends to their embryological development. For example, as embryos, they all have a post-anal tail, somites (segmented blocks of mesoderm lying on either side of the notochord), and paired pharyngeal pouches and bordering gill arches. In aquatic animals, these pouches and arches become functional gills (Fig. 18.5). In humans, the first pair of pouches becomes the cavity of the middle ear and auditory tube, the second pair becomes the tonsils, and the third and fourth pairs become the thymus and parathyroid glands.

Figure 18.5   Vertebrate embryos.
During early developmental stages, vertebrate embryos have certain characteristics in common.

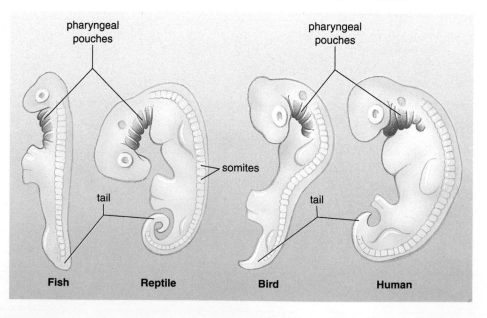

Observation: Chick and Pig Embryos

1. Obtain prepared slides of vertebrate embryos at comparable stages of development. Observe each of the embryos using a binocular dissecting microscope.

2. List five similarities of the embryos:

a. _____

b. _____

c. _____

d. _____

e. _____

Conclusion: Vertebrate Embryos

Vertebrate embryos resemble one another because _____

_____.

18.3 Molecular Evidence

Almost all living organisms use the same basic biochemical molecules, including DNA, ATP, and many identical and nearly identical enzymes. In addition, living organisms use the same DNA triplet code and the same 20 amino acids in their proteins. There is no obvious functional reason these elements need to be so similar. Therefore, their similarity is best explained by descent from a common ancestor.

Protein Differences

According to the **protein clock theory,** the number of certain amino acid changes between organisms is proportional to the length of time since two organisms began evolving separately from a common

ancestor. Why should that be? _____

 The sequence of amino acids in **cytochrome c**, a carrier of electrons in the electron transport chain found in mitochondria and chloroplasts, has been determined in a variety of organisms. Figure 18.6 lists the number of differences between amino acid sequences in cytochrome c for several of these organisms.

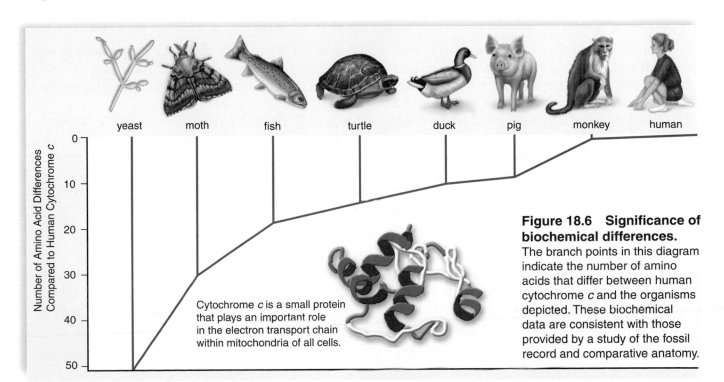

yeast moth fish turtle duck pig monkey human

Number of Amino Acid Differences Compared to Human Cytochrome c

Cytochrome c is a small protein that plays an important role in the electron transport chain within mitochondria of all cells.

Figure 18.6 Significance of biochemical differences.
The branch points in this diagram indicate the number of amino acids that differ between human cytochrome c and the organisms depicted. These biochemical data are consistent with those provided by a study of the fossil record and comparative anatomy.

Protein Similarities

The immune system makes **antibodies** (proteins) that react with foreign proteins, termed **antigens.** Antigen-antibody reactions are specific. An antibody will react only with its particular antigen. In today's Laboratory, this reaction can be observed when a precipitate, a substance separated from the solution, appears.

Biochemists have used the antigen–antibody reaction to determine the degree of relatedness between animals. In one technique, human serum (containing human proteins) is injected into the bloodstream of a rabbit, and the rabbit makes antibodies against human antigens. Some of the rabbit's blood is then drawn off, and the sensitized serum that contains the antibodies is separated from it. This sensitized rabbit serum will react strongly (determined by the amount of precipitate) against a new sample of human blood serum. The rabbit serum will also react against serum from other animals. The more closely related these animals are to humans, the more the precipitate forms (Fig. 18.7).

Figure 18.7   Antigen-antibody reaction.
When antigens react with antibodies, a complex forms that appears as a precipitate.

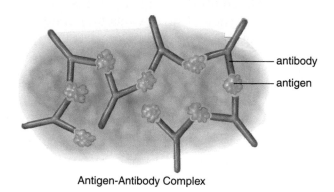

Antigen-Antibody Complex

Experimental Procedure: Protein Similarities

1. Obtain a chemplate (a clear glass tray with wells), one bottle of synthetic *human blood serum,* one bottle of synthetic *rabbit blood serum,* and five bottles (I–V) of *blood serum test solution.*
2. Put two drops of synthetic rabbit blood serum in each of the six wells in the chemplate. Label the wells 1–6. See yellow circles in Figure 18.8.
3. Add 2 drops of synthetic human blood serum to each well. See red circles in Figure 18.8. Stir with the plastic stirring rod attached to the chemplate. The rabbit serum has now been "sensitized" to human serum. (This simulates the production of antibodies in the rabbit's bloodstream in response to the human blood proteins.)
4. Rinse the stirrer. (The large cavity of the chemplate may be filled with water to facilitate rinsing.)
5. Add 4 drops of *blood serum test solution III* (tests for human blood proteins) to well 6.

   Describe what you see. _____

   _____

   This well will serve as the basis by which to compare all the other samples of test blood serum.
6. Now add 4 drops of *blood serum test solution I* to well 1. Stir and observe. Rinse the stirrer. Do the same for each of the remaining *blood serum test solutions (II–V)*—adding II to well 2, III to well 3, and so on. Be sure to rinse the stirrer after each use.

Micropipette, 19
Microscopes
    electron, 11
        vs. light, 10–11
        scanning, 11
        transmission, 11, 11*t*
    field of view, 17–18
    focusing of, 12–13, 16
    image, inversion of, 16
    light
        compound light, 10, 11*t*, 13–20
        vs. electron, 10–11
    magnification, total, 17, 17*t*
    observation with, 18–20
    parts of, 11–12, 14
    resolution, 11
    rules for, 15
    stereomicroscope, 10, 11–13, 13*f*
    use of, 13–20
Microscopic studies
    adipose tissue, 33, 33*f*, 55, 55*f*
    blood, 57, 57*f*
    bone, 55, 55*f*, 152*f*, 153
    cardiac muscle, 58, 58*f*
    Euglena, 20, 20*f*
    hay infusion cultures, 260*f*
    human epithelial cells, 20, 20*f*, 51–53, 51*f*, 52*f*, 53*f*
    hyaline cartilage, 56, 56*f*
    loose fibrous connective tissue, 54, 54*f*
    muscle tissue, 57–59, 58*f*, 59*f*
    nervous tissue, 59–60, 60*f*
    ovary, 129–130, 130*f*, 211, 211*f*
    potato starch, 29, 29*f*
    red blood cells, 85
    sea star embryos, 182, 182*f*
    skeletal muscle, 58, 58*f*, 160, 160*f*
    smooth muscle, 59, 59*f*
    spinal cord and spinal nerves, 170, 170*f*
    squamous epithelium, 51–52, 51*f*
    testis, 127–128, 128*f*, 212, 212*f*
    white blood cells, 85
    whitefish blastula, 197–198, 198*f*
Microtubules, 38*f*
Microvilli, epithelial, 51
Midbrain, 166, 167*f*, 187*f*
Middle ear, 175*f*, 176*t*
Milk, 103*t*
Milligram (mg), 267
Millimeter (mm), 17*t*, 267
Miocene epoch, 244*t*
Mitochondrial disease, 47
Mitochondrial DNA, 47
Mitochondrion, 38*f*, 39*t*, 161*f*

Mitosis
    cancer and, 213
    in cell cycle, 196–198, 197*f*, 197*t*
    cytokinesis and, 200, 200*f*
    vs. meiosis, 206–207, 206*f*, 207*f*
    model, 197–198
    overview, 195
    phases of, 198–200, 198*f*–200*f*
    in whitefish blastula, 197–198, 198*f*
Mitral (left atrioventricular; bicuspid) valve, 79
Molecular evidence, for evolution, 255–257, 255*f*, 256*f*, 257*f*
Molecular genetics, 213
Monocytes, 57*f*, 84*f*
Monosaccharides, 30–31, 30*t*, 31*t*
Morula, 182*f*, 183*f*, 184*f*
Motor neurons, 59, 60*f*, 169, 170*f*
Mouth cancer, 213
mRNA. *See* Messenger RNA (mRNA)
Mucosa, 50, 50*f*
Multiple births, 131
Muscle(s)
    in antagonistic pairs, 151, 151*f*, 158–159, 159*f*
    cardiac, 58, 58*f*
    contractions of, 160–163, 160*f*, 161*f*
    insertion of, 151, 151*f*
    involuntary, 58
    movement types, 159*f*
    naming of, 157
    origin of, 151, 151*f*
    skeletal, 58, 58*f*, 157–160, 158*f*, 159*f*
    smooth, 59, 59*f*
    visceral, 59, 59*f*
    voluntary, 58
Muscle fiber, 57, 161*f*
Muscular action, 151*f*
Muscularis, 50, 50*f*
Muscular tissue, 50, 57–59, 58*f*, 59*f*
Musculoskeletal system
    axial skeleton in, 154–156, 154*f*, 155*f*
    long bone in, 152–153, 152*f*
    overview of, 151
Myelin sheath, 60*f*, 165*f*
Myofibrils, 161, 161*f*
Myosin, 162
Myosin filaments, 161, 161*f*

N

Naming, of muscles, 157
Nanogram (ng), 267
Nanometer (nm), 17*t*, 267
Nasal bone, 154*f*, 155, 253*f*

Pancreatic duct, 94f
Pancreatic juice, 94f
Pancreatic lipase, digestion of fat with, 94–95, 94f
Papa John's, 104t
Papillary muscles, 79, 80f
Pap test, 21, 21f
Paramecium, 260f
Parathyroid gland, fetal pig, 68f
Parental cell, 196
Parfocal, defined, 16
Parietal bone, 154, 154f, 155f, 253f
Parietal lobe, 167f, 168
Particulate genetics, 215
Patella, 155f, 156
Patellar tendon, 171
Peanut butter, 103t
Peas, 103t
Pectoral girdle, 155f, 156
Pectoralis major, 158f
Pedigrees, 222–224, 222f, 223f
Pelvic girdle, 155f, 156
Penis
    anatomy, 129, 129f
    fetal pig, 67, 122, 123f
    human, 121f
Pepsin, digestion of proteins with, 92–93, 92f
Peptide bond, 25, 25f
Peptides, 24–25, 24f, 25f
Pericardial cavity, fetal pig, 72
Pericardium, human, 77f
Periosteum, 152f, 153
Peritoneum, 73, 119
Peritubular capillary network, 143, 143f
Permafrost, 265
Permeability, selective, 41
Permian period, 245t, 247f
Personal DNA sequencing, 241
pH
    balance, 146
    catalase and, effect of, 46–47
    effect on enzyme activity, 46
Phalanges (foot), 155f, 157
Phalanges (hand), 155f, 156
Pharyngeal pouches, 254f
Pharynx
    fetal pig, 67–68, 67f, 68f
    in torso model, 64f
Phenol red, 95
Phenotype, 215f
Phenylketonuria (PKU), 219
Philodina, 260f
Photomicrographs (light micrographs), 10, 10f
Pie, 103t

Pinna, 175f, 176t
Pituitary gland, 146, 168f
PKU. *See* Phenylketonuria (PKU)
Placenta, 181, 189–190, 189f, 190f, 192f
Plasma, blood, 57, 57f
Plasma membrane, 38f, 39t
    diffusion across, 41–43, 41f
Platelets, 84f
Pleistocene epoch, 244t
Pleural cavity, fetal pig, 71–72
Pliocene epoch, 244t
Polar body, 210
Polypeptides, 25
Polyribosome, 38f
Polysaccharides, 27, 27f
Poly-X syndrome, 209
Pons, 166, 167f
Population, 243
Poriferans, 247f
Portal system, 88
Posterior, 65
Potassium hydroxide (KOH), 25
Potassium permanganate ($KMnO_4$), 40
Potato, microscopic study of, 29, 29f
Precambrian time, 245t
Precapillary sphincter, 86f
Prehypertension, 89
Presumptive notochord, 184f
Primary follicle, 129, 211f
Primary oocyte, 130f
Progesterone, 124
Proline, 235t
Prophase, 198f
    in meiosis, 202f, 206f
    in mitosis, 198–199, 199f, 206f
Prophase I, 202f
Prostate gland
    fetal pig, 122
    human, 121f, 122
Protective eyewear, 46
Protein(s)
    amino acids and, 24–25, 24f, 25f
    antibodies as, 24
    carrier, 41, 41f
    digestion of, 25, 92–93, 92f
    enzymatic, 24
    in foods, 33f, 103t
    functions of, 24
    in molecular evidence for evolution, 255, 255f
    pepsin and, 92–93, 92f
    regulatory, 24
    R group in, 24, 24f
    similarity in living organisms, 256, 256f

Tongue
    fetal pig, 67f
    in fetal pig, 66f
    human, 64f
Tonicity, 43
Tooth
    fetal pig, 67f
    human, 64f
Torso model, 64–65, 64f
Total magnification, 17, 17t
Touch receptors, in skin, 177
Trabeculae, 152f, 153
Trachea(e)
    fetal pig, 68f, 70, 71
    human, 64f
Transcription, 232, 233, 233f
Trans fatty acids, 31
Transfer RNA (tRNA), 232, 234, 234f
Translation, 232, 234, 234f
Translocation, chromosomal, 208
Transmission electron micrographs (TEM), 10, 10f
Transmission electron microscope, 11, 11t
Transplant tissues, 61
Transport proteins, 24
Trapezius, 158f
Triassic period, 244t, 247f
Triceps, in body composition, 112
Triceps brachii, 151, 151f, 158f
Tricuspid (right atrioventricular) valve, 79, 80f
Triplet code, of DNA, 234
Triplets, 183
Trisomy 21, 208, 208f
tRNA. See Transfer RNA (tRNA)
Trophoblast, 183f
Tubular reabsorption, 144, 144f, 145
Tubular secretion, 144, 144f, 145
Turner syndrome, 209
T wave, 81
Twins, 183
Tympanic membrane, 175–176, 175f, 176t
Typing, energy cost for, 106t

U

Ulna, 155f, 156
Umbilical artery, 72f, 123f, 126f, 192, 192f
Umbilical cord, 189–190, 189f, 190f
    around baby's neck, 193
    fetal pig, 70f, 72f, 120f, 126f
    in fetal pig, 66f
    functions of, 189
    human embryo, 188f, 190f, 192f
Umbilical vein, 69, 72f, 192, 192f

Unattached earlobe, 215f
Unsaturated fatty acid, 31
Uphill walking, energy cost for, 106t
Uracil (U), 231, 231f
Urea, formation, 139
Ureter
    fetal pig, 119, 120f, 123f, 126f
    human, 118f, 121f
    in urinary system, 118, 119
Urethra, 64f
    fetal pig, 119, 120f, 122, 123f, 126f
    human, 118f, 121f, 122, 124f
    male, 118
    in urinary system, 118, 119
Urethral sphincters, 119
Urinalysis, 147–148, 148f
Urinary bladder
    artificial, 61
    cancer, 213
    fetal pig, 72f, 119, 120f, 123f, 126f
    human, 118f, 121f, 124f
    in torso model, 64f
    in urinary system, 118, 119
Urinary system, 64f, 75
    anatomy of, 118–119, 118f, 120f
    in fetal pig, 119, 120f
    in homeostasis, 133f
    human, 118f
    kidneys in, 118–119
    overview of, 117
Urine, production of, 144, 144f
Urogenital opening, fetal pig, 66f, 67
Urogenital orifice, fetal pig, 123f
Urogenital papilla, fetal pig, 66f, 67, 126f
Urogenital sinus, fetal pig, 120f, 125, 126f
Urogenital system. See Reproductive system;
        Urinary system
Uterine horns, fetal pig, 125, 126f
Uterus
    fetal pig, 126f
    human, 124f, 125
Utricle, 176t
Uvula
    fetal pig, 67
    human, 64f

V

Vagina
    fetal pig, 125, 126f
    human, 124f, 125
Valine, 235t

Valves, in heart, 78
Variability, of subjects, 5
Variables, in experimentation, 4
Vas deferens, 128f
    fetal pig, 122, 123f
    human, 121, 121f
Vegetable, 103t
Vegetal pole, 184f
Veins
    anatomy of, 86f
    cardiac, 78f, 79
    in circulatory system, 3f, 85
    in dissection, 65
    dorsal, of penis, 129f
    hepatic, 88f, 138, 138f
    hepatic portal, 88f, 138, 138f, 192f
    iliac, 88f
    jugular, 88f
    ovarian, 126f
    pulmonary, 78f, 79, 80f, 88f, 192f
    renal, 88f, 118f, 142f
    subclavian, 88f
    umbilical, 69, 72f, 192, 192f
    vitelline, 187, 187f
Vena cava
    in circulatory system, 79
    fetal pig, 120f
    inferior, 78f, 80f, 118f
    superior, 78f, 80f, 88f
Venous duct, 192f
Ventral, 65
Ventral horn, of spinal cord, 170f
Ventricles
    brain, 166, 168f
    in human heart, 78, 78f, 79, 80f
Venules, 85, 86f
Vernix caseosa, 191
Vertebrae
    cervical, 156
    lumbar, 156
    thoracic, 156
Vertebral column, 155f, 156
Vesicles, 38f, 39t
Vesicular follicle, 211f
Vestibular nerve, 175f

Vestibule, 175f, 176t
Villi, intestinal, 98, 98f
Visceral muscle, 59, 59f
Vision, 172–175, 172t, 173f, 174f
Vitelline arteries and veins, 187, 187f
Vitreous humor, 172t, 173f
Volume, metric units, 19, 267
Voluntary muscle, 58
Vomer bone, 154f
Vorticella, 260f

W

Walking, energy cost for, 106t
Weight, ideal
    body composition and, 112–115, 113t, 114t
    body mass index and, 111, 111t
    for females, 110t
    for males, 110t
    overview of, 101
Weight units, 267
Wet mount, 19, 19f
White blood cells, 19, 57, 57f, 84, 84f, 85
Whitefish blastula, mitosis in, 197–198, 198f
White matter, 170, 170f
Women, Pap test in, 21, 21f
Wrestling, energy cost for, 106t
Wrist, of fetal pig, 66f, 70f
Writing, energy cost for, 106t

X

X-linked disorders, 220–221

Y

Yellow bone marrow, 152f
Yolk sac, 189, 190f

Z

Zoom mechanism, of stereomicroscope, 12
Zygomatic arch, 253f
Zygomatic bone, 154f, 155, 155f
Zygote, 181, 182, 182f, 183f